WONDERS of the LAND

WONDERS of the LAND

Kendall Haven

Merging Earth Myth with Earth Science

Illustrated by Julie Stringer

Wonders of Nature: Natural Phenomena in Science and Myth

A Member of the Greenwood Publishing Group

Westport, Connecticut • London

Library of Congress Cataloging-in-Publication Data

Haven, Kendall F.
  Wonders of the land / by Kendall Haven.
      p. cm.—(Wonders of nature : natural phenomena in science and myth)
  Includes bibliographical references and index.
  ISBN 1–59158–318–7 (pbk : alk. paper)
  1. Geology—Popular works. I. Title.   II. Series: Wonders of nature (Libraries Unlimited)
QE31.H38 2006
550—dc22   2006000376

British Library Cataloguing in Publication Data is available.

Copyright © 2006 by Kendall Haven

All rights reserved. No portion of this book may be reproduced, by any process or technique, without the express written consent of the publisher.

Library of Congress Catalog Card Number: 2006000376
ISBN: 1–59158–318–7

First published in 2006

Libraries Unlimited, 88 Post Road West, Westport, CT 06881
A Member of the Greenwood Publishing Group, Inc.
www.lu.com

Printed in the United States of America

The paper used in this book complies with the Permanent Paper Standard issued by the National Information Standards Organization (Z39.48–1984).

10 9 8 7 6 5 4 3 2 1

Special Thanks

I owe a special thank you to a number of people and groups who helped me either with the stories or the science information for this book. In particular, a huge thank you to Dan Keding, a good friend and owner of the most extensive and comprehensive private collection of myths and fables in the country.

I also owe a big thank you to the librarians and the Sonoma State University library and to a number of people at the University of California, Berkeley, for their help in gathering and verifying the science information in this book.

A personal thank you goes to Sharon Coatney for initially connecting me with this book and for her visionary work in shaping and steering this series to completion. Finally, I owe countless thanks to my ace proofreader Roni Berg, the love of my life, and the best litmus test I know of a story's success.

Contents

ILLUSTRATIONS		xi
INTRODUCTION		xiii
I	**FORCES THAT CREATE THE LAND**	**1**
1	THE ORIGINS OF LAND	3
	Myths about the Origins of Land	3
	"The Making of the World," A Myth from the Huron Tribe of the Upper Great Lakes Region	4
	The Science of the Origins of Land	6
	Topics for Discussion and Projects	18
	Suggested Reading for Teachers	21
2	VOLCANOES	23
	Myths about Volcanoes	23
	"The Fire Goddess," A Myth from the Big Island of Hawaii	25
	The Science of Volcanoes	27
	Topics for Discussion and Projects	44
	Suggested Reading for Teachers	47
3	CREATING ROCKS	49
	Myths about Creating Rocks	49
	"The Goddess of Mahi River," A Myth from the Gujarat Region of India	50
	The Science of Creating Rocks	52

CONTENTS

	Topics for Discussion and Projects	65
	Suggested Reading for Teachers	68
4	CREATING GEMS AND CRYSTALS	69
	Myths about Creating Gems and Crystals	69
	"Mountains of Gold and Jewels," A Myth from Borneo	71
	The Science of Creating Gems and Crystals	73
	Topics for Discussion and Projects	81
	Suggested Reading for Teachers	83
5	CREATING MOUNTAINS	85
	Myths about Creating Mountains	85
	"Mountain Making," A Myth from the Modoc Indians of California	86
	The Science of Creating Mountains	89
	Topics for Discussion and Projects	98
	Suggested Reading for Teachers	101
II	FORCES THAT CHANGE THE LAND	103
6	WATER	105
	Myths about How Water Shapes the Land	105
	"The Gift of the *Menehune*," A Myth from Kauai, Hawaii	107
	The Science of How Water Shapes the Land	110
	Topics for Discussion and Projects	122
	Suggested Reading for Teachers	126
7	WIND	127
	Myths about How Wind Shapes the Land	127
	"Sun, Water, and Wind," A Myth from Russia	129
	The Science of How Wind Shapes the Land	131
	Topics for Discussion and Projects	142
	Suggested Reading for Teachers	145
8	GLACIERS	147
	Myths about How Glaciers Shape the Land	147
	"The Touchy Ibis," A Myth from the Yamana People of Tierra del Fuego	148
	The Science of How Glaciers Shape the Land	150
	Topics for Discussion and Projects	164
	Suggested Reading for Teachers	167

9	EARTHQUAKES	169
	Myths about How Earthquakes Shape the Land	169
	"The Lion's Earthquake," A Myth from India	170
	The Science of How Earthquakes Shape the Land	172
	Topics for Discussion and Projects	184
	Suggested Reading for Teachers	187
10	LIVING THINGS	189
	Myths about How Living Things Shape the Land	189
	"How Beaver Stole Fire from the Pines," A Myth from the Nez Percé People of the Pacific Northwest	190
	The Science of How Living Things Shape the Land	192
	Topics for Discussion and Projects	201
	Suggested Reading for Teachers	204
APPENDIX: ADDITIONAL RESOURCES		205
INDEX		211

Illustrations

1.1 • The Plates of Earth's Crust   11

1.2 • What Happens at Plate Boundaries   12

1.3 • Inside the Earth   15

1.4 • Holmes's Conveyor Belt   16

2.1 • Active Volcanoes   32

2.2 • The Three Types of Volcanoes   35

3.1 • The Rock Cycle   60

4.1 • Elements in the Crust   74

5.1 • Forming Mountains   90

6.1 • The Water Cycle   112

7.1 • Global Air Currents   132

7.2 • The World's Deserts   136

7.3 • The Shape of Sand Dunes   139

8.1 • Valley Glaciers   153

9.1 • California Fault Lines   175

9.2 • Earthquakes around the World   177

Introduction

I have lived all my life on Earth. More precisely, I have lived all my life on the continental land of Earth. Most likely, so have you. We often take land and rocks and dirt for granted. We save our gaze of awe and wonder for comets, solar eclipses, and lumbering whales.

But a rock can be—*should* be—equally fascinating. Think of how hard it is to make a rock. Can you? No, you cannot. There are rocks that have survived for 3 billion years! That's 3,000 times a million years. Not only has no living organism survived nearly that long, no *species* has survived that long. The dinosaurs, as a whole, lasted only 150 million years from the first two-legged thecodonts (the creatures dinosaurs descended from) to the last dying stegosaurus. Cockroaches (and they seem impossible to exterminate) have survived for only 500 million years. Individual rocks have lasted six times that long!

Imagine what creatures have lumbered past these very rocks and what events have come and gone while they sat. How many dinosaurs have tripped over rocks that still sit on the ground for us to take our turn and sit on? How many giant ice age glaciers have covered the land, only to retreat in melting defeat as the planet warmed and these rocks still exist? How many volcanoes have belched fire and ash into the sky and then quietly gone extinct while these same rocks sat and watched?

Rocks endure. They're survivors. Rocks withstand constant attacks by the greatest destructive forces on Earth. And they get by. They make do. We could learn a thing or two from rocks.

Many people think that rocks and land forms are boring. The problem is that we learn about rocks through lectures. It's the lectures that

INTRODUCTION

are mostly boring. We should do what traditional cultures have done and tell stories to teach about rocks. Stories engage, enthuse, excite. Stories are a delight, a gift, a treat. Why not use the power of myth and story to engage students in serious science discussion and research?

Do myth and science belong together? Absolutely. What we now call myth represented, at one time, the best explanation available for the nature of the world that surrounds us. Much of what we now call science may, in some future eon, be regarded as myth and fantasy by those whose understanding goes far beyond our own. Gazing from ancient myth to modern science allows us to chart our human progress. It shows us where we have come from and helps us understand who we *are* by showing us who we *were*. It gives us a perspective from which to appreciate the benefits and majesty of the sciences that have led us to where we are.

Myths and science both attempt to answer the grand mysteries of nature—where things and beings came from, how they got here, why they act as they do, and the purpose of life. Myths explain things through story. Science explains them through empirical observation, controlled experiments, and precise calculation. Science provides factual information and understanding. Stories create context and relevance for that information within the human mind. Stories inspire, captivate, and open the door to follow-on science activity.

By definition, a myth is a traditional story or legend, especially one concerning fabulous or supernatural beings, giving expression to early beliefs and perceptions and often explain natural phenomena or the origins of some aspect of a people or nature. Myths were created as entertainment with a serious purpose. They were supposed to explain some origin or instruct community members in essential beliefs, attitudes, behavior, history, and values.

We do not yet know all there is to know about our planet. As of this writing, an unmanned space probe has intentionally been smashed into a comet so that scientists can gain a few new clues about the origin and early life of our planet by studying the aftermath of that collision. No human has ever ventured or drilled more than a few miles into the Earth's crust. The Earth's radius is around 4,000 miles. We have scratched only the top two.

We can guess at what lies underneath that shallow bed of knowledge. But imagine what mysteries await us as we invent new ways to explore deeper into the heart and soul of our Earth!

We are like the early civilizations, still piecing together our best guesses about the structure and origins of our planet. Our myths are more sophisticated and rooted in stronger scientific knowledge than theirs. But who is to say how humans 1,000 years in the future will view the stories our science tells us? Will they snicker at our ignorance? Will they look at our science and call it ancient myth?

I wrote this book to introduce and explain some of the major concepts of modern Earth Science by gazing at them through the wonders and intrigue of myths. This book forms a bridge between the exciting world of mythic story and science's logic and precision. I want to merge the power and delight of myth with the factual data of modern science.

To do that, I have picked ten aspects of Earth Science that lend themselves to myth and are also important to a science curriculum study of the Earth and its land. One chapter is devoted to each of these ten aspects. The first five, as a group, address the forces and processes that create land and the various parts and features of the land. The last five describe the forces that act to change, erode, and weather the land. The first half of the book is about building the land up. The second half is about tearing it down. And we get to live in the middle of this magnificent and global battle between the builders and the eroders!

For each chapter, I have selected one myth that embodies that aspect of Earth Science and attempts to explain it. I sifted through many hundreds of myths and traditional stories before selecting those ten that I present here. None of these ten stories comes from a single source. I have tracked multiple sources for all and have tried to fashion the common elements of those various versions into a unified version to present here. In several cases, as individually indicated, I combined several similar traditional versions from different groups or countries all from the same geographic region. I shortened several stories to fit within the physical constraints of this book. By presenting the stories at the beginning of each chapter, I get to compare the beliefs inherent in the myths with our current scientific understanding of the Earth's land masses.

Use this book as a block introduction for Earth Science studies. Use it to expand and enhance specific lessons and subunits of Earth Science. Students can use it for individual research. Teachers can use it for reference. I have tried to make this book a fun read as well as an informative one.

Enjoy these mythic stories. Marvel at the science and reality of the land we live on. Revel in the glorious mysteries that still lurk deep within our planet. Then seek out your own mysteries and myths to explore, to share, and to revel in.

1 — FORCES THAT CREATE THE LAND

1 — The Origins of Land

—— MYTHS ABOUT THE ORIGINS OF LAND

We live on the *land*. Our houses are made of materials that come from the land. Most of our food comes from the land. Humans are one of the many species that need solid land under our feet. We couldn't survive in an all-water world. Land is one of the three big elements we depend on for our existence: land, water, and air.

How our land came to exist quickly became an important subject for myths. How long has the Earth's land been here? Has it always been here? How long is always? What was here before that? Where did the land come from? How did it get here?

The questions of where the land came from and how it formed are also key to understanding Earth Science. What is land made of? Why did dry land push up above the seas? Why doesn't it all sink back down into the molten mantle? Why isn't the Earth not a smooth, round ball? Why the ups and downs, the low spots and high spots, the mountains and valleys and deserts? Why is the land shaped the way it is? How did it get that way?

Most traditional cultures felt obligated to explain the origin of land as part of their core creation myths. The creation of humans was viewed inseparable from the creation of the Earth. Modern science has the Big Bang theory as its creation story—a detailed accounting of how the universe (and the Earth) was formed and how it evolved into its current condition over its 16-billion-year span of existence. Traditional cultures didn't have giant telescopes, ultraviolet and infrared deep-space sensors, radio telescopes, satellites, space probes, and shuttle flights to gather data for them. They had to build their mythic visions from what they could see around them.

Two fundamental types of creation myths emerged: myths in which water came first, and those in which land came first. People and animals typically came from either overcrowded homes in the sky or from lower levels of the Earth—underground levels. However, there are many, very inventive variations on these central themes. In an Inuit myth, Raven harpoons a massive whale floating through a watery world. The whale dies and forms the land.

In many creation myths, some cultural hero arrives either in canoe or on a raft and instigates the creation of land. A Russian myth begins, "At first the God Ulgen created water. Soon Ulgen saw mud floating on the water." (Water came first.) Ulgen then forms land from this mud.

A Nigerian tale begins, "In the beginning, the earth was all watery, just a marshy place, a waste." A Mayan myth begins, "There was no one at first: no animals, no birds, fish, or trees. There was no rock or forest, no wind, no canyon or meadow. There was just the sea, so calm and all alone."

On the other side, an intriguing South American myth has the seas trapped in a greedy pelican's egg. A curious boy climbs a mountain to reach the pelican's nest and then slips and drops the egg. It cracks open and out flow the oceans and fish.

In the myth that follows—typical of many—a woman falls through a hole in the sky to a watery world. Her fall causes land to be created. While other animals actually create the world, this woman is *responsible* for its creation and development. Some cultures call her Gaia, Mother Earth. Some call her Mother Nature. She is called Prithvi in India, Papa in Polynesia, and Ki in ancient Mesopotamia. The Earth existed and was covered by water. Woman caused the land to form.

"THE MAKING OF THE WORLD," A MYTH FROM THE HURON TRIBE OF THE UPPER GREAT LAKES REGION

In the beginning there was nothing but water, a wide sea, peopled by various animals of the kind that live in and upon the water. It happened one day that, with a loud rumble from above, a woman fell down from the upper world and through the sky.

Two loons that happened to be flying over the water and near

The Origins of Land

that spot happened to look up and see the woman falling. To save her from drowning, they hastened to place themselves beneath her, joining their soft bodies together to form a cushion for her to land on and to rest on.

In this way, the loons held her up while they cried in a loud voice to summon the other animals to their aid. The cry of the loon can be heard a great distance and soon many animals of all kinds assembled to hear the cause of the alarm.

The animals clustered about peering at the woman. "Can she fly?" asked a gull.

"No, she fell through the sky," answered one of the loons.

"Can she swim?" asked an eel.

"No. She would have drowned if we hadn't caught her," the loons answered.

"Can she at least float?" demanded a toad.

Again the loons shook their heads, no.

"Then how can she live?" asked the muskrat.

A great debate began that was interrupted when a mallard asked, "*Why* did she fall from the upper world?"

Some believed that the woman's husband had accidentally pushed her through a hole in the sky because it was growing too crowded up there. Some thought that she had fallen as a gift from the gods to the people below. Some argued that she had been cast out of the upper world because she was evil.

The loons said that, while this debate was both interesting and important, they were growing exceedingly tired. The tortoise agreed to carry the woman while the animals decided what to do.

The woman said that she couldn't live on the back of a turtle forever and needed land. But there was no land. There never had been any land.

A new great debate began among the animals. In the end they decide that the woman must have Earth to live on—even though none of them knew where any such thing was to be found.

Seal volunteered to swim over the entire surface of the ocean to search for land. She swam in growing circles until, at last, she had covered the entire surface of the ocean. There was no land.

Toad said that there was land at the bottom of the ocean and that someone should dive down and bring some up to start a land for the woman to live on.

Many tried. Beaver, Egret, Muskrat, and many others dove, but without success. Some remained below so long that when they rose again they were dead. The tortoise searched their mouths but could find no trace of earth. At long last *Dayunisi*, Beaver's grandchild, the tiny water beetle, volunteered to try. Deeper and deeper she went. Harder and harder she swam until she reached the bottom.

When at last she returned to the ocean's surface she was exhausted and nearly dead. On searching her mouth, Tortoise found a tiny bit of sand and mud from the bottom. Tortoise gave these to the woman. She carefully placed sand and mud around the edge of the tortoise's shell. When thus placed, it became the first beginnings of dry land. The land grew and extended on every side forming at last a great country. The entire Earth was supported on Tortoise's back as it still is.

The animals were all impressed that the woman had created such a vast land, but the land lay flat and barren. Eagle flew low over the land. Where he dipped his wings low to the ground, valleys formed. Where he lifted up his wings toward the sky, mountains rose. The land was beautiful, but still nothing but barren rock and mud.

The woman, it turned out, had been pregnant when she fell. Soon it was time for her to give birth. She died while giving birth to twins. However, from her body arose all of the plants, grasses, trees, and animals that the land and her twin boys needed in order to develop.

(The myth continues focusing on the two sons, one of whom represents good, the other evil. However, this first part of the myth concludes the description of how land was first formed.)

— THE SCIENCE OF THE ORIGINS OF LAND

The following beliefs are either directly stated or strongly implied in the presented myth. Here is what modern science knows about the aspects of the land explained by each belief.

BELIEF: First came air (sky), then sea (water), and then some god created the land.

This myth implied that sky (more correctly, the atmosphere) and water (oceans) existed for some time before land was first created by being dredged up from the bottom of the sea. Is it true? Which came first? Land or water? (The chicken or the egg?) And how can scientists possibly know?

From studying our own planet, other planets, and nearby stars and nebula, here is our planet's history as scientists currently believe it to be. Six billion *years ago* (YAG) our solar system was a nebula—a cloud of space dust and gas. Most of this nebula condensed into the growing protostar (our sun). Over millions of years, some of the remaining space

The Origins of Land

dust and granules condensed into clumps of rock—planetisimals. Gravity pulled more space dust to these planetisimals and pulled those planetisimals into slamming collisions with each other.

A few of the planetisimals grew larger than the rest and combined with comets. Over millions of years they formed into the planets that still circle our sun. By 4.8 billion YAG the Earth had formed into one of these planets. Sixty million tons of meteorites and planetesimals slamming into our forming Earth every day! (Still over 100 tons of new material fall on Earth every day.)

The planet's core began to heat up. Heat came from the collisions with hurtling planetisimals (accretion), from radioactive decay in the core (like in a nuclear power plant), and (especially) from the growing pull of gravity that squeezed the material of Earth tighter and tighter together. As the Earth's core material was compressed, collision between adjacent atoms and molecules increased. Each collision produced heat. The Earth—including the surface—was a molten, seething inferno.

As the fiery planet slowly churned and boiled, the various elements tended to separate. Different elements in the Earth formed different chemical compounds with different melting points and densities. In this molten and semimolten Earth, they tended to sort themselves into layers in a process called *differentiation*. Heavy iron and magnesium concentrated in the core. Lighter aluminum, oxygen, and silicon sifted outward into the mantle and surface of the planet. Hissing gases reached the surface and were expelled from the plane to form an early atmosphere—nitrogen, carbon dioxide, water vapor, hydrogen, but virtually no oxygen.

Slowly the outer surface of Earth began to cool. By 3.8 billion YAG some solid crust must have formed covering the Earth like a thin layer of scum that forms on a boiling pot of milk or in a saucepan of boiling fudge. Rocks 3.8 billion years old, the oldest rocks ever discovered on Earth, have been found in Canada.

Even though the crust had cooled to well under 1,000°C (1,830°F) and had solidified, Earth's innards were still a fiery furnace. Contrary to the notions presented in movies like *Journey to the Center of the Earth*, it is impossible to travel, or to survive, very far under the surface—and certainly not at the center of the Earth. Temperatures at the Earth's core hover above 4,000°C (7,230°F), and can be as high as 5,000°C (9,030°F). The pressure in the core is a crushing 1,000 times that of the surface. The core remains a radioactive inferno and the mantle (the semimolten layer between the core and the crust) isn't much better.

Between 2.0 and 0.5 billion YAG even Earth's surface wouldn't have attracted many vacationing tourists. It was a violent time on our planet. The thin outer shell was still steamy hot. Volcanoes spewed ash, fire, and dust into the air. The surface was shrouded by thick clouds of dust and ash. Moving in the dense atmosphere of carbon dioxide (CO_2), water vapor, hydrogen, and nitrogen would have felt like walking through a dripping sauna. (Many scientists think that the water reached Earth from comets that merged into the planet as it formed.) Rain fell in unending torrents as volcanoes spewed more ash and gas into the atmosphere.

Sometime around 3 billion YAG, life began. Simple one-cell organisms spread across the growing oceans. Around 800 million YAG, some of those mosses, plants, or lichens crawled out of the ocean and onto solid rocks—the first life on solid land. There was no dirt, only layers of rock and sand. It must have been a most inhospitable and uninviting world that these plants found. But life is powerful and seems always to find a way to survive. Life spread across the land. The profusion of plants began to pump oxygen into the atmosphere.

The myth is wrong. The land formed billions of years before the oceans and before the sky (atmosphere). The myth had the order backward. Water was the last of these three basic elements to form.

BELIEF: Land formed all at once.

The myth implies that the land was formed all at once and has remained unchanged ever since. Has it?

First, let's define what we mean by "land." *Land* is that part of the continental crusts (plus scattered islands) that rises above sea level. *Land* is the top part of the crust of the Earth. We think of land as what we live on, walk on, build on, grow food in, dig in, and drill oil wells in. That sense of "land" describes only the top, tissue-thin layer of the Earth's rigid crust. The crust is the top layer of the Earth. While Earth's insides are still hot enough to melt rock, the crust has cooled enough to become solid.

The crust didn't "form" as a separate structure. As patches of Earth's fiery hot surface cooled, they solidified into solid rock that we call the crust. But there are two kinds of crust. They differ in thickness, in chemical composition, and in how they move.

Oceanic Crust

Oceanic crust is the parts of the crust that lie under the world's oceans. Oceanic crust is denser and thinner than continental crust. Oceanic crust is only 5 to 7 km (3.1 to 4.2 miles) thick and is mostly dense volcanic rock. There is one chemical compound that is especially important because it affects the density and physical properties of rock and of the crustal plates. That compound is called *silicon dioxide*. Oceanic crust contains less than 40% silicon dioxide. (The chemical formula for silicon dioxide is SiO_2: one part silicon, Si, and two parts oxygen, O.) Finally, oceanic crust contains far more calcium, iron, and manganese than continental crust.

Continental Crust

Continental crust is the part of the crust that contains the land continents. Continental crust is thicker than oceanic, with an average depth of about 28 km (17 miles), but it can reach 70 km (42 miles) under mountain ranges such as the Andes or Himalayas. Continental crust is less dense and lighter than oceanic crust and contains over 60% SiO_2. Continental crust has more granite, sandstone, and sedimentary rock than oceanic. Continental crust also contains more aluminum and sodium.

The Earth's crust formed quickly—over about 100 million years. (That's "quick" in geologic time.) Then the crust began to move, change, shift, expand, and contract. The crust is still changing today. Land is still being formed, still being destroyed. That process will go on for hundreds of millions of years to come.

The first life on land took root 800 million to 1 billion YAG. That marked the beginning of dirt and soil. Soil is a mixture of decomposed organic material with bits of rock and clay. You can't have soil until there is plant life to decompose to form soil. Until then, the Earth's surface was pure rock.

The myth is both right and wrong. Most of the continental crust (land) formed rather quickly between 3.5 and 4 billion YAG. Most of that continental crust still exists. However, our planet is continually creating new land at the margins of continents and as islands. Continents stretch and compress as they move. Earth's land looks very different today than it did 3 billion YAG.

BELIEF: Land is as it originally was and always has been. Once formed, land doesn't change.

People used to believe that the Earth's crust was one solid, unmoving piece. That belief is very wrong. The first scientist to propose that continents moved was German scientist Alfred Wegener in 1911 with his theory of Continental Drift. He found that fossils from South America matched those from Africa, even though the species present on the two continents in 1911 were different. He noticed that South America and Africa seemed to fit together like pieces of a jigsaw puzzle.

Other scientists scoffed. The public laughed at him. It sounded preposterous to claim that massive continents could move.

However, oceanographic research in 1968 proved that Wegener was right. The newly built ship *Glomar Challenger* collected core samples from the bottom of the Atlantic Ocean between Africa and South America. These samples showed that the oceanic crust was youngest near the middle of the Atlantic and grew steadily older toward either continent. Then scientists noticed the mid-Atlantic ridge running from north to south like a 6,000-mile backbone down the middle of the ocean. New crust oozed from countless volcanic fissures and cracks along this ridge and slowly spread out east and west as the Atlantic stretched wider and wider. The ocean floor (crust) was moving and spreading.

Continents didn't have to plow through the oceanic crust to move. Ocean crust simply moved and dragged the continents with it. Continents grew as new continental crust piled up along the leading edge of each continent as it moved.

Scientists have studied the current motion of the various continents and have pieced together theories on where they were and how they moved in the past.

The Earth's crust is broken into plates—like fragments of a dinner plate dropped on the kitchen floor and shattered. There are seven major plates and a dozen smaller ones. (These plates are shown in Figure 1.1.)

Of the seven major plates, six contain the major continents and portions of the ocean floor: the North American plate, the South American plate, the African plate, the Eurasian plate, the Antarctic plate, and the Indian-Australian plate. The seventh is the only purely oceanic plate: the Pacific plate. All the smaller plates are oceanic, many including island chains such as the Caribbean plate.

These plates glide independently across the surface of the Earth like bumper cars racing along the polished floor of a county fair amusement park ride. Some pull away from each other. Some scrape past each other. Some smash headlong into each other. Some drift in straight lines; some pivot and turn. Their speeds and directions vary and change over time.

The Origins of Land

FIGURE 1.1 • The Plates of Earth's Crust

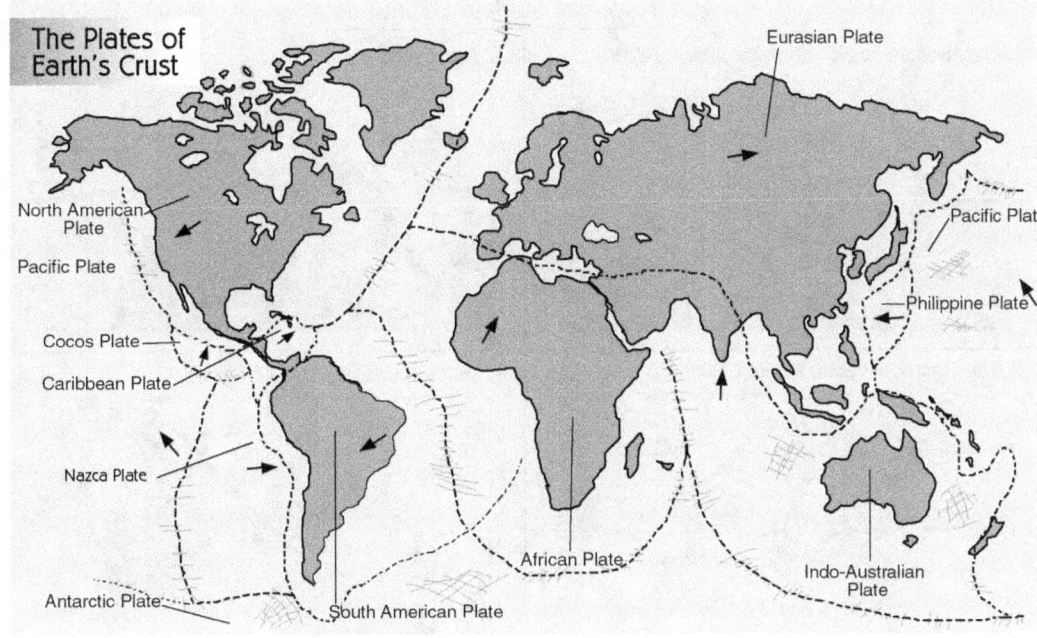

As Figure 1.2 shows, there are several possible interactions between moving plates. When a continental plate collides with an oceanic plate, the lighter continental plate rides over the dense, thin oceanic plate. The continental plate lifts and buckles like the hood of a colliding car, forming new mountains. The oceanic plate is forced back down into the mantle in what scientists call a *subduction zone*.

When two plates separate, a gap, called a *rift valley*, forms in the crust between them. New magma floods up from the mantle to fill this gap. When two continental plates collide, it is like a head-on collision between two cars. Neither plate subducts back into the mantle. Neither rides up. Both crumple into tall, thick mountains. (More details on these plate collisions and examples of each type of interaction are provided in later chapters.)

The movement of these crustal plates is called *tectonic* movement. The forces that drive plates are called *tectonic* forces.

Around a billion YAG, all the continents were jammed together into one supercontinent (called *Pangaea*). Five hundred million YAG, one southern supercontinent (*Gondwanaland*) contained modern South America, Africa, India, and Australia and had drifted apart from the

FIGURE 1.2 • What Happens at Plate Boundaries

What Happens at Plate Boundaries

1. Ocean Plate and Continental Plate Collide

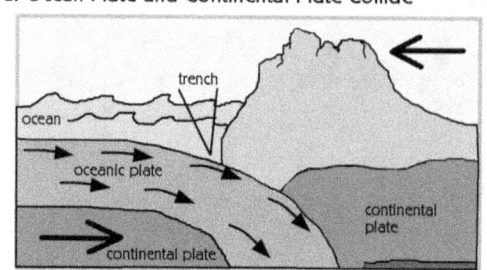

2. Plate Seperates

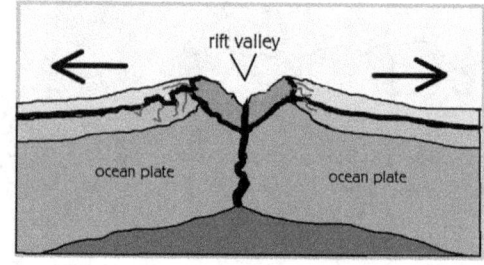

3. The Two Continental Plates Collide

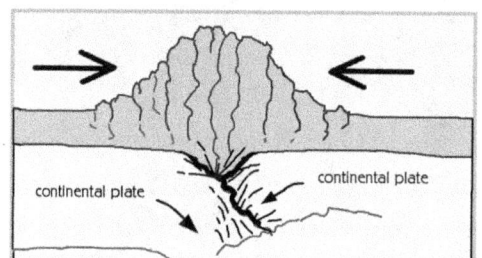

4. Plates Slide Past Each Other

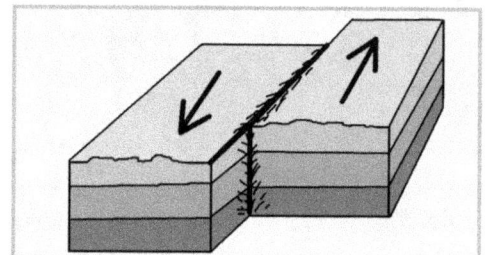

northern continents (North America, Europe, Asia, and Greenland). Three hundred and fifty million YAG tectonic forces reunited the continents and reformed them into Pangaea—a vast land of barren mountains and rock, sand and dust.

Pangaea began to break up about 180 million YAG as a rift formed between southern Africa and South America. North America broke from Europe only 65 million years ago. About 120 million YAG, the Indian plate broke free and (about 65 million YAG) slammed straight into the Asian plate to start the Himalayan Mountains, home of the world's highest mountains.

Around this same time, the Pacific plate also changed directions about 20° counterclockwise as it continued it drive toward Asia. North America has picked up an additional 300+ miles of land along the Pacific coast over past 40 million years as it grinds it way west and over the various oceanic plates along the eastern edge of the Pacific Ocean.

These various plates sprint along at up to 6 inches a year. That may not seem like much, but that's 9,400 miles in 100 million years—almost halfway around the world. The North Atlantic has grown 3,500 miles wide in 65 million years. In another 50 million years the Red Sea, which is just starting to spread, will be as wide as the Atlantic is now.

The continents move and change position. We can guess, but do not know where they will be and how they will be shaped in another 50 million years. We just know that they will change and be different.

But does the land itself change once it is formed? The answer is absolutely yes! Many forces act in concert to lift, twist, fold, bend, tear down, and move all land.

Collisions between plates often push up towering mountain ranges along the border between the plates—the Andes, Alps, Sierras, Himalayas, and so on. (Later in this book is a chapter devoted to the formation and growth of mountains.) The process still occurs today as the Himalayas and the Andes continue to rise because the surrounding plates continue to crumple into each other.

Tectonic forces lift some plates and lower other. What had been seabed 200 million YAG could now be a wide mountain plateau (as with the Colorado-Wyoming plateau). Wide valleys the dinosaurs walked across are now 800 feet below sea level. What was coastal marsh 30 million YAG is now a landlocked prairie with an altitude of 1,500 feet.

Sea level itself rises and falls over time, exposing or covering wide stretches of land. During the ice ages, the continental shelves were exposed land. You could have walked straight from Long Island to Rhode Island (if you could have cut through the thick glacial ice).

Over time wind, water, and gravity tear mountains apart and pull them back down. Three hundred and fifty million YAG, the Appalachian Mountains were as tall and ragged as the front range of the Rockies are now. Sixty million years ago, the Himalayan Mountains were just forming into gentle peaks. In another 100 million years, the Rockies will be as low, gentle, and rounded as the Appalachians are now.

Rivers grind out canyons from what had been smooth plateaus. Hillsides wash away. Coastal bluffs collapse into the sea. Floods, slides, water, and wind tear down and move the surface layer of the Earth.

Finally, islands appear and disappear over time as volcanic actions pushes them above the waves, and as those same waves combine with tides, water, and wind to tear them back down. Peninsulas exist one day. Then a tsunami or a hurricane blasts over them and turns them into a ragged island or partially submerged marsh.

The belief is wrong. The land is always changing. The shape and location of the continents, and of the land itself, are forever changing as a

WONDERS OF THE LAND

dizzying array of forces act to build up and to tear down the land. (Later chapters of this book examine these forces in greater detail.)

While the land looks today as it did yesterday and last month and ten years ago when you were young, it is actually different today than yesterday. It will be new and different tomorrow—though the change over so short a time as one day or one year or one human lifetime is so small you can't notice it.

BELIEF: All of Earth is the same—down to the center of the Earth.

The myth implies that land is land, and that the Earth (once you dive below the oceans) looks the same all the way to its middle. But what do the innards of the Earth really look like?

If you slice the Earth in half you'd find three distinct layers inside: the core, the mantle, and the crust. (These are shown in Figure 1.3.) However, each of these three layers must be broken in half to make sense of its composition and action.

CORE. The core contains a solid inner core and a liquid (molten rock) outer core. The pressure, density, and temperature of the core are all significantly higher than in the mantle. The inner core is mostly iron and is kept in solid form by the immense pressure there. The outer core is similar in composition but is as fluid as the glowing lava flowing down an Hawaiian hillside.

Scientists now believe that the inner core also contains a concentration of radioactive elements (primarily uranium and thorium) that act like a nuclear reactor and produce enough heat to keep the core temperature between 4,000°C and 5,000°C (7,230°F and 9,030°F).

CRUST. The crust is the rigid, solid, outer surface of the Earth. We have already seen that there are two kinds of crust, oceanic and continental. However, there is a very thin (30 km to 50 km thick) semisolid layer along the top of the mantle that moves with, and is attached to, the crustal plates. The crust and this top layer of the mantle are called the *lithosphere*. The lithosphere (the word literally means rocky sphere) is up to 200 km (130 miles) thick and represents only 0.1% of the mass of the Earth. The crust represents only 15% of the mass of the lithosphere. Over two thirds of the mass of the crust is in dense oceanic crustal plates. The continental crusts—including all our continents, countries, mountains, valleys, deserts, and the crust beneath them up to 40 miles beneath the surface—represent only 0.0005% (five one-millionths) of the mass of the Earth!

FIGURE 1.3 • Inside the Earth

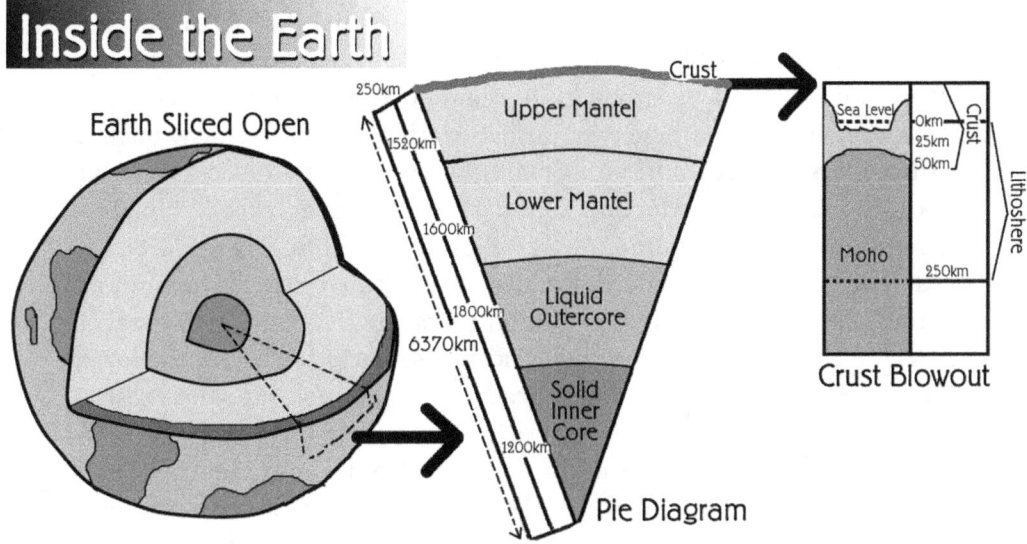

MANTLE. The mantle contains 83% of the volume of the Earth and lies between the core and the crust. Silicon and oxygen are found there in great abundance. There you'll also find concentrations of aluminum and sodium. The temperature of the mantle drops from about 3,500°C (6,330°F) at its boundary with the core to around 1,000°C (1,830°F) at its outer edge.

The lower mantle is quite uniform in composition and is thicker (more semi-solid) than the upper mantle. The transition between these two parts of the mantle occurs at a depth of around 450 to 550 miles beneath the surface. The upper mantle is a liquid churning mass that is the source of the magma that rises to the surface in volcanoes.

Strong currents slowly churn mantle material from the core boundary outward just as boiling fudge in a sauce pan on the stove slowly rises, rolls across the surface and dives back into the boiling depths as it cools. These currents transport heat from the fiery heat engine of the core out toward the crust and space.

There is a distinct boundary between the mantle and the lithosphere. The chemical composition and physical properties of the material on either side of that boundary are distinct and different. That boundary is called the *Moho* (named for its discoverer, Polish scientist Dr. Mohorovicic, and officially called the Mohorovicic Discontinuity). Ongoing research into the Moho and into how heat and energy transfer across the Moho should reveal important secrets about Earth's inner structure in coming years.

In the lithosphere the strong currents of the mantle flatten out and run in shallow ovals like the treads on a tank. Magma rises toward rift valleys and descends at subduction zones. Oceanic crust moves like a conveyor belt between these two, pushed by the upwelling of new magma at rift valleys between spreading plates, and pulled by old crust diving back into mantle at subduction zones. This movement, called "Holmes's Conveyor Belt" (see Figure 1.4), is believed to be the driving force behind plate tectonic movement. Because of this conveyor belt motion, no oceanic crust is older than 200 million years. By that time, it is dragged across the top of the conveyor belt and pulled back down into the lower lithosphere, where it melts and is ready to erupt back into the crust as new magma.

If no one has ever drilled more than a few miles into the crust, how do we know about the mantle and core? The answer is seismic waves. (These will be more fully explained in the chapter on earthquakes.) Earthquakes create natural seismic waves. Underground explosions set off artificial ones. Seismic waves travel at different speeds through different kinds of material. Just as radar waves send back an echo blip every time they hit metal objects, seismic waves send back echoes when they reach a boundary between two different materials. Scientists watch the

FIGURE 1.4 • Holmes's Conveyor Belt

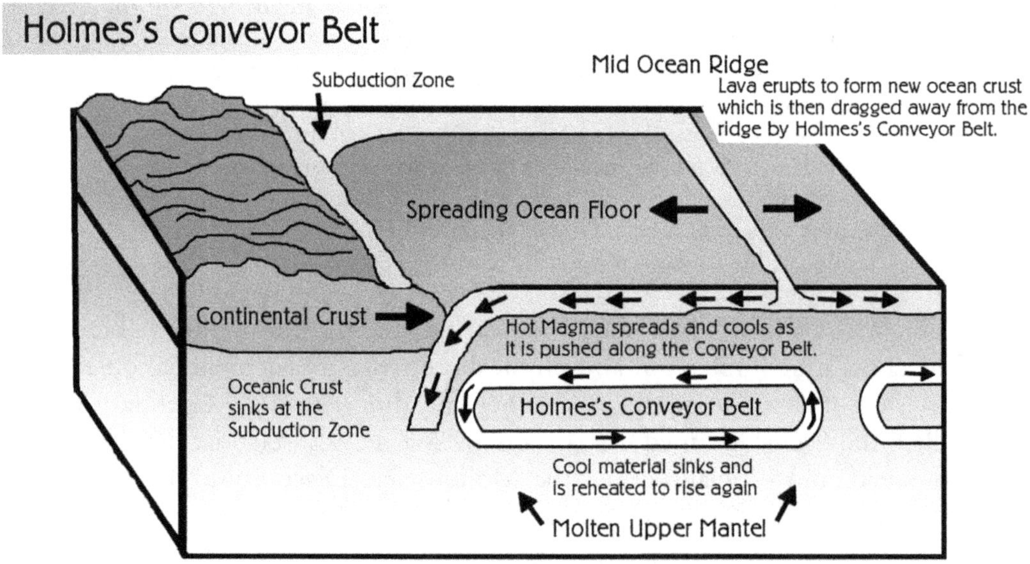

echo of these waves as they race through the mantle and core and reflect echoes back to listening stations around the world.

Allied countries built the first stations in this seismic net in the mid-1960s to enforce the Nuclear Test Ban Treaty with the Soviet Union. One hundred and twenty-five worldwide stations were dedicated to listening for the seismic shock waves of an underground nuclear test. Since the 1980s these stations have concentrated on using seismic waves to study the interior of the Earth.

> BELIEF: Changing land is a sign of a problem in the planet, a sign of something going wrong.

Just the opposite is true. A moving, churning crust and an ever-changing landscape are completely natural parts of the systems that makes our planet uniquely habitable. A dynamic volcano- and earthquake-riddled crust is part of the system that created an atmosphere and water as well as the plants and animal life. That same churning, fiery system is what concentrated the elements in the crust that we depend on for our existence.

If the internal churning of our planet should ever stop, if the crust stopped shifting, if volcanoes stopped pouring new crust to the surface, life would probably end on Earth. Earth would become a barren rock like Mars.

However, Earth formed at just the right distance from the Sun and developed at just the right temperature so that hydrogen and oxygen (water) collected in abundance in our Earth. Conditions in our forming planet were just right for the creation of the right mix of heavy, light, and radioactive elements to allow for the right amount of crystallization to form the core and mantle of a vibrant planet. Earth sat far enough away from the Sun to hold onto an atmosphere, but close enough to develop the life that enhanced the atmosphere and created a rich layer of soil (dirt) over the planet.

The belief is wrong. Conditions on Earth (including the constant and fractured changes to the land) were perfect for the development of advanced life forms like ours.

WONDERS OF THE LAND

— TOPICS FOR DISCUSSION AND PROJECTS

Here are activities, research topics, and discussion questions you can use to expand upon the key science concepts presented in this chapter.

Research and Discuss. Why do stars (the Sun) and planets (the Earth) get to be thousands of degrees hot in their cores when space and the material they were formed from are freezing cold? What produced enough heat inside the Earth to melt rocks? Does the same thing happen on Venus? Mars? Mercury? Why or why not?

An Activity. Make a cross section model of Earth the size of a basketball. Assume that the radius (distance from center to outer edge) is 4,000 miles. Research the size of the core, mantle, and crust. In your model, how big will each of these elements be? Can you find information to let you accurately size the inner core and the outer core? The solid and liquid parts of the mantle? How deep (in your model) will the Pacific Ocean be if its average depth is 15,500 feet (approximately 3 miles)? How tall will Mt. Everest (29,000 feet tall, or about 5.5 miles) have to be on your model? If continental crust varies from 17 to 50 miles thick, how thick will it be on your model?

Research and Discuss. Research the concepts of continental drift and plate tectonics. How are the continents moving? Where were they 65 million years ago? What did the world look like then? What will the world look like 65 million years from now if all plates continue to move as they now are?

An Activity. On a global map, mark the boundaries between all twenty major plates that form Earth's crust. Label each with its name, and show the direction and speed of its current movement. Draw red lines between colliding plates and green lines between plates that are moving apart. Compare your red and green lines with maps of global volcanoes, earthquakes, and mountain ranges. Why are they similar or dissimilar?

An Activity. Does land really change? Make a series of maps showing the changes in your local area over the past 100 years, 1,000 years, 50,000 years, and 500,000 years. How different was the area 1 million years ago? Guess at how this area will look in another million year.

Research and Discuss. Research modern scientists' beliefs about the origin of, and early period of, our planet. Where did the mass that constitutes our planet come from? How did it gather together? Why is Earth's core still molten? Where did the fire come from? When did Earth's atmosphere begin to form? When did the first water vapor erupt into

that fragile atmosphere? What did land look like for the first 2 billion years?

Include the following question in all your research: *How do we know?* No one has been deep inside the Earth. No one has seen it. How could anyone possibly know what it looks like now, much less what it looked like billions of YAG.

A Research Activity. Compare the continents. Compare their size, mountains, rivers, lakes, populations, deserts, and resources. Compare the history of their plate movements. Prepare a chart or diagram with your findings.

An Activity. Develop your own myth about the creation of land on Earth. In your myth who will create land? Why? What existed before land was created? How was the land created? What will make your story exciting? Answer the following questions about the character who creates land: What are his or her talents and abilities? What are his or her frailties and shortcomings? What is he or she afraid of? What does this character want? Is he or she struggling against anyone or anything? Who? Why?

SUGGESTED READING FOR STUDENTS

Ahrens, L. *Distribution of Elements in Our Planet.* New York: McGraw-Hill, 1995.

Ballard, Robert. *Exploring Our Living Planet.* Washington, DC: National Geographic Society, 1993.

Cattermole, Peter. *Encyclopedia of Earth and Other Planets.* Oxford: Andromeda, 1998.

Cole, Joanna. *The Magic School Bus Inside the Earth.* New York: Scholastic, 1999.

Deneke, Edward. *Let's Review Earth Science.* Hauppauge, NY: Barron's Educational Series, 2001.

Dixon, D. *The Planet Earth.* Chicago: World Book Encyclopedia of Science, 1999.

Erickson, Jon. *Plate Tectonics.* New York: Facts on File, 2001.

Gallant, Roy. *Dance of the Continents.* Salt Lake City, UT: Benchmark Books, 2000.

George, Linda. *Plate Tectonics.* New York: Thomson Gale, 2002.

Gibbons, Gail. *Planet Earth: Inside Out.* New York: William Morrow, 1998.

Gregory, K. J. *Earth's Natural Forces.* Oxford: Andromeda, 2000.

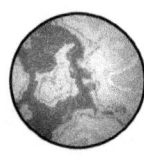

Jackson, Kay. *Plate Tectonics*. New York: Thomson Gale, 2005.

Meissner, Rolf. *The Little Book of Planet Earth*. New York: Copernicus Books, 1999.

Walker, Sally. *Inner Earth's Fire*. Minneapolis, MN: Carolrhoda Books, 1996.

Weiner, J. *Planet Earth*. New York: Bantam Books, 1996.

Willie, Peter. *The Way the Earth Works*. New York: Wiley, 1996.

── SUGGESTED READING FOR TEACHERS

Andel, T. van. *New Views of an Old Planet*. New York: Cambridge University Press, 2001.

Garner, H. *The Origins of Landscapes*. New York: Oxford University Press, 1994.

Keary, Philip. *Global Tectonics*. Malden, MA: Blackwell Science, 1996.

———. *An Introduction to Geophysical Exploration*. Malden, MA: Blackwell Science, Inc., 1995.

Lutgens, F. *Essentials of Geology*. London: Allen and Unwin, 2001.

Meissner, Rolf. *The Continental Crust*. San Diego, CA: Academic Press, 1996.

Montgomery, C. W. *Earth: Then and Now*. New York: William Brown Co., 2001.

Phinney, Robert, ed. *The History of Earth's Crust*. Princeton, NJ: Princeton University Press, 1993.

Press, Frank. *Earth*. New York: W. H. Freeman & Co., 1997.

Skinner, Brian. *The Dynamic Earth*. New York: John Wiley & Sons, 2000.

Wilson, J. *Continents Adrift and Continents Aground*. San Francisco: W. H. Freeman, 1996.

2 Volcanoes

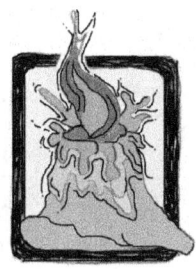

MYTHS ABOUT VOLCANOES

There are over 1,500 active volcanoes on Earth—rumbling, deadly volcanoes. Sixty of them are stuffed into the island chain of Japan alone. Kilauea volcano in Hawaii is currently the most active. The Earth's major volcanoes, among them Vesuvius (Italy), Mt. St. Helens (Washington), Kilauea (Hawaii), Mt. Fuji (Japan), Mt. Pinatubo (Philippians), Krakatoa (Indonesia), and Mt. Etna (Italy), are well know to most people.

Most likely there were many more active volcanoes in past eras than there are today. Early cultures had to deal with the constant threat of volcanic devastation. Prayers and sacrifices were offered to appease apparently angry fire gods. The name *volcano* comes from the Roman god of fire, Vulcan, and from the island of Vulcanus, where he had his giant forge for the gods.

The word volcano conjures images of massive explosions, streams of deadly fire, molten rock, giant plumes of gas and ash, and of the Earth literally ripping itself apart in fiery explosion. Whole mountains vaporize in a giant ball of ash and gas rising 5 or more miles into the air. Flows of unstoppable lava destroy everything in their path. Boiling flows of dust and ash bury whole towns in seconds. Like hurricanes, lightning, tornadoes, and earthquakes, volcanoes were experienced as frightening freak events that seemed to materialize unannounced and undeserved. Certainly, volcanoes are the most impressive, frightening, and unforgettable of all of nature's terrifying spectacles.

The notion that the Earth deep under our feet is not solid rock but molten fire seemed both unimaginable and terrifying to early cultures. Where does the fire to melt rocks and cause volcanoes come from? Why does it erupt onto the surface? Why are many volcanoes so explosive? Are volcanoes a sign of instability in our planet, a warning of ultimate disaster? Do they represent something going wrong in the Earth's system? Why do volcanoes happen where they happen? Do modern volcanoes relate to the fiery origins of the Earth? What do volcanoes tell us of Earth's history and physiology?

These questions have plagued humans for thousands of years and still engage the best research techniques and abilities of modern science.

How could early cultures explain such ferocious and unpredictable violence? A mountain sits quietly for hundreds of years and then explodes with no warning. How could mere humans make sense of such awe-inspiring and aweful upheavals? Humans needed to understand who (or what) was responsible for volcanoes and what caused that supernatural force to explode when and how it did. Such violence was the perfect subject for myths.

Most myths blame these frightening displays on an angry god or demon. Some myths explain them away as the result of underground metal forges for the gods (Vulcan, Odin, etc.). Some myths explain volcanoes as the result of brawls between gods representing different aspects of nature—thunder and lightning, for example. In a myth from the African nation of Madagascar, volcanic eruption represents fighting between Flames of the Sun and Thunder.

A Pacific Northwest myth uses a fight between two warring chiefs who can spit fire. In a Maori (New Zealand) myth, the spirit of Taranaki (now Mount Egmont) fought with the spirit of Ruapehu over the love of another volcano. The two warring spirits each swallowed and melted their own mountaintops and spit it at the other. The mountain they fought over fled out to sea to get away from both of them, and there she remains as an offshore island while the two rivals smolder and plot their revenge.

Pele, Hawaiian goddess of fire, is the most famous of the wide variety of worldwide fire gods. Her stories are usually stuffed with intrigue and drama mixed with big-budget-movie special effects. The myth that follows includes arrogant boasting, challenges, vicious competition, jealousy, and revenge. It also demonstrates and explains the capricious nature of volcanic eruptions.

"THE FIRE GODDESS,"
A MYTH FROM THE BIG ISLAND OF HAWAII

Once, long ago, it was a festival day on the Island of Kilauea (now called Hawaii). There was plenty of food to eat and music to sing. And there were games—ball games and races. Most exciting of all were the sledge (large wooden sleds) races down the long, grassy slopes of the mountain. Brave young men would carry their sledge high up the mountain, either sit or lie on their sledge, hold tight to the wooden rails, and shoot down the mountain so fast that they were a blur.

Kahawali, the young chief from the village of Puna, and his friend Laka were two of the sledge racers. They carried their sledges higher up the slope than any other racers and placed them on a tiny ledge near the summit. Far below the dancers and swimmers looked like the tiniest of dots.

"It's a long way down," said Kahawali. "Be careful or we'll be dashed to pieces on one of those big boulders in the middle of the valley."

Laka laughed, "Oh, I'll be careful, alright—careful to get to the bottom first!"

Both men dove onto their sledges and pushed off the ledge as a great crowd gathered below to watch them speed down the steep slopes.

But at that moment a tall woman covered in a flowing black hood and robe stepped from behind a bush and stood in their path. Her eyes seemed hard as lumps of coal. Both men stopped their sledges and stared at her with a deep shiver.

The woman gazed from Laka to Kahawali and then pointed at Kahawali. "You are the high-born one and the strongest," she said. "Will you match your strength and skill against mine?"

Kahawali stammered, "I am a chief and do not compete with women."

"Were you not about to race your sledges?" she scoffed.

"Yes."

"Then race against me," she commanded. "If you dare."

Now Kahawali was angry. No woman could talk to him that way. The woman turned her glare on Laka, snapped her fingers, and pointed at his sledge. At her command, Laka climbed off and handed her the rope.

Laka leaned close to his friend and whispered, "Be careful. This woman frightens me."

"No woman will beat the chief of Puna," Kahawali answered and turned to the woman. "It takes years of practice to learn how to race a sledge. This is the longest, steepest course I have ever seen and there are giant and deadly boulders in the path. You will never reach the finish line and should leave now while you still can."

The woman's eyes began to glow as she answered, "If your sledge can race as fast as your tongue, you might stand a chance."

She knelt on Laka's sledge holding tight to the steering peg and pushed herself down the steep slope with Kahawali following close behind. They plunged down ravines and gullies, soaring into the air over each bump and rise. Crashing through bushes and down the rough and rocky mountainside, the riders had to cling with all their might to the wooden handles.

The huge boulders that Kahawali had warned about loomed ahead. The sledges, now side by side, sped straight for them. The woman screamed and threw her body to the left, bringing her sledge almost to a standstill.

Kahawali laughed aloud as he swayed to the right. His sledge shot up the side of the valley, slowed slightly, and then roared like a diving hawk back down toward the thick trees and watchers below.

The villagers shouted and danced with joy seeing their chief leave the strange woman far behind and streak across the finish line. The woman stopped far short of the finish, picked up Laka's sledge, and started to climb back up the mountain.

Kahawali grabbed his sledge and ran after her. He caught her near the top of the sledge course. "I told you it was a dangerous course and that you would never finish."

"Not on this worthless sledge," she answered.

As they reached the top, Laka said, "Now it's my turn. I'll show you what real speed looks like!"

The woman said, "We will race again, Kahawali. But this time I will use your sledge and you will use Laka's. Then I'll show you who is the better racer."

Again Kahawali grew angry. He didn't want to keep racing with this strange woman. "Come on, Laka. Ignore her," he ordered and jumped onto his sledge. Laka dove onto his and the two men sped off down the mountainside ignoring the cries of the woman.

The woman was furious. Her coal-black eyes began to glow the red-yellow of bubbling lava. "Fools!" she shouted. "Don't you know who I am?"

The woman's eyes glowed like burning embers radiating heat that withered nearby bushes and trees. She stomped her foot and a great gash opened along the mountainside. At her command, boiling lava gushed out, spurting high into the cloudless sky. "I am Pele, the goddess of fire and volcanoes, and you shall pay for ignoring me!"

Steam and lava swirled around Pele and raced down the mountain ever gaining on Kahawali and Laka, who now sped down the steep slope in terror.

The two men reached the bottom but no one watched their race. Every person stood frozen with awe and fear watching the roaring river of fire thunder down the slope burning trees, grass, huts, and everything else that stood in its way. Rocks hissed and exploded from the heat. Trees burst into flames like kindling.

The people screamed and ran. But the lava flowed faster. One by one Pele's river of fire caught and killed each of the people—except for Kahawali, the fastest runner of all.

Kahawali raced on, swift as the wind. But the churning lava raced ever closer and closer. He reached his house and paused only long enough to snatch up a long, broad spear. Then he raced on.

Kahawali came to a great chasm in the rocks. It was too wide for him to jump. He couldn't turn back for the lava was right behind him. Kahawali laid his long spear across the chasm and crossed by tightrope walking across the sturdy shaft.

With a roar, a crackle of flames, and a great billow of steam, the lava poured over the lip of the chasm and down to the churning ocean below.

When the steam was blown aside by the wind, Pele saw that Kahawali had escaped. Her fury rose to explosive rage. Again she stamped her foot. New jets of lava flared into the sky and hurled giant boulders at the fleeing chief.

Kahawali leapt into a canoe and paddled furiously to escape as the rocks crashed down around him sending geysers of water into the air.

Soon Kahawali was far out to sea and beyond the reach of the angry goddess. As he paddled, his beloved island of Kilauea slowly disappeared beneath the horizon and the towering peaks of Maui rose before him.

Kahawali made a new home for himself there, far away from the island he loved with all his heart. But just as he never forgot his island of Kilauea, so, too, Pele never forgot Kahawali. Every time Kahawali paddled his canoe toward Kilauea, hoping to return, Pele would stomp her foot and the volcano would explode into a fiery eruption. Lava and rocks would burst from the mountainside and race in glowing rivers toward the sea to drive him away.

And to this very day, Pele sits brooding on her mountainside waiting for Kahawali to return and periodically stomps her foot just to show how angry she is that he refused her a second sledge race.

THE SCIENCE OF VOLCANOES

The following beliefs are either directly stated or strongly implied in the presented myth. Here is what modern science knows about the aspects of volcanoes explained by each belief.

BELIEF: The heat that creates volcanoes comes from some outside source (a god) rather than from the Earth itself.

In the myth, Kilauea crater is quiet and cool until Pele, goddess of fire, stomps her foot and turns it into raging fountains of fiery lava. If not from a god, then where does the heat come from that melts rock and creates volcanoes?

We see only the tissue-thin outer surface of our planet and so forget that what's normal on our planet's outside does not represent what happens on the inside. As we saw in the past chapter, the Earth's core is a heat engine. Nuclear decay of radioactive elements produces enormous amounts of heat (as it does in a nuclear reactor). Gravity's compression force also produces heat by squeezing the molecules and atoms of the core ever tighter. By 5 billion YAG, the core of our planet grew hot enough to melt iron and most other elements (2,500°C or 4,530°F). By 4.5 billion YAG, the core temperatures topped 4,000°C (7,230°F). In just 2 billion years, the Earth had progressed from freezing cold space dust to a 4,000°C churning inferno.

Solids (rocks) expand when heated just as gas does. As they expand they become lighter and rise. In the liquid and semi-liquid outer core and mantle, this super-hot material rose, cooled, and then settled back toward the core. This flowing motion started giant currents away from, and then back toward, the core. The same vertical currents happen when you heat any liquid on the stove. Liquid at the bottom of the pan heats, expands, and then rises toward the top. There, it glides across the surface, cools, condenses (making it heavier), and so sinks back toward the bottom. Gravity pulls cooler, denser material down. Heat expands it and pushes it back up.

In the Earth's mantle, these currents stir huge plumes of molten rock outward and cooler plumes back toward the core. This process moves heat toward the outer layer. But Earth's outer edge (the crust) is cooled by space and has become solid. The rising heat is trapped below the crust, trying to escape. Wherever there is a weak spot in the crust (especially along plate boundaries) hot magma from the mantle rises forming magma pockets under the surface. These magma pockets erupt onto the crust's surface as volcanoes.

The Earth is like a giant furnace that stretches from the almost 5,000°C (9,000°F) solid core out to gushing volcanoes, hissing steam vents, geysers, and bubbling mud pots dotted across the surface and that vent Earth's excess heat out to space. This same kind of planetary furnace also has occurred in the other terrestrial planets and on several moons. The process is still happening on Earth, on Venus, and on Jupiter's moon Io.

The myth is wrong: the heat to power volcanoes doesn't come from some outside source (like a god). It comes from deep within the fiery furnace of the planet's core.

> BELIEF: Volcanoes aren't important to the Earth's crust.

The myth makes volcanoes sound like something for a god's trivial revenge and of little importance to the Earth's surface. Is that true? Are volcanoes important to the formation, history, and current structure of the land?

There are over 1,500 active volcanoes on Earth. Eighty-three of them erupted during the last century. The biggest volcano in the solar system is Olympus Mons on Mars. It rises 17 miles (27 km) high and 450 miles (700 km) wide. It's over three times as high as Mount Everest, Earth's tallest mountain. On average, one volcano erupts on Earth every year. Many volcanoes are small and harmless. Some are giant killers. Some, like the Kilauea volcano in Hawaii, erupt regularly. Many lie dormant for hundreds—even thousands—of years before blasting back to life.

What do volcanoes contribute to the Earth's crust? Simple. Almost everything. Virtually all of Earth's crust and almost all of Earth's water, plus virtually Earth's entire atmosphere, reached the surface through volcanic eruptions. Volcanoes are how our planet naturally creates new crust and brings new gases to the surface. Volcanoes are how the Earth gives off excess heat to space and maintains the proper core and mantle temperatures.

Volcanoes create new land—and not just in the distant past. They still do so today. In 1963 the island of Surtsey was created off the coast of Iceland by an undersea volcanic eruption. The Hawaiian Islands are all volcanic islands. A new island in the Hawaiian chain is currently forming and is close to breaking above sea level off the southeast side of Hawaii's Big Island.

Volcanoes also deliver many commercially important elements and minerals to the surface for us to mine and use. The dirt around volcanoes is the richest and most fertile soil in the world. The belief is wrong. Volcanoes play a central and indispensable part in the process that makes our planet work.

BELIEF: Gods create volcanoes and geysers.

Natural, essential processes of the Earth create volcanoes. Continental drift and plate tectonics were described earlier. All of Earth's crustal plates are in continual motion. Below the plates lies a seething sphere of molten magma—always pushing outward, wanting to escape higher.

Cracks, fissures, gaps, or joints in the crust form weak spots that the magma pushes through to reach the surface. The word *magma* literally means "melted rock." Magma is characterized by three properties: its temperature, the amount of trapped gas it holds, and its SiO_2 (silicon dioxide) content. Magma that flows across the surface is called lava.

The amount of SiO_2 in magma determines how willing the magma is to flow. There is a term, *viscosity*, that indicates a substance's willingness to flow. The higher the viscosity of a substance, the stickier it is and the less willing it is to flow. The lower the viscosity, the more easily and rapidly it will flow. Water has a low viscosity. It flows readily. Cold molasses and sticky bread dough have high viscosities. Motor oil is rated by its viscosity.

Magma with more SiO_2 has a higher viscosity. SiO_2 easily forms crystal fragments that stick to rock walls like gluey sludge. It is harder for the forces of the Earth to push this magma up through the crust. Low SiO_2 (low viscosity) magma tends to flow faster and more smoothly up through fissures and vents in the crust and out across the land.

As magma rises through the lithosphere, two things happen. First, it begins to cool. Second, pressure on that magma is decreased. As magma cools, it begins to solidify, forming tiny crystals within the molten mass. This increases viscosity. The farther magma has to travel through the crust to reach the surface, the cooler it becomes and the higher its viscosity.

As pressure is decreased, gases trapped inside the magma (nitrogen, carbon dioxide, sulfur, hydrogen, etc.) tend to separate from the magma and form bubbles—just as happens when you open a carbonated soda. This gas is buoyant and exerts tremendous upward pressure on the rocks above. If enough gas builds up before the magma reaches the surface, the pressure can literally rip a mountain apart in an explosive volcanic eruption.

Everywhere under the crust hot magma pushes upward searching for weak spots. What makes a spot in the crust weak? Primarily weak spots occur at the boundaries between plates in the crust. Since all Earth's plates are moving, these boundaries are also changing as the plates either collide, scrape past each other, or pull apart (separate). Each type of boundary creates different types of volcanic action.

Separation

Some plates are pulling apart. Examples include the North American plate pulling away from the Eurasian plate, the South American and African pulling away from each other, and the Arabian and African plates pulling away from each other as they widen the Red Sea.

When two plates pull apart along an undersea boundary, the ocean floor spreads from that plate boundary. A rift valley forms along the seam between the two plates. The seam becomes a thinner, weaker line in the crust. Magma pushes up from the mantle, bulging the crust into a mid-oceanic ridge along the boundary between the two plates. Lava erupts along this seam to fill the growing gap in the crust. These under-the-ocean plate separations produce massive amounts of low SiO_2 basalt rock (a kind of volcanic rock described in Chapter 3) for new crust. Plate separations are characterized by chains of small volcanoes that tend to be nonexplosive.

Because the lava has had to push up through only a thin crust, it hasn't cooled off and arrives at the ocean floor hot and molten. It spreads easily down the slopes of the mid-ocean ridge and fills in the crust as the plates move apart. Few earthquakes happen along this type of plate boundary.

Twenty million YAG, the North American plate began to split in two. The western half began to pull away. Like pulling a lump of taffy apart, the middle sagged into a wide rift valley, then, 4 or 5 million years later, the separation stopped. The plate resolidified as a single plate. The depression, stretching south from Minnesota, never stretched low enough to dip below sea level and start a new sea. Over time, sediment filled in the rift valley. But periodic earthquakes still rumble through the region as a reminder of the time when, long before the Civil War, North America wanted to divide.

Collision

Sometimes plates collide, smashing headlong into each other. This is when Mother Nature puts on her grandest and most explosive fireworks show.

FIGURE 2.1 • Active Volcanoes

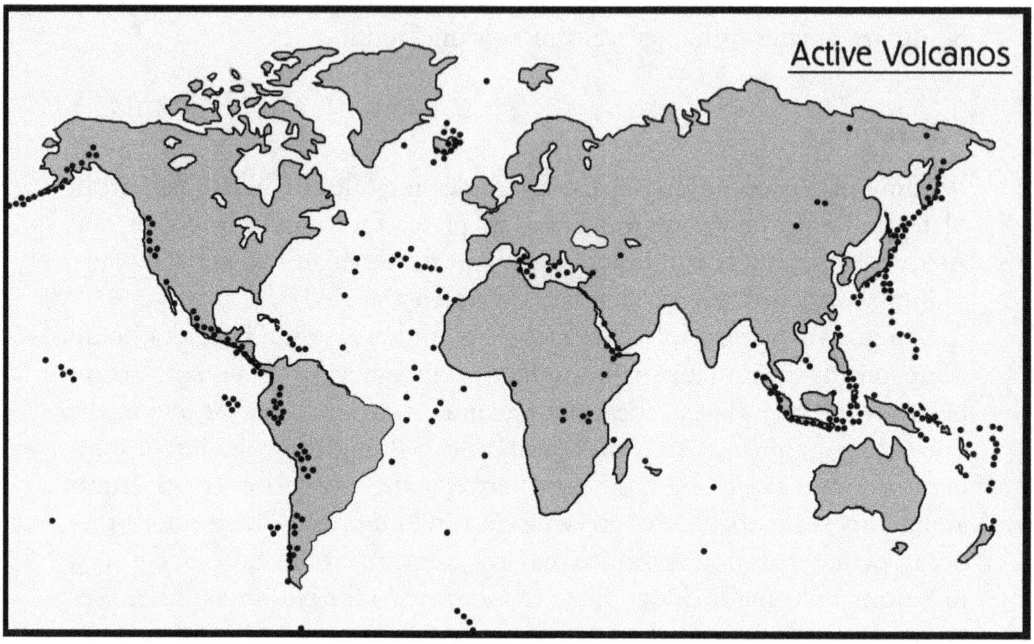

Oceanic vs. Continental

When oceanic crust collides with continental crust, the oceanic crust is pushed down (it's more dense) and the continental crust rides up and over it. It's like a sports car colliding with an eighteen-wheeler. The sports car will always wind up on the bottom with the eighteen-wheeler on top.

Where the oceanic plate is pushed down toward the mantle (see Figure 1.2), it is said to be *subducted*. Earthquakes abound along this *subduction zone*. The continental crust buckles into a mountain range as it lifts over the oceanic plate. Volcanoes also abound along this boundary. The dense ocean crust is melted as it re-enters the mantle and turns back into magma. As it melts, it expands, becomes buoyant, and surges up through the thick, fractured continental crust. As it slowly rises, this magma cools and viscosity increases. The magma also releases gas as the pressure rapidly decreases. This gas buildup tends to turn these volcanoes into explosive eruptions when the magma finally reaches the mountainstops.

Seventy percent of the Earth's active volcanoes line the fringes of the Pacific Ocean along plate collisions involving a subduction zone (see Figure 2.1 for the locations of active volcanoes). This area is often called "The Ring of Fire." Mt. St. Helens, Mt. Pinatubo, Mt. Fuji, and Krakatoa are a few examples of the deadly, exploding volcanoes that ring the

Pacific Ocean where oceanic plates are being subducted under continental plates as the Pacific slowly shrinks to make room on the Earth's surface for the growing Atlantic Ocean and Red Sea. These volcanoes belch plumes of ash and dust into the upper atmosphere as they explode in classic eruptions. Often entire mountaintops—millions of tons of dirt and rock—vanish into a plume of ash when these monsters erupt.

Continental vs. Continental

If two continental plates collide (India slamming north into Eurasia, for example), they create a continental fender bender. Neither plate is subducted. They mash and crumple into each other. The result is jagged mountain ranges lifted high into the sky. The Alps and Himalayas were created this way. Earthquakes abound along this collision front, but there is little volcanic action.

Scraping

Some plates don't hit head on. They strike in a glancing blow. Partly they scrape past each other. Partly they collide. This is happening along the west coast of the United States and Canada as the North American plate scrapes past several small oceanic plates in the Pacific Ocean. Scraping produces earthquakes—lots of earthquakes—and buckling as the plates grind past each other. The collision subducts the oceanic plates and creates the Sierra and Cascade mountain ranges and the line of volcanoes that dot their way up these rugged chains.

Hot Spots

Volcanoes don't happen only along plate boundaries. Sometimes a volcano pops up in the middle of one of the Earth's plates. These volcanoes seem to be random and to support the idea that there is no logic or reason to volcanoes. El Chichón in Mexico is such a volcano. The Hawaiian Islands are another.

These volcanoes form over what are called *hot spots*. What are hot spots? They are weak points—small thin spots—in the Earth's crust laced with wide fissures and cracks through which magma can rapidly rise. Large magma chambers build up in the lower crust under these hot spots. From there it's easy for magma to push up to the surface. Most hot spots lie under thin oceanic crustal plates.

Lava tends to arrive at the surface hot and with low viscosity. The lava flows easily down the slopes of these volcanoes. Most commonly, only small amounts of gas spew out of oceanic hot spot volcanoes (as is true in Hawaii), since the magma rises quickly through the crust.

Once a hot spot forms, the volcano over it typically lasts for a million years or so before the hot spot fades. (The Hawaiian hot spot is an exception that has been active for over 100 million years.) Some volcanoes erupt frequently over that period. Some sit dormant for thousands of years and then erupt with no warning. Some rumble and shake (earthquakes) for months, burp a little steam and ash, but never really erupt.

Types of Volcanoes

I have just described the places where volcanoes tend to occur (plate boundaries and hot spots). Are all volcanoes the same once they exist and erupt? No. The hills and mountains that form around volcanoes can be grouped into three types: turtle (shield) volcanoes, teapot (composite) volcanoes, and soufflé (caldera) volcanoes (see Figure 2.2).

Turtle Volcanoes

Picture the rounded sloping shell of a turtle. Turtles are gentle. Turtles are playful. If that turtle were a volcano, magma would rise to the surface from magma chambers just underneath the shell and would spread as low viscosity lava evenly over the gently sloping dome formed by previous eruptions. Scientists call these *shield* (or basaltic shield) volcanoes. They mostly occur along mid-ocean ridges where plates are separating and over oceanic hot spots. Hawaii, the Galapagos Islands, the mid-Atlantic ridge, and Iceland are all turtle shell volcanoes. In this sense, the myth presented in Chapter 1 was right. Much of the Earth's crust is built over turtle shell volcanoes, as if the land were resting on a turtle's back.

The magma that rises into this type of volcano tends to have low (less than 50%) SiO_2 content and low viscosity. Because it rises through weak spots in the Earth's crust, it rises quickly from magma chambers through wide fissures and feeder pipes to the surface. Turtle shell volcanoes produce hot, low viscosity lava that flows out with minimal explosion, much like a mountain spring. These volcanoes create almost entirely basalt rock. Commonly, the lava emerges from fissures and cracks in the side of the volcanic mountain instead of emerging from the central cone in the mountain's top.

The gas held in this type of lava (mostly waver vapor, carbon dioxide, and sulfur) hasn't had time to come out of solution and form gas bubbles by the time the magma reaches the surface. The gas tends to pass

FIGURE 2.2 • The Three Types of Volcanoes

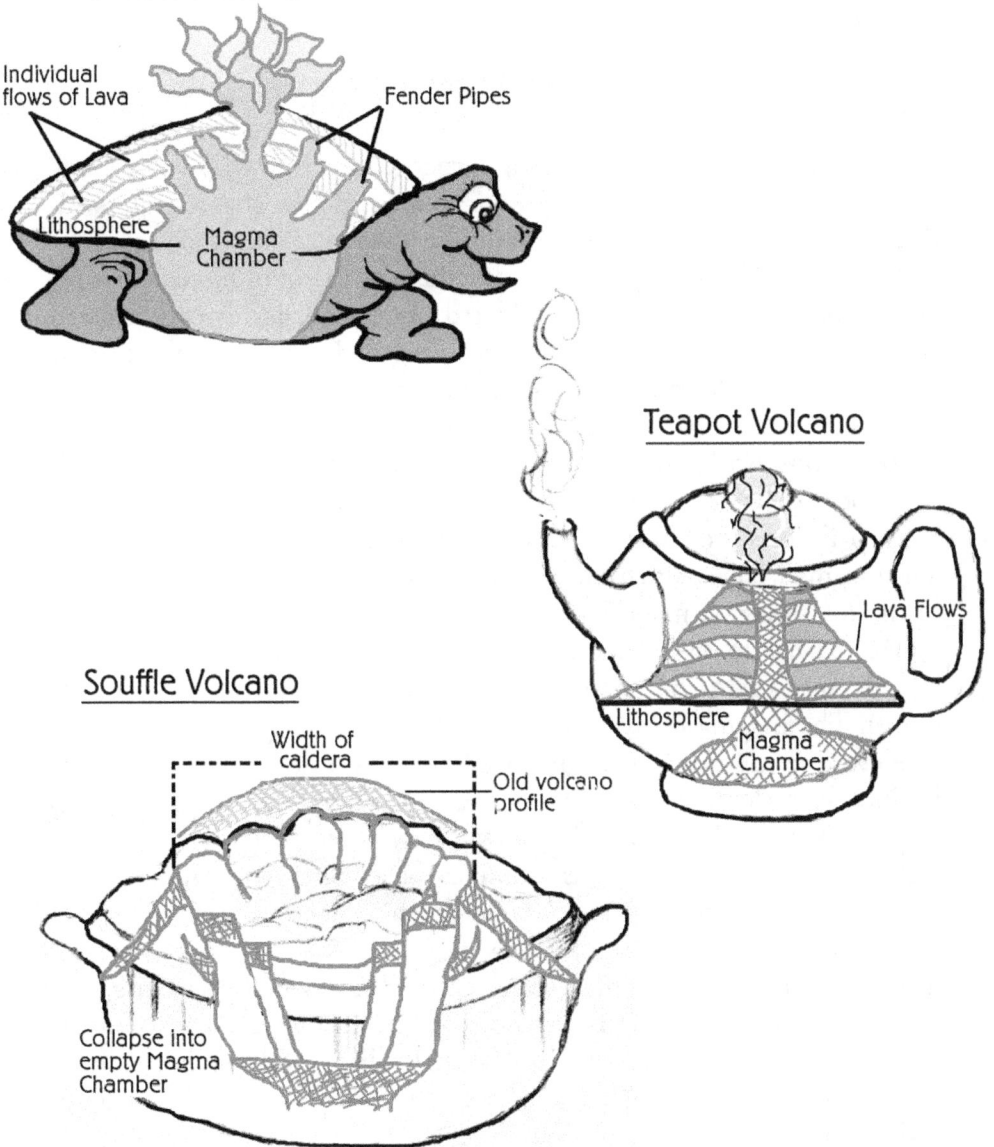

out of the lava slowly after it is cooling on the surface and tends to leave porous rocks with Swiss cheese–like holes behind.

Because they don't explode, turtle shell volcanoes often build up, lava layer by lava layer, into some of the world's tallest mountains. Mauna Loa (on the island of Hawaii), for example, rises 30,000 feet from its base on the floor of the Pacific Ocean, making it taller than Mt. Everest. (Only the top 13,685 feet rises above sea level.) It took thousands of eruptions over a million years to build up that giant volcanic shield one layer of lava at a time.

Teapot Volcanoes

Picture a teapot on the stove with burner roaring below. Slowly the pot's water begins to boil. Gas (steam) pressure builds, and the pot's warning whistle blasts. Teapot volcanoes tend to steam, whistle, and blow their tops a lot.

Teapot volcanoes happen on land, either over a colliding plate boundary where one plate is being subducted under another or over isolated, land-based hot spots. Teapot volcanoes are called *composite* volcanoes because lava both flows out of side fissures and is blown out of the volcano's top. Most of the eruption of a teapot volcano comes out of the central spout as the volcano blows vertically into the sky.

Teapot volcanoes often come in chains (like those around the Pacific Ring of Fire) as they mark the long boundaries between colliding plates. The magma in these situations tends to contain more SiO_2 (60% or more of the total magma mass).

Magma has to rise much farther through thick and fractured continental crust to reach the surface of a teapot volcano. The trip takes longer. The magma cools as it rises through low temperature, low pressure crust. Some minerals begin to solidify into minute crystals. Viscosity increases, slowing the magma's rate of rise. Pressure decreases as the magma rises and, because it rises slowly, gases have plenty of time to separate from the magma and form bubbles—even large pockets of gas. Gas pressure builds as the magma struggles inch-by-inch upward.

Seismic activity usually increases near the volcano as the gas and magma rumble upward. Far more often than not, gas pressure triggers a vertical explosion that starts the flow of lava. Those explosions can be huge (as with Mt. St. Helens in 1980). It's like suddenly popping the cap off of a warm and well-shaken bottle of soda—only multiplied several hundreds of millions of times bigger.

If the magma's viscosity rises too high, it will stall on its upward journey, sticking like almost-firm concrete to the sides of the fissures and feeder pipes it is following. The flow of magma grinds to a halt like blood trying to pass through a clogged artery. A plug of solidified magma forms inside the mountain.

If that magma contained little water vapor and other gases, the volcano will never erupt. This central plug often long outlives the rock layers around it that slowly weather away, leaving the exposed plug standing alone. Ship Rock in New Mexico and the Devil's Tower in Wyoming are excellent examples of such ancient volcanic plugs.

Mount Pinatubo, Mt. St. Helens, Mt. Fuji, Vesuvius, Hekla, and Queen Maries Peak (in South America) are all teapot volcanoes located over colliding plate boundaries. A few teapots also occur over terrestrial hot spots.

Teapot volcanoes rarely reach the impressive height of a turtle shell volcano because teapots tend to blow their tops off when they erupt. (Mt. St. Helens lost the top 1,500 feet of the mountain during the 1980 eruption.) Teapot eruptions often send ash, smoke, and dust plumes billowing 5 or more miles into the sky—often a half-mile thick. Ash cover darkens the sky. Ash rains down thick enough to clog and stall car motors. Teapots often dozens of square miles with an ash layer thick enough for people to have to shovel it up like a heavy snowfall.

But teapot volcanoes aren't through with the grand show yet. Often the scalding steam and hot gas turn the mountain's snow and ice into water in a flash, triggering landslides and deadlier mud slides. Walls of mud and debris rocket down slopes at speeds most cars couldn't outrun.

Soufflé Volcanoes

Picture a soufflé in the oven rising fluffy light and golden brown. Just as you gingerly ease it out of the oven, someone dashes through and slams a door. With a deep sigh, all the hot air trapped in your soufflé hisses out the top and escapes. The vibration collapses your delicate soufflé. The center fizzles and collapses, leaving a ring with a deeply sunken middle where once stood a glorious, domed dinner masterpiece. That's what happens in a soufflé volcano—but only after its gigantic explosive eruption.

Soufflé volcanoes are actually the stickiest, nastiest, gassiest of the lot. The recipe for these soufflés calls for high SiO_2, high viscosity magma that is super-saturated with gas. Because of the high viscosity, gas has plenty of time to build the necessary pressure for earth-shattering explosions. These volcanoes are found in the same areas where teapot volcanoes exist. Soufflés, however, contain more gas, more SiO_2, and higher viscosity, than normal teapots.

Soufflé eruptions are earth-shattering, often exceeding the explosive power of many nuclear bombs. Thick plumes containing millions of tons of ash and dust can be shot as high as 60 miles into the upper atmosphere, where particles linger for years and drift back to cover the entire planet in their ash. Some of the most beautiful, intense sunsets ever seen occur in the months and years following a soufflé eruption. The increased ash in the upper atmosphere reflects more of the deep reds and oranges that produce vivid sunset colors.

Soufflé volcanoes erupt so much rock and lava so fast that they leave giant, empty magma chambers beneath the volcano with insufficient rock above to support the roof of these gaping caverns. The rocks that form the top of the volcano collapse into this giant hole that geologists call a *caldera*.

Typically, calderas are steep-walled, circular depressions usually a kilometer or more in diameter. Crater Lake (Oregon) is a collapsed soufflé volcano whose caldera stretches 6 miles across and over 1,200 feet deep. (Most of that depth is now under the water of the lake.) However, by soufflé standards, that's almost puny. Yellowstone Valley in Wyoming (28 × 46 miles) and Long Valley in eastern California (25 × 12 miles) are extremely big soufflé volcano calderas. The Long Valley caldera sank over a mile deep after its explosive eruption 700,000 YAG.

Nature hath no furry like a soufflé volcano. First, these volcanoes are often hidden from view because they blow themselves away with each eruption. A few thousand years later there exists little or no volcanic mountain, exposed lava flow, or other volcanic clues for anyone to identify. Soufflés sit quietly until—blamo!—the Earth cracks open and all hell breaks loose in a total surprise. The Yellowstone eruption (600,000 YAG) showered ash as thick as a Big Mac 1,400 miles away in Texas. When the island of Krakatoa (Indonesia) blew itself up (1883), over a foot of ash landed like a blizzard 80 miles away.

Soufflés often begin with a swarm of violent earthquakes that crack open the ground like a watermelon dropped out the window. Soufflés also generate their share of landslides and mudslides. Forests are incinerated in giant fireballs. More deadly, however, these volcanoes typically produce *pyroclastic flows*—dense clouds of boiling, super-hot gas, ash, and semi-melted rock that can flow along the ground at up to 400 mph. The word *pyroclastic* comes from the Greek words meaning "hot or fire" and "broken." Pyroclastic flows are made of hot, broken fragments.

Pyroclastic flows can sweep across the ground for 150 miles from the volcanic site, burying and torching everything (and everyone) that stands in their path. When Vesuvius had its famed eruption, pyroclastic flow swept down its slopes with 1,000°C (1,830°F) of lung-searing, flesh-burning ash and gas destroying whole cities that lay buried in pyroclastic sediment until they have been slowly excavated from the thick ash and mud in recent years.

If these terrors are not enough, soufflés often create tremors strong enough to trigger tsunamis, the silent killers that race across oceans at speeds of up to 600 mph and pounce with no warning on distant coastal populations. Nature spares nothing when she decides to serve up a soufflé volcano.

Geysers

Are geysers different than volcanoes? The answer is yes and no. No magma reaches the surface in a geyser. However, magma chambers trapped in the crust heat the near-surface rocks enough so that they will boil groundwater that trickles over them. This steam surges through fissures, fractures, and cracks to the surface as a geyser. Some geysers spew steam continuously. Some do it periodically (like Old Faithful Geyser in Yellowstone Park, Wyoming) taking a fixed amount of time to draw in and heat enough water to send another burst of steam hissing toward the surface. Some geysers bubble through swampy mud pots that seem to boil like thick chocolate oatmeal on the stove as the steam swirls and mud plops.

The belief is wrong. Volcanoes and geysers are not created by some external force such as a god. Very natural and understandable forces and processes within the Earth create volcanoes and geysers.

BELIEF: Volcanoes are a sign of something going wrong in the Earth. They are abnormal occurrences, something out of balance.

As we have seen, volcanoes are a normal and essential part of the successful operation of our planet. Volcanoes release heat from the mantle. They create new crust to replace crust that has been pulled back down into the mantle and maintain the crustal plates that cover the Earth. They replenish surface water and supply many of the gases of our atmosphere. They bring essential elements and minerals to the surface. Volcanoes maintain Earth's natural balance.

However, volcanoes are still unpredictable. The problem is that we humans need more time precision for our predictions than nature can provide. For example, let's say that you get up around 7:00 A.M. every morning. If you only needed to measure time to the nearest hour, you could accurately predict that you will get up at 7:00 tomorrow morning. Your time of rising is predictable. However, if you needed to predict when you'll get up to the nearest second, you couldn't do it. On that scale the actual time that you get out of bed varies too much from day to day to be predictable.

In the same way, nature works on a time scale of hundreds of thousands of years or millions of years. If we only needed to predict volcanoes to the nearest 10,000 years, we could, and would say that volcanoes are predictable. But we humans want prediction on a time scale of days and hours (or even years). This is like trying to predict to the nearest second when you'll get up tomorrow. You can't be that accurate.

There is, however, considerable worldwide effort being made to monitor and predict volcanoes. Scientists have installed seismometers in the craters and along the slopes of major volcanoes to detect the swarms of tiny earthquakes that could signal an upcoming eruption. Scientists use sensitive laser systems to detect even the slightest bulging of volcanic mountains that would indicate a buildup in the magma chambers below. Satellites shoot infrared film of volcanoes to detect any temperature change in the volcanoes' dirt and rock. Scientists still can't predict exactly when a volcano will erupt, but they can provide much improved warning of a possible or probable eruption.

BELIEF: Volcanoes are the source of Earth's rocks.

The three main types of rock and their characteristics are described in Chapter 3. One of the three types of rock—igneous rocks—comes from volcanoes. However, that doesn't mean that volcanoes contribute only one third of the Earth's rock.

Sedimentary rocks are created after some other rock is worn and weathered down. Metamorphic rocks are created when heat and pressure change the chemical and physical properties of some other rock. Both of these types of rocks require that some rock already exist to be changed into either sedimentary or metamorphic rock.

Magma, the source of all of Earth's crust, reaches the surface through volcanoes. Originally, then, all of Earth's crust had to come from volcanoes and had to have been igneous rock. Over time these rocks weathered and, grain by grain, became sedimentary rock. Some of the sedimentary rock folded and lifted. Some sank back into the mantle. Some was transformed by heat and pressure into different chemical structures and became metamorphic rock.

The belief is right—sort of. Magma from the Earth's mantle is the *original* source of all rock. That magma reached the surface through volcanoes. Volcanoes create igneous rock. Sedimentary and metamorphic rocks do not come directly from volcanoes. But in this version of which-came-first-the-chicken-or-the-egg, the answer is clear. Volcanic igneous rocks came first. Sedimentary and metamorphic rocks came second.

BELIEF: Volcanoes are dangerous and evil, intent on destroying humanity.

In the myth, Pele orders a volcano to destroy all the people (and especially Kahawali). Is it possible for volcanoes to target humans?

Volcanoes can be as dangerous as any of nature's furies. However, rather than volcanoes being out to destroy humanity, humans seems determined to put themselves in harms way by living and working in the deadly shadow of dangerous volcanoes.

Why do we do it? Volcanoes are covered with rich soils that grow bountiful crops and with many of the elements and minerals modern industry and commerce find most valuable. Besides, graceful volcanic mountains (Mt. Fuji, Mt. Shasta, Mt. Pinatubo, etc.) are beautiful to look at. That is, until they erupt.

Not all volcanoes are truly dangerous. Turtle shell volcanoes are relatively safe. Although their lava flows can and do destroy property, they are easy to outrun (contrary to what was said in the story) and so rarely claim any lives. Those who do die from turtle shell volcanoes are more likely to die through carelessness than through the volcano's viciousness.

However, majestic teapot and those often-disguised soufflé volcanoes create some of the world's greatest disasters. Examples will help.

El Chichón, an unimpressive soufflé volcano located over a previously unknown hot spot hundreds of miles from the nearest plate boundary, is tucked into a remote section of Mexico. El Chichón's cone-shaped mountain rose only 1,260 meters (4,000 feet). Before its 1982 eruption, it lay dormant for over 1,000 years.

On March 28 of that year, a mild earthquake was followed by a violent explosion that ejected a column of ash and smoke 11 miles into the sky. A few deaths resulted. The few people who fled soon returned in the calm and quiet of the next few days.

On April 3, seismographs recorded over 500 tremors that built in intensity until a powerful blast shook the region at 7:32 that evening. Many people ran outside but then returned to their houses as the tremors quickly tapered off.

At 5:20 the next morning the major blast erupted. It blew out the core of the volcano and most of the mountain as easily as a champagne bottle blows out a loosened cork and shot 500 million metric tons of ash 60 miles into the upper atmosphere. The 12 million tons of ash that lingered in the upper atmosphere cut down incoming solar radiation enough to affect worldwide weather patterns. Five years later satellites could record that this ash cloud still blocked and reduced incoming sunlight to Earth.

The explosion caused hundreds of instant deaths from flaming debris and ejected rocks that whistled to Earth as fast and deadly as glowing solid shot from a Napoleonic canon. If it had happened in a more heavily populated area, that explosion would have killed tens of thousands. The high sulfur content of the ejected gases formed sulfuric acid in droplet form that rained down for 50 miles around the volcano killing whole forests and poisoning lakes and streams.

And then, as if content, El Chichón went quietly back to sleep as if nothing more serious than a disturbing dry cough had happened.

As of 1990, Mt. Pinatubo on the Philippine Island of Luzon had stood quietly for over 600 years. However, steam venting from several fissures on the mountain's flanks spurred scientists to set up detailed monitoring equipment. Four days before Pinatubo exploded in 1991, they knew the mountain was set to erupt and evacuated 200,000 people out of the danger zone.

Beginning in late June and continuing for almost a month, Pinatubo blew. The initial explosive eruption lasted 20 hours. A series of massive explosions deep inside the volcano sent billowing clouds mushrooming high into the atmosphere. Day turned dark as night for the Philippine population. Hot ash rained down over a wide area, starting countless fires—many of which were snuffed out by the thick layer of ash that fell blizzard-thick across the island. Runways on the United States' Clark Air Base were quickly clogged with several feet of ash. The base declared whiteout conditions, zero visibility, and had to close.

Pyroclastic flows raced down two slopes of Pinatubo, flattening trees and several villages. In minutes they destroyed 42,000 houses and 100,000 acres of crops. Even with all the warnings and precautions, almost 1,000 people died from the eruption that first day.

But the effects of Pinatubo's blast traveled far beyond the Philippine Islands. Astronauts in space said they had never seen the Earth appear so hazy. Within weeks, a thin ash cloud encircled the Earth. During the next two years, average temperatures worldwide fell almost two degrees below normal.

When Krakatoa (actually Krakatau, a tiny island between Java and Sumatra in the South Pacific) blew itself up in 1883 in the biggest volcanic explosion ever recorded, it was not the first time this volcano had thundered to life. A similar explosion of this soufflé volcano in A.D. 416 left a gaping caldera over 5 miles wide.

Then on August 27, 1883, Krakatoa's cataclysmic explosion rocked the world. The thunder of this explosion was heard almost 4,000 miles away! Thick ash fell 3,500 miles away. The collapse of the caldera created a tsunami. This monster wave towered almost 450 feet high as it funneled through the narrow Sunda Straight. It regularly reached heights of 150 feet as it slammed across shorelines hundreds of miles away. A Dutch cargo ship was tossed half a mile inland. The tsunami destroyed almost 200 coastal villages and all inhabitants. That wave was the only tsunami wave to literally travel around the world. Two days after the explosion, it raised sea levels in the English Channel (15,000 sea miles away) by 3 to 5 inches.

The island of Krakatoa virtually vanished below the waves, having blown itself out of existence. Ash and pumice fell so hard and fast from this explosion that it formed a carpet on the ocean thick enough for a man to walk across. Many harbors were closed because they were clogged with mounds of floating pumice. Krakatoa's ash created sunsets whose reds were so intense and vivid that fire alarms were turned in every night for a week in New York—halfway around the world!

Scientists had discovered unusually high levels of SiO_2 in the pumice from previous eruptions of this volcano and had warned of Krakatoa's explosive potential. No one listened and over 100,000 were dead.

Krakatoa still grumbles through regular, minor eruptions. It is likely only a matter of time until the volcano again prepares its soufflé feast to terrorize the South Pacific.

The belief is half right. Volcanoes can be as deadly and dangerous as any natural force on this planet. Humans would be well advised to stand clear. But there is no evil intent in volcanoes. They have a job to do to maintain a healthy planet and are impressively good at doing it.

WONDERS OF THE LAND

— TOPICS FOR DISCUSSION AND PROJECTS

Here are activities, research topics, and discussion questions you can use to expand upon the key science concepts presented in this chapter.

Research and Discuss. Research destructive volcanoes. What makes them dangerous? Why? Are there any volcanoes that aren't dangerous? Why? What's different about these volcanoes? Walk through the sequence of an eruption and explain the dangers as they arise. Give real examples of each step as you go.

An Activity. There are places near Kilauea volcano (Hawaii) where you can stand in the middle of a recent (3- to 5-year-old) lava flow and you will be the oldest thing you can see. The lave flow destroyed every tree, grass blade, and ant. Now as plants begin to regrow, they are all younger than you are. Being the oldest thing in sight is not something humans get to experience often. Imagine what it would feel like to be the oldest thing in the general area where you are now. Decide what you think the oldest thing nearby is (a tree, rock, stream, hill, etc.) and imagine what you would feel like if you were that oldest thing. Imagine what you have seen, watched, experienced. What would be your attitude toward animals? Weeds? Humans? Time? Automobiles? As this oldest thing, write a page describing your views on the world since you were first created.

Research and Discuss. Research past explosive volcanic eruptions. How much damage did they do? How many people did they kill? What, exactly, killed them (mud, lava, pyroclastic flow, ash, explosion, tsunami, etc.)? Make a chart comparing the dozen deadliest volcanic eruptions you can find. How powerful was each eruption? What type of volcano was it?

An Activity. Build a model of one of the three types of volcanoes— turtle, teapot, or soufflé. As an alternate, draw a detailed profile of the volcano. Try to build into your model or drawing some details that will uniquely show which type of volcano you are depicting. Include an underground magma chamber and feeder pipes and tubes for the magma to use on its rise to the surface.

An Activity. On a map, mark the locations of turtle, teapot, and soufflé volcanoes. For your map choose either the whole world, one of the Pacific Rim countries, or just the United States (be sure to include Alaska and Hawaii on a U.S. map). Use different symbols to indicate the location of turtle, teapot, and soufflé volcanoes. Do the lines and concentrations of volcanoes match any other Earth Science phenomena? What?

An Activity. Select and research a real volcano somewhere in the world. Then imagine an eruption by this volcano. Describe in as much detail as you can what happens to people in different areas around the volcano. What they experience, feel. Describe the eruption and how they react to it.

Research and Discuss. What is magma? Is all magma the same? How does it vary from place to place? Is there any difference between magma and lava? How much magma is there in the world?

Research and Discuss. Research geysers. What's the difference between a geyser and a volcano? Where do geysers get the heat they need to turn groundwater into steam? Why is there no lava in a geyser? Why do some geysers (like Old Faithful in Wyoming's Yellowstone National Park) erupt at regular intervals? Do all geysers do that? Why not?

SUGGESTED READING FOR STUDENTS

Arnold, Eric. *Volcanoes! Mountains of Fire.* New York: Random House, 1997.

Blong, R. J. *Volcanic Hazards.* New York: Academic Press, 1994.

Bolt, T. A. *Inside the Earth.* San Francisco, CA: Freeman, 1999.

Francis, Peter. *Volcanoes.* New York: Pelican Books, 1996.

Ganeri, Anita. *Eruption: The Story of Volcanoes.* New York: DK Publishing, 2001.

Greenwood, Rosie. *I Wonder Why Volcanoes Blow Their Tops.* New York: Houghton Mifflin, 2004.

Gregory, K. J. *Earth's Natural Forces.* Oxford: Andromeda, 2000.

Herman, Gail. *The Magic School Bus Blows Its Top.* New York: Scholastic, 1996.

Macdonald, G. *Volcanoes.* Englewood Cliffs, NJ: Prentice Hall, 2001.

Matthews, William. *Volcanoes and Earthquakes.* New York: Harvey House, 1995.

Moores, Eldridge. *Volcanoes and Earthquakes.* New York: Barnes and Noble Books, 2003.

Morton, Ron. *Music of the Earth: Volcanoes, Earthquakes, and Other Geological Wonders.* New York: Plenum Press, 1996.

Palmer, L. *Mt. St. Helens: The Volcano Explodes.* Seattle, WA: Caroline House Publishers, 2000.

Simon, Seymour. *Danger! Volcanoes!* New York: Chronicle Books, 2002.

———. *Volcanoes.* New York: William Morrow, 1999.

Walker, Sally. *Volcanoes.* Minneapolis, MN: Carolrhoda Books, 1998.

Willie, Peter. *The Way the Earth Works.* New York: Wiley, 1996.

SUGGESTED WEB SITES

Volcano World News. http://volcano.und.nodak.edu/vwdocs/vw-news/vw-news.html

—— SUGGESTED READING FOR TEACHERS

Alexander, David. *Natural Disasters*. London: UCL Press, 2003.

Brown, G. C. *Understanding the Earth*. New York: Cambridge University Press, 2002.

Decker, R. *Mountains of Fire*. New York: Cambridge University Press, 2001.

Harris, S. *Fire Mountains of the West*. Missoula, MT: Mountain Press, 1999.

Krafft, M. *Volcanoes: Earth's Awakening*. Maplewood, NJ: Hammond, 2000.

Lauber, Patricia. *Volcano: The Eruption and Healing of Mt. St. Helens*. New York: Simon & Schuster, 1996.

Skimkin, T. *Krakatau 1883: The Volcanic Explosion and Its Effects*. Washington, DC: Smithsonian Institution, 1993.

Stokes, W. Lee. *Essentials of Earth History*. Englewood Cliffs, NJ: Prentice Hall, 2002.

Van Rose, Susan. *Volcano and Earthquake*. New York: Knopf, 1998.

3   Creating Rocks

MYTHS ABOUT CREATING ROCKS

Rocks seem like a totally uninteresting sidelight. Rocks just . . . *are*. Studying rocks seems as dull as watching paint dry. Yet, rocks form the most basic and fundamental structure of the Earth. Without rocks, there is no land. Rocks are almost *too* basic to be the subject of myths. It's impossible to imagine an Earth without rocks. People believed that rocks did nothing but just sit—right where they were and had always been. They were so much a part of the landscape—seemingly never growing, moving, or changing—that they were often overlooked.

To most cultures, rocks seem, at best, to represent the permanence and unchanging, solid reliability of the Earth. Civil War Confederate general Thomas Jackson rallied his troops to stand and not retreat during the first battle of Bull Run and so was ever after called Stonewall Jackson because he did not move. Two years later Union general George Thomas stubbornly held his ground during the Battle of Chickamauga and gained the honorary nickname "The Rock of Chickamauga." If rocks just sit there, how can rocks be significant to study? How can they reveal anything? Rocks just . . . *are*.

However, modern science has come to appreciate the importance of rocks to the Earth. Rocks represent the oldest things (some are 3.8 billion years old) and newest things (current lava flowing from Kilauea volcano in Hawaii is only seconds old) on Earth. Rocks represent and even record the history of this planet. Indeed, rocks are the record book in which nature has written the history of the planet.

There are few myths about rocks. Most that do exist, explain the creation of a particular rock face or large and prominent rock outcropping. Such specific landmarks were typically explained in two ways. First, the rock came to be when a troll or other mean giant was turned to stone. Second, the rock was created as a monument to (usually) noble lovers who were denied joy in life and honored in death by being made into giant stone cliffs or rock faces.

Many early cultures connected reverence toward rocks with reverence for the Earth Mother (Gaia, Mother Nature, etc.). In some myths huge gods or giant beings emerge from rock. In a Papago Indian myth, boulders on the mountaintops were once people who asked the Great Spirit to save them from the flood. In a Greek myth, Queen Niobe turned to stone while grieving the murder of her children. So did a woman in several North American myths who grieved for her lover, who married someone else.

A myth from Latvia, along the Baltic Sea, calls stones "the devil's turnips." A few myths attribute life to stones. A Hawaiian myth says that solid rocks are male, porous ones are female, and when they bump together, the females give birth to pebbles. In many myths, rocks are considered to be the bones of the Earth, or of the Earth Mother.

The myth that follows, originating in India, is one of the few that attempt, in part, to explain the original creation of rocks. In addition, this is a grand story of spurned love, revenge, battle, and cowardice—all the elements of a good soap opera or a great myth.

"The Goddess of Mahi River,"
A Myth from the Gujarat Region of India

The eastern part of Gujarat contains the lovely Satpura Hills. The Mahi River flows from these hills and winds its way to the sea. The river flows wide and strong and black as the dirt of the hills from which it springs.

Myths say that the Mahi River is the daughter of the Satpura Hills and that the hills are her father. This myth—as do many myths—gives human form and qualities to both river and hills in order to explain why the river is as it currently is.

Long ago, when the Mahi River first matured, she wanted to marry the sea. However, Mahi's father, the hills, never favored such a marriage for his daughter and would not even listen to her reasons or try to know her heart.

Still, Mahi was a strong and independent woman. Even without her father's permission, she left his house in the hills and vowed to find her way to the sea without his help and marry her true love. First she traveled to the west, but this way was strewn with thorns and deep canyons. Her progress was blocked by thick jungles. She was attacked by ferocious tigers and leopards.

Tattered, dirtied, but still determined, Mahi turned back to find a different path. She wandered east of her father the hills, always confident that she would soon find a path to the sea. At night she dreamed of the warm reception she would have when she finally reached the sea. She dreamed of his handsome smile and of his tender kisses.

Mahi crossed wide wastelands where dust blew in the howling wind. Nettles stung her legs and thorn bushes tore at her clothes. But she refused to turn back.

When Mahi finally found the sea, she was exhausted from the struggles of her long journey. Her face was streaked with dirt and mud. Her hair was blown into wild and dirty clumps. Her beautiful clothes were stained black and in tatters. Mahi didn't care for she had found the sea!

But the sea turned his face away and laughed when she proposed marriage. The sea would not even talk to her.

Filled with rage, Mahi stormed back through the dust, thorns, and dangers of her long trek. Soon she reached her father's house, and he was dismayed at the forlorn look of deepest woe on her face. He wrapped his arms around her and tried to comfort her saying, "Oh daughter, the center of my heart, do not look dejected. Tell me what you have experienced on your long journey."

Tears began to tumble from Mahi's eyes. The droplets sparkled like dew as they dripped onto the cotton leaves in the warm morning light. But Mahi concealed her bitter rage from her father. She asked only for an army.

When her father demanded to know why she wanted an army, River Mahi said only that she needed to wage war on the sea and would not say any more. He piled questions upon her and then heaped more questions on top of those questions. She would only answer, "Father, if you love me even a little, then you must lend me your army and ask me no more of these questions."

With a deep and sorrowful sigh, the hill father finally decided that he must give in to his daughter. He assembled the dirt of the hills and said, "This, daughter, is my army. They are yours."

But Mahi scoffed, "Father, these soldiers cannot defeat the sea. My soldiers must be hard and vicious. They must be made so that water will not harm them."

"But who has ever heard of such soldiers?" asked her father.

Again Mahi commanded, "You must make these soldiers *hard*."

Using his mighty hands, Mahi's father squeezed and compressed his soldiers into the first stones—some big as boulders, some small as pebbles. The rock soldiers yelled ferocious cries and crashed against each other, raising a thunderous noise, and Mahi was mightily pleased.

Mahi marched at the head of her warriors as she again began the long trek to the sea, proudly storming across the parched Earth like the general of a terrible invading horde. Rock soldiers banged and rumbled behind her, a vast and fearsome force.

Finally Mahi reached the sea. She stood at the shore with her army arrayed behind her and cried out, "Hateful Lord of the Sea, be ready with your army. Come forth and accept my challenge of war!"

Her stone army was now excited and in the fevered pitch of battle. They roared and smashed against each other, raising a frightful thunder. Confident that in victory she would get to humiliate the Lord of the Sea, Mahi looked forward to battle and screamed her challenges along with her army.

But the sea trembled in terror. Never had the sea seen such a ferocious army. The sea quickly surrendered and agreed to marry Mahi. She accepted—for this was her original desire—and had no further need of an army. They stopped their crashing and shouting and dropped—like stones—right where they were.

To this day, great piles of jumbled stones lie at the mouth of the Mahi River where it dumps into the sea—Mahi's army standing like good soldiers right where they were left. Except, on a few nights each year, Mahi remembers her bitter rage and roars down her channel. On those nights, her soldiers come back to life, ready to begin the battle they were denied so many years ago. On those nights, anyone standing near the mouth of the Mahi River can hear the crashing and pounding of Mahi's soldiers, eager for battle.

THE SCIENCE OF CREATING ROCKS

The following beliefs are either directly stated or strongly implied in the presented myth. Here is what modern science knows about the aspects of rocks explained by each belief.

BELIEF: All rocks are the same. Rocks were originally formed from dirt.

First, what is a rock? Giant boulders dot the hills and mountains. We hide behind rocks during games of hide-and-seek. We skip stones across a pond. We spread pebbles and gravel in driveways. Boulders, rocks, stones, pebbles, gravel, and sand—are they all the same? What makes a rock a rock?

Here is what the dictionary says. *Rock:* "a lump or mass of hard, consolidated mineral matter; material consisting of the aggregate of minerals like those making up the Earth's crust." The key words in that definition are *aggregate* and *mineral.*

Rocks are made up of *minerals*. In the next chapter we'll look inside rocks and decide what a mineral is. For now we want to focus on the rocks themselves—solid clumps created by sticking bits of different minerals together. *Aggregate* means "a grouping of similar things (minerals, in this case) considered as a single whole." Rocks are aggregates (groupings) of different minerals all fused together into a solid whole. Rocks are not uniform. They aren't the same all the way through.

It's like sticking wads of different colored Play-Doh® together. They'll form a single, solid ball of Play-Doh, but one part will be blue, another red, another yellow, and so on. Change Play-Doh to mineral, and that's a rock.

When we humans picture the world, we picture dirt and plants. That's what we walk on, play on, dig in, and grow things in. You might climb on a rock or pick up and throw a rock, but it's dirt we live in. Rocks seem like the exception. Dirt seems like the rule.

We forget that dirt is found only on the thinnest top lining of the crust, which, itself, is only the thinnest top lining of the planet. If you were to walk from the center of the Earth to the surface, you would have to walk a little more than 4,000 miles. You would find dirt only during the last 40 feet of your hike.

What is that like? Imagine a sphere that is just 1 mile in diameter. Now lay one thickness of tissue paper on the outside. The tissue paper is like the dirt that covers our planet. Not counting water, 99.9995% of the Earth is rock!

To study or to understand the Earth, you will need to understand some basic concepts about rocks. If you wanted to study human biology, you would need to pay some attention to blood to understand how the human body works. Rocks are the lifeblood (and muscle, and bone) of this planet.

Minerals aren't skattered at random through all rock. Certain kinds of minerals are found in certain kinds of rock. Many of these thousands of natural minerals are worthless. Several hundred, however, are extremely valuable for industrial and commercial use. Some lead geologists to oil and gas. Some to coal deposits. Diamonds and rubies are each found in layers of rock with certain specific minerals. Bauxite (where we get aluminum), limestone (cement), hematite (iron ore), ilmenite (titanium), and potash (potassium) are all valuable, sought-after minerals. They can each be found in specific kinds of rocks.

Precious fossils and artifacts of past life exist in only one kind of rock. An archeologist who doesn't know a little about rocks will never know where to search for clues to the animal, plant, and human past. Know a little about the rocks, and you can begin to understand why diamond mines and oil wells and coal mines are where they are.

More important for a study of Earth Science, if you understand how different rocks are formed, then you can begin to understand how our planet was formed and how it changes.

So let's look—for one chapter—at these amazing rocks.

To scientists, rocks are amazingly important. Rocks have been studied in minute detail because they are the roadmap to the history of our planet and of its formation and changes. Their structure, texture, and composition provide a record of the geologic events that existed when they were created. Minerals are often called nature's notebook. That makes rocks nature's library—a collective history of the events that led to the creation of each rock and of the events it has experienced since its creation.

We won't go into much detail here about the kinds of rocks and their minerals. But anyone who is interested can find detailed information in the local library.

Which rocks are best for scientists to study? Old rocks. The older the rocks are, the more they reveal about the early history of Earth. Luckily, the oldest rocks are found on continental crust plates. Continental plates ride up and over oceanic plates when the plates collide. It is oceanic plates that are subducted (pushed down) back into the mantle while continental plates are lifted up and remain part of the crust and surface.

It is rare for the rock in an oceanic plate to survive for 180 million years. The average continental crust rock survives for over 650 million years. In some geologically stable areas rocks have survived for billions of years. As mentioned at the beginning of the chapter, the oldest rock ever found is 3.8 billion years old and was found in northern Canada.

Rocks can be divided into three general groups according to how the rocks were formed. Knowing how the rocks in some spot on Earth formed gives clues about the history of that place. The three rock groups are igneous, sedimentary, and metamorphic rock. Let's look at the origin and general characteristics of each group.

Igneous Rocks

Igneous rocks are formed from magma—melted rock—in the upper sections of the mantle at temperatures over 1,200°C (2,200°F—water boils at 212°F). Magma becomes igneous rock when it cools and solidifies. The word *igneous* comes from the Latin word *igneus* and literally means "fire rock." Igneous rocks are born of fire and arrive at the surface through volcanoes. But magma doesn't have to reach the surface to become an igneous rock. Sometimes magma tubes and chambers cool enough to solidify into rock while still underground. These kinds of underground igneous rocks are called *magma plugs*, since they plug up the fissures and tubes magma would otherwise use to reach the surface and flow out as lava.

Most igneous rocks are dense and extremely hard. They weather slowly and often remain standing while softer rock around them are eroded and washed away over the eons. Examples of these dense igneous rocks include granite (beautifully colored granites are popular for countertops because they won't be scratched or marred) and basalt (the hard rock found around most volcanoes that is used for road stone, basaltic rocks are also a good source of iron ore, sapphires, and copper). Obsidian, a rock that looks (and cuts) like glass—only black—is also an igneous rock formed in volcanoes. The first knives and medical operating tools were made from chips of glass-sharp obsidian.

Quartz (source of many gemstones and commercial crystals), gabbros (formed deep underground and not commercially used), and peridotite (a source of platinum, nickel, garnets, diamonds) are other common examples among the dozens of specific, dense igneous rocks.

All magma has gas dissolved in it. That was mentioned in the last chapter. Usually this gas separates from magma before it hardens into rock. Hard dense rocks can't have a lot of gas pockets in them. However, if the magma is saturated (loaded) with gas and reaches the surface quickly, and if the lava then cools quickly, tiny gas bubbles are trapped in the lava rock as it hardens. The rock will be brittle and stuffed with more holes than a fine Swiss cheese. Pumice is a good example of this type of rock. So is much of the lava flowing from the Kilauea volcano in Hawaii.

Sedimentary Rocks

Sedimentary rocks are the result of erosion. Wind, water, ice, earthquakes, oxygen, waves, gravity, and living organisms begin to wear down, break up, and tear down rocks as soon as they are exposed on the Earth's surface. Over time, a large rock face is worn down to boulders, stones, pebbles, gravel, sand, clay, and silt. Wind and water carry the flakes, chips, grains, and pebbles down wind and down stream and eventually deposit them. They might be deposited in an alluvial fan, in a river delta or lake bottom, on low-lying farmland, in a marsh or swamp, or on the ocean floor. But eventually these tiny bits of rock will be deposited as sediment—somewhere. There the sediment builds up and is slowly squeezed—compressed—into rock. These are sedimentary rocks.

Sedimentary rocks come from other rocks mixed with bits of dirt, bone, and shell fragments as they are deposited, grain by grain, as sediment. Thus, sedimentary rocks are called "secondary" rocks. Sedimentary rocks are how other rocks are recycled.

For 4 billion years volcanoes have been spewing new igneous rocks onto the surface of the Earth. Tectonic forces have lifted and folded rock layers into mountains and high plateaus. For those same 4 billion years, the forces of erosion have been tearing those rocks down. The Earth would be as smooth and round as a billiard ball if tectonic forces stopped wrinkling, lifting, and warping its surface.

Every one of the mountain ranges, every one of the volcanoes, every one of the hills that the erosion has worn down over those 4 billion years, turned into sedimentary rock—layer upon layer upon layer. The top 8,000 to 10,000 feet of the entire Appalachian Mountains have been eroded and worn down in just 100 million years. Imagine how much rock has been worn down and deposited as sediment in 4 *billion* years!

Over billions of years the Earth has been covered thick with sedimentary rocks. Of course, over those same billions of years volcanoes have deposited new igneous rock. Tectonic forces have pushed up new mountain ranges to be worn down, and much of the sedimentary rock has itself been eroded, deposited, and turned into new sedimentary rock. Some of the rock has been pushed back down into the mantle and melted back into magma.

Most scientists and engineers who study rocks focus on sedimentary rocks because sedimentary layers reveal the most clues about millions of years of Earth's history just as tree rings reveal clues about tens and hundreds of years of history. Plus, sedimentary rocks contain fossils and most of the commercially important minerals, hydrocarbons, petroleum, gas, and coal that drive modern industry.

What, then, are the common characteristics of sedimentary rock? First, sedimentary rocks are layered. The characteristics of each layer change as the content of the sediments change over time. The great variety of minerals contained in any given slab of sedimentary rock depends on the characteristics of the upstream and upwind rocks that were eroded to create that sediment.

A second general characteristic of sedimentary rocks is that they are weaker (less dense and less strong) than igneous or metamorphic rocks. Sedimentary rock crumbles and weathers far more easily than rock of the other two groups.

Terrestrial (continental) sedimentary layers can be many miles thick. When deposited and then uplifted (as happened to the Colorado plateau, for example), the raised sedimentary rocks are subject to rapid weathering. The results can be spectacular as these thick sedimentary layers are worn away. The Grand Canyon and Bryce Canyon are examples of the weathering of sedimentary rock layers.

A third characteristic of sedimentary rock is that these rocks tend to have a low melting point (700°–1,260°F, or less). Examples of common sedimentary rocks include sandstone, oil shale, chalk, and limestone. Limestone is created most often on the ocean floor, where an abundance of fossil shells in the sediments provides enough calcium carbonate to form limestone. Limestone found on land is an indication that at one time the land was on the bottom of the ocean.

Metamorphic Rock

In science fiction stories, a character who can change from one physical form into another is called a *metamorph*. Like such a character, a metamorphic rock is a rock that has been changed from one form into another. *Metamorphic* comes from the Greek words *meta*, meaning "change," and *morphe*, meaning "form." When rocks change form, they become metamorphic rocks.

It can happen to any kind of rock—igneous, sedimentary, or even metamorphic rock. If a rock is subjected to enough heat (over 500°F) and/or enough pressure (generally the weight of at least 2 miles of rock pushing down above it), it will physically and chemically change into a new rock structure. Metamorphic rocks are still rocks. The change happens while they are still solid rocks. They do not melt. They are still composed of aggregates of minerals. But they are chemically and physically different from the original rock.

Where does a rock find enough heat and pressure to change? Deep under the surface or near magma pockets and chambers tucked into the crust. A rock reaches those fiery regions by being subducted. Usually it is oceanic crust (and the sedimentary layers that have piled on top of that crust) that is subducted. But some continental crust is also subducted when two continental plates collide.

Temperatures and pressures rise as the rock is pushed deeper into the lithosphere. Chemical changes in the rock begin to take place. Some elements escape from the structural bonds of the mineral crystals and leave the rock. Some new elements are captured and added to the rock's crystal matrix. Minerals in the rock are reformed and recrystallized. New granular bonds form and the rock is changed on a fundamental level.

This process is similar to what happens to potter's clay when it is fired. A potter molds the clay into the shape of a graceful bowl. Then he slides it into a kiln, where it is cooked at high temperature. The tiny mineral grains in the clay undergo a series of chemical reactions driven by the intense heat. New compounds are formed, and the formerly soft clay changes into a new chemical and mineral form that is rigid and brittle.

Limestone is metamorphosed into marble. Slate is the metamorphic version of the sedimentary rock, shale. However, the nature of the metamorphic rock will also vary depending on the amount of pressure, the temperature, and the amount of time that the rock was subjected to these conditions. If the same shale were placed under higher temperatures and pressures and left for a longer time, it would eventually morph into high-grade schist (a kind of rock) and would have an abundance of the mineral garnet (a precious gemstone). There are some minerals that only exist in metamorphic rock, since they only form under high pressure and temperature.

The mineral and physical characteristics of a metamorphic rock depend on the nature of the source rock that underwent the metamorphic change. Metamorphic rocks tend to have a "grain," a specific direction that all mineral grains are aligned to and elongated along. But every metamorphic rock retains some vestige, some hint, of its former self. This makes metamorphic rocks the most complex rocks.

The majority of all rock in the Earth's continental crust is sedimentary. Metamorphic is the least common of the three groups. Metamorphic rocks are most often found around volcanoes where rocks have been heated by their proximity to magma chambers and in uplifted mountains where tectonic forces have compressed and then lifted large regions of one plate.

The belief is wrong. Rocks are definitely not all the same. And in their differences lie the clues to help scientists read the past history of the Earth.

> BELIEF: Rocks were formed by the gods and for the gods' pleasure.

As we have seen, rocks are formed from minerals by the natural processes of the Earth. Igneous rocks are solidified magma and so are formed in the upper mantle and delivered to the surface by volcanoes. Sedimentary rocks form on the surface as other rocks erode. Metamorphic rocks form deep inside the crust where heat and pressure alter the composition and structure of solid rock.

One kind of rock is created on the planet's surface. Another kind is created within the crust. And a third kind is brewed below the crust in the liquid mantle.

There is a natural cycle for rocks—just as there is for water. (The rock cycle is shown on Figure 3.1.) The cycle begins as magma is carried toward the surface to create new igneous rock in the crust. That igneous rock will either reach the surface and be attacked by the agents of weathering or it will be pushed deeper into the crust by tectonic forces. There either it will continue downward and remelt or it will linger inside the crust and be subjected to the heat and pressure that brings on metamorphic change.

Weathered rock becomes sediment and is recycled into sedimentary rock. One of three things can happen to a sedimentary rock. It can be uplifted and reach the surface (and begin to be eroded). It can be subducted and melt in the mantle to become magma and eventually be reborn as new igneous rock. It can undergo metamorphic change inside the crust of the Earth.

Rocks that have undergone metamorphic change either will be pushed down into the mantle and melt or will be uplifted to eventually reach the surface, where they, too, are weathered and eroded.

And so the cycle goes, on and on, as old rock is exchanged for new and as one kind of rock slowly changes into another.

Again, the belief is wrong. Rocks were not formed for the pleasure and amusement of the gods. Rocks are part of the normal and natural cycling of heat and material through our planet.

WONDERS OF THE LAND

FIGURE 3.1 • The Rock Cycle

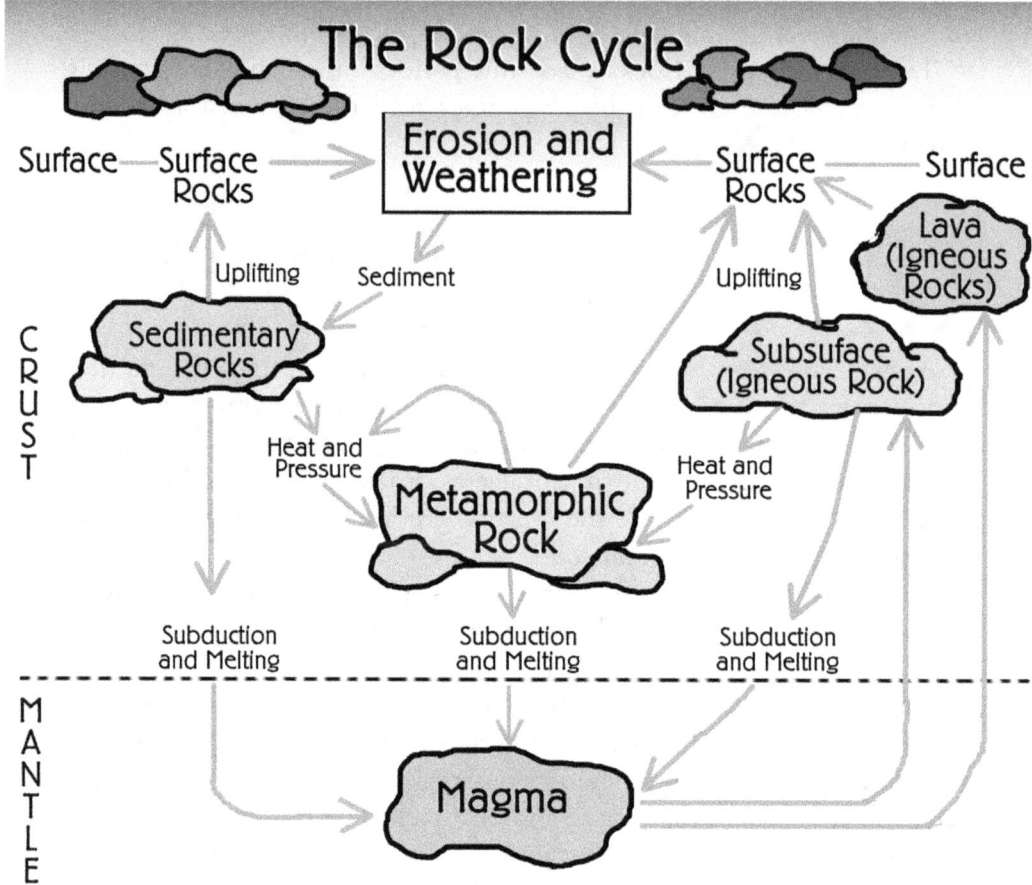

BELIEF: All rocks formed at the same time when the Earth was new.

The myth implies that all rocks were created at once (to be Mahi's army) and have not changed since. Not true. There has never been a period on Earth when rocks were not being created and destroyed.

Some new rock was created today—as you read this chapter. Somewhere on this planet a volcano splattered lava onto the surface of the crust. Maybe it happened in Hawaii, maybe in Iceland, maybe along one of the mid-ocean ridges. Somewhere today sediments on the ocean floor or in a thick alluvial fan put enough pressure on the layers of sediment deep below to compress them into sedimentary rock. Somewhere today some rock completed its metamorphic transformation and emerged as a new kind of metamorphic rock. Maybe it happened near the magma chamber growing under the Krakatoa caldera. Maybe it happened along the margin of the collision of the India and Eurasian plates and deep under the growing Himalayan Mountains. But somewhere—today—each of those events happened.

The process of creating, changing, and destroying rocks is a never-ending cyclical process in the crust of our planet. The average continental crustal rock exists for 650 million years. However, some rocks have lasted as long as 3.8 billion years. Some igneous rock hardened along the Hawaiian shore are pulverized by crashing waves in a matter of months and turned to sediment gently drifting toward the ocean floor 15,000 feet below.

Once a rock reaches the surface and is subject to the forces of weathering, its life expectancy drops dramatically. Few rocks can withstand the onslaught of wind, rain, water, living organisms, and ice for even 1 million years.

Even this summary presentation of the life of a rock brings up an important question. How do scientists know? How can they pick up one rock and tell that it is 500 million years old and know that another is only 200,000 years old? There has to be a little chemistry in this explanation, thus far kept as simple as possible.

The answer is that, over time, the atoms of certain elements change in very precise and predictable ways. In the heart of every atom lies a nucleus. Inside the nucleus sits a cluster of protons and neutrons. Every atom of any given element has exactly the same number of *protons* in its nucleus as does every other atom of that element. Every oxygen atom has eight protons in its nucleus. Every carbon atom has six. Every gold atom has seventy-nine, and every hydrogen atom only one. This is like the number of players different kinds of teams put on the field for a game. If nine players are on the field, you know that it's a baseball team. Why? Because every baseball team has nine players on the field. Just as every team of the same sport puts the same number of players on the field, every atom of the same element has the same number of protons in its nucleus.

However, atoms of the same element can have different numbers of *neutrons* in their nucleus. This is a lot like the numbers of players a team has on the bench. One baseball team could have twelve players on the bench during a game. Another team might have fifteen. They are both still baseball teams. They will both put exactly nine players on the field. But they can have a different number of players on the bench. Thus, whereas every atom of carbon has exactly six protons in its nucleus, some carbon atoms have six neutrons, some have seven, and some have eight.

The *atomic number* of an atom is the sum of the protons and neutrons in its nucleus. A carbon atom with six protons and eight neutrons has an atomic number of 14 (6 + 8). It is written like this: C^{14}. C is the chemical symbol for carbon. The superscript 14 represents the atomic number of that atom of carbon. Atoms of the same element but with different atomic numbers are called *isotopes*.

What's the point of all this chemistry? Simple. Scientists have learned that certain percentages of different isotopes of several elements will be present in certain kinds of rocks when the rock first forms. They also have learned that these particular isotopes break down (decay into some other isotope or into some other element) at very precise and consistent rates. This rate is measured in *half-lives*. That is, scientists measure how long it will take for exactly half of the total number of atoms of that isotope in a given sample of rock to decay. That length of time is called one *half-life*. In the next half-life's worth of time exactly half of the remaining atoms of that isotope will decay. And so on.

One isotope of uranium, U^{238}, has a half-life of 4.5 billion years. (In 4.5 billion years half of the U^{238} atoms in any rock sample will decay into something else. In another 4.5 billion years, exactly half of the remaining atoms will decay.) U^{238} decays into one specific isotope of lead, Pb^{206}. Another isotope of uranium, U^{235}, has a half-life of 713 million years and decays into a different isotope of lead, Pb^{207}. C^{14} has a half-life of 5,730 years and decays into an isotope of nitrogen, N^{14}.

Scientists can measure how much of these specific isotopes exist in a sample of rock. Then they can calculate how old the rock is because they know how much of each of these isotopes the rock had to have when it first formed.

Once scientists know how old selected rocks in a large rock face are, they can determine how old each of the rock layers is and study individual layers to determine what was going on when that layer of rock was created. Soon they have pieced together an accurate history of an area that dates back many millions of years.

The belief is wrong. For the past 4 billion years, rocks have continuously been created, changed, weathered, and remade. The process still continues today. Scientists' studies of the isotopes in rocks have proved it.

> BELIEF: Rocks don't reveal important information
> about our planet's past.

What can scientists learn from a hunk of rock? Plenty. Scientists learn the most from sedimentary rocks. The composition of the different layers in these rocks reveals conditions at the different time periods in Earth's history when the sediment was deposited and compressed as well as the environment in which the sediment accumulated (under the ocean or on land, for example). The presence of hydrocarbons or other specific minerals tells scientist what kind of animal and plant life existed in that area. So do the fossil fragments present in the various layers.

Ripple markings in a layer of sandstone or limestone indicate that this sediment was once on the deep ocean floor. If you find one of those sedimentary rocks on land, you know that tectonic forces have lifted that section of crust.

Some layers contain unique elements, isotopes, or minerals that can indicate a major regional or global event (such as a meteorite impact). Layers with these unique elements can be located in other sites and used to compare sediment rates and continental movements over long time periods. Mud leaves a specific signature impression once it hardens into sedimentary rock. Scientists know that sedimentary rock layers with that pattern of depressions were deposited on a wide mud flat—probably along the shore or in a swamp. All these clues and many more are written into the layers of sedimentary stone.

Metamorphic rocks, although not as common, are also quite revealing. Because different types of metamorphic rock are produced by different amounts of heat and pressure, and because metamorphic rocks are created under specific circumstances (plate collisions, or around volcanoes and magma chambers in the crust), their presence can be used to identify old plate boundaries as well as the types of plate collisions that occurred in the past. Continental-to-continental plate boundaries produce pressure but lower temperatures for metamorphic change while continental to oceanic plate collisions produce much higher temperatures and pressures—and, thus, different kinds of metamorphic rock.

Different kinds of metamorphic rock present in a metamorphic rock sample can indicate the changing temperature and pressure conditions over tens of thousands of years within the crust during the period when that rock underwent metamorphic transformation.

The composition and type of igneous rock reveals whether it hardened on the surface or deep underground. The gas content of the rock tells much about how it cooled. This information about conditions when the rock was created can be compared to conditions at the rock's present location.

For example, rocks have been used to support the case that fabled Atlantis *could* have existed. In 1984 Dr. Maria Klenova, Soviet Academy of Sciences, reported that ocean-bottom igneous rocks taken in samples from a 6,000-foot depth north of the Azores Islands (on the mid-Atlantic ridge) had to have been formed at atmospheric pressure less than 15,000 YAG. Dr. Pierre Termier, French oceanographer, studied ocean-bottom rocks about 500 miles southeast of the Azores in the early 1990s and discovered that they were a type of igneous lava called tachylite that is formed only in the presence of air and that will dissolve in seawater in 15,000 to 20,000 years. Both of these small studies used the characteristics of igneous rocks to show that what is now deep ocean floor in the mid-Atlantic (exactly where Atlantis was supposed to have been) had to have been dry land until around 12,000 to 15,000 YAG—just when Atlantis was supposed to have sunk.

The belief is wrong. Rocks tell us so much about the past that scientists have been able to create an accurate picture of much of the Earth's history over the past 3 to 4 billion years. Rocks reveal so much that scientists know as much about the world as it was a *billion* YAG as they do about human culture only 8,000 or 9,000 YAG.

— TOPICS FOR DISCUSSION AND PROJECTS

Here are activities, research topics, and discussion questions you can use to expand upon the key science concepts presented in this chapter.

Research and Discuss. Recall an experience you have had with rocks. Pick one particular incident and describe it. What size was the rock(s)? How did you think about the rock at that time? Did you *think* about the rock at that time, or just use it? What did you do with the rock?

Compare your memory with those of other students. Did all stories involve the same size rocks? How did different students use rocks? As tool? As weapons? How did they think about the rocks? As an annoyance? As something helpful? Did anyone pause to study and appreciate the rocks? Was it difficult to remember an incident centered around a rock? Considering their importance to Earth, why do you think we don't hold rocks in a higher regard?

An Activity. Make a chart of the rock cycle and a separate map of the water cycle. Now compare the two. Can you find similarities between these two cycles? What are they? What do you think is the significance of those similarities?

Research and Discuss. Pick one of the three types of rocks—igneous, sedimentary, or metamorphic—and research that one type of rock. Look for common physical and chemical properties. Where is that type of rock found? How common are such rocks? How are they produced? Destroyed? Are there specific kinds of rock within this general type that are valuable and commonly used? What are they and what are they used for?

An Activity. Let's try to make a metamorphic rock. Find a layered, sedimentary rock and ask someone with a rock-cutting saw to cut your sedimentary rock in half. Sedimentary rocks are turned into metamorphic rocks with heat and pressure. Let's see if heat alone works. Put half of the sedimentary rock into the oven and bake it at 550°F for 3 hours. Take the rock out and let it cool. Study this rock and compare it to the half you did not bake. Can you detect any differences? Has baking changed the rock? Is its grain structure different? Its composition? If you didn't notice any difference, why not?

Let's try pressure. Place heavy books, boards, bricks, and other objects on top of the half of the sedimentary rock that you have already baked. Let this weight (pressure) stand on the rock overnight. Again compare it to the half that was neither baked nor subjected to pressure.

Did you notice any difference *this* time? Why not? The process of making rocks is a slow one. If you left your rock in the oven for 1,000 years,

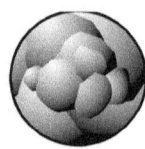

you might begin to notice some effect (not to mention an enormous energy bill).

Write a page describing why your experiment failed to transform a sedimentary rock into a metamorphic one.

An Activity. Sedimentary rocks reveal the most history of any rock type. Find local sedimentary rocks and chip out a hunk of one to study. Mark the spot this rock came from in case any question arises later. Can you clearly see layers in the rock? Are they of different colors? Why the color changes? What do you think is in it? Does it crumble? Does it have dirt content, or is it just made of ground-up rock? Can you find any fossils in this rock sample? If you have access to a chemistry lab, wash this rock in a carbonic acid solution. Does it begin to dissolve? Research sedimentary rocks to see which types dissolve most readily.

Research and Discuss. What are the commercial uses for rocks? Research the industries that use rock. Which industries use rocks? Where do they get it? What do they do with rocks? What rock products do they produce? Write a paper describing one of these industries and the uses they make of rocks.

SUGGESTED READING FOR STUDENTS

Blobaum, Cindy. *Geology Rocks!* Nashville, TN: Ideals Publications, 1999.

Bown, Deni. *Rocks and Minerals*. New York: DK Publishing, 2002.

Christian, Peggy. *If You Find a Rock*. San Diego, CA: Harcourt, 1999.

Cole, Joanna. *The Magic School Bus inside the Earth*. New York: Scholastic, 1999.

Dietrich, R. V. *Stones: Their Collection, Identification, and Use*. Prescott, AZ: Geoscience Press, 1994.

Dussling, Jennifer. *My First Field Guide: Looking at Rocks*. New York: Penguin Putnam Books for Young Readers, 2001.

Flashkids Editors. *Rocks and Minerals*. New York: Flashkids, 2004.

Fuller, Sue. *1001 Facts about Rocks and Minerals*. New York: DK Publishing, 2003.

———. *Rocks and Minerals*. New York: DK Publishing, 2003.

Gans, Roma. *Let's Go Rock Collecting*. New York: HarperCollins Children's Books, 1997.

Parker, Steve. *Rocks and Minerals*. New York: DK Publishing, 1997.

Ricciuti, Edward. *National Audobon Society First Field Guide to Rocks and Minerals.* New York: National Audobon Society, 1998.

Staedter, Tracy. *Rocks and Minerals.* New York: Reader's Digest Books, 2004.

Stewart, Melissa. *Igneous Rock.* Portsmouth, NH: Heinemann, 2003.

———. *Metamorphic Rock.* Portsmouth, NH: Heinemann, 2003.

Symes, R. F. *Eyewitness Rocks and Minerals.* London: Natural History Museum, 2004.

SUGGESTED READING FOR TEACHERS

Dickin, Alan. *Radiogenic Isotope Geology*. New York: Cambridge University Press, 1997.

Lutgens, Frederick. *Essentials of Geology*. Englewood Cliffs, NJ: Prentice Hall, 2002.

McGraw-Hill Editors. *McGraw-Hill Dictionary of Geology and Minerology*. New York: McGraw-Hill, 2002.

Murk, Barbara. *Geology: A Self-Teaching Guide*. New York: John Wiley & Sons, 2001.

SparkNotes Editors. *Geology and Earth Science*. New York: Spark Publishing, 2004.

Tarbuck, Edward. *Earth: An Introduction to Physical Geology*. Englewood Cliffs, NJ: Prentice Hall, 2004.

4 ·· Creating Gems and Crystals

MYTHS ABOUT CREATING GEMS AND CRYSTALS

Sparkling gems are always the highlights of fabled mounds of treasure. Kings and pirates hoard dazzling gems—rubies, emeralds, sapphires, and diamonds. Dazzling gems must be different than ordinary rocks. Gems are precious and special. Rocks are close to worthless. These glowing, translucent treasures—buried at random and scattered across the Earth—seem otherworldly, as if they had been brought to our drab planet by a god or other supernatural force from some distant glittering world.

Often more precious than gold, these rubies, emeralds, diamonds, and other gems are brilliant wonders mixed in with dreary and ordinary rock and dirt. Early people had to wonder: where did they come from? Why are they here? Sparkling, glowing, radiating as if alive, wonder and awe inspiring, these brightly colored treasures must have been placed (or dropped) by the gods. Surely, the same processes that created ordinary dirt and rock can't have created them.

Many also believe that crystals hold supernatural powers and convey healing abilities, enable seers to tell the future, and connect to the invisible worlds of the afterlife. Gems and crystals have been prized as long as humans have existed and were believed to have value far beyond their sparkle and dazzling beauty.

Several early cultures believed that they should grind rubies into powder and eat the powder to dispel fear and to gain strength and courage.

Ground emeralds were believed to create wisdom and cure illness. Hindus and early Christians associated sapphires with health, joy, energy, and divine favor. Early cultures in China, Mexico, and Egypt often placed a piece of jade in the mouth of a corpse to represent the heart when the heart was buried separately. Jade is still believed to create luck in China.

Pearls are a traditional gemstone created out of, and by, living organisms (oysters). Since this one precious stone was created by a living being, many cultures assumed that living beings created *all* gems and crystals. Credit was usually given to the gods.

The term *minerals* is a newer designation and a newer human concern. People have used minerals for thousands of years but never thought of them as a single group of chemical structures until modern times.

Treasure hunters seek gems and precious metals. But geologists spend more effort searching for minerals and the rock formations that predict the existence of oil and commercially valuable minerals. Should serious scientists care about gems—the brilliant, glowing blocks of color that ordinary people covet? Do gems, crystals, and minerals reveal the processes of rock formation and the chemical process of the Earth? Is there scientific value in studying the process of forming crystalline structures?

In most mythic references, gems exist and are used or sought. Yet only a few myths described the processes of their original creation. In one Indian myth of Bali, the demon monster-king, great God Indra smacks Bali on the head. Bali shatters. The first diamonds sprang from the bones of the demon king, Bali. Pearls first came from his teeth. Drops of his blood formed the first rubies. And so on. A Mayan (South American) myth featured Vucub Caquiz (Seven Macaw), a great braggart and vainest of all gods. In the myth, hero twins trick Seven Macaw and strip him of all gems. Seven Macaw realizes that he has been tricked and flies into a rage. During the ensuing battle, all of the gems are scattered across the Earth.

The Southwest Casa Grande tribe tell of Chief Morning Green, who horded all the pieces of precious turquoise after a blue lizard helped him to find them. A clever parrot from a tribe to the east tricked Morning Green's daughters into feeding it all the turquoise. It flew off and Morning Green flew into a rage, sending an endless rain and a great flood over the lands to the east. All the turquoise pieces were rescattered by the raging floodwaters and buried, waiting to be found again.

In the myth that follows, the gods first created the gems—in this case, for petty rivalry in an attempt to outdo each other. One-upmanship turns to violent war, and the gems, along with all the Earth's gold, are scattered ("where the winds carry them").

"Mountains of Gold and Jewels," A Myth from Borneo

In the very beginning, longer ago than even the rocks and the sea can remember, the land was flat and all people walked easily anywhere they wanted to go. There were no uphills or downhills. There was only the flat ocean to paddle on and the flat land to walk on. And all the people were content.

The supreme god of the upper regions, however, was most dissatisfied. "Why should I have to live and walk at the same level as the people and animals? Why should they live in houses built at the same height as mine? Aren't I better? Shouldn't I be above them?"

This god of the upper regions was deeply vexed, for there was nowhere in all the wide, flat land that he could build his house and be *above* all of the people and animals. The god pondered the problem for long weeks and ages with his brow furrowed into deep ridges and folds that made him appear both ugly and fierce.

Then the answer came to him. He should live on a mountain. A mountain would place him high above the ordinary people. But what kind of mountain? What should his mountain be made out of? He gazed about and saw rocks and dirt and grasses and green bushes and waving trees. Certainly none of these were worthy enough to be made into his mountain and home.

The god finally decided on gold. Gold sparkled and dazzled. It was sturdy and beautiful. It was believed to be precious by the people. Certainly a gold mountain would be worthy for his home. And so, the god of the upper regions built a golden mountain. He scraped together all the gold on Earth and shaped it into one towering mountain, more dazzling in morning light than the sun, itself.

The people were deeply impressed and sang chants of praise and bowed low toward the god's mountain. This pleased the god of the upper regions greatly.

On top of his golden mountain he built a magnificent house that radiated such brilliant light that it hurt the eyes and even outshone his golden mountain. The radiance of that house made the sun and moon pale in fear.

The people gasped in awe and admiration and trembled at the magnificence of god's house.

This pleased the god of the upper regions even more. But it did not please the god of the lower regions. The god of the lower regions was outraged and in the dark recesses of his mind he plotted revenge. "Who does he think he is? What did he ever do to merit his own mountain and a fancy house? If he deserves a gold mountain, I deserve one, too."

WONDERS OF THE LAND

The god of the lower regions searched for gold to build his own mountain—higher, fatter, and more brilliant than the god of the upper region's. But there was no more gold to be had.

The god of the lower region glared at the towering mountain and he fumed and he muttered and he cursed. Finally he could stand it no more and decided to build his mountain out of whatever was handy—dirt and rocks.

The god of the lower regions built a fantastic mountain—higher than the clouds, perfectly shaped and pleasing to the eye. But it did not sparkle with the brilliance of gold. It did not dazzle the eye. So the people shrugged and then they laughed.

The face of the god of the lower region turned as red as glowing lava. He shook with rage. He knew that making his mountain *big* had not been nearly enough. He had to make his mountain more stunning and beautiful than that of the god of the upper regions.

In his anger he snatched up several of the rocks left over from his mountain building and squeezed them in his hands. He squeezed them and ground them between his fingers with the strength of a furious god. When he opened his hands, he was startled to find that the rocks had turned into rubies, emeralds, sapphires, and diamonds. But still the god was not satisfied. He breathed fire and ice deep into these sparkling gems to turn their luster into radiant beauty.

The god of the lower regions placed these glowing gems across the outside of his mountain. Then he squeezed and ground more rocks and breathed fire and ice into them until his mountain was covered top to bottom with the most beautiful gems of every color and description imaginable.

Now the people gasped in wonder, awe, and joy. They cheered and bowed low to the mountain of the god of the lower regions, and he smugly crossed his arms and sneered at the god of the upper regions, glaring from the porch of his golden house.

The two gods began to argue, shouting insults back and forth across the flat land between their two mountains. Thunder rumbled and shook the trees. Following the will of their gods, the two mountains leaned closer and then crashed into each other. Over and over, they smashed against each other trying to tear the other mountain apart.

And then the two mountains exploded in a fiery eruption that filled the sky with dark ash and clouds. Lava ran shimmering red down the stubs of the remaining mountains. The stubby remains of these mountains formed the Island of Borneo. But the precious gold and gems were blown high into the sky by the explosion and carried in the dust cloud that billowed all the way up to heaven. The jewels were scattered across the Earth wherever the winds carried them. There they rained down and were buried deep in the soft Earth. There they have waited 1,000 generations for humans to dig and find them.

THE SCIENCE OF CREATING GEMS AND CRYSTALS

The following beliefs are either directly stated or strongly implied in the presented myth. Here is what modern science knows about the aspects of gems, minerals, and crystals explained by each belief.

> BELIEF: Gemstones were formed by the gods and for the gods' own pleasures.

The myth makes it sound as if gems were created as ornaments for the gods. Is that how and why they were formed?

First we must be sure we know what we are talking about. What is a mineral? What is a crystal? And what is a gem?

We'll start by defining a mineral. In the last chapter we found that rocks are mixtures (aggregates) of minerals. But what is a mineral? A true mineral must meet four criteria. First, a mineral must be naturally formed. There are 3,500 naturally formed minerals that have been found in the crust of this planet plus a few others that have been found in moon rocks and in meteorites. (There are also over 50,000 artificially formed minerals that have been created in the laboratory.)

Second, a mineral must be solid. Third, it must have a specific chemical composition that can be expressed as a chemical formula. A *chemical formula* (SiO_2 for example) is a listing of the number of atoms of each element needed to make one molecule of this mineral. Saying that the mineral must have a specific chemical formula says that every molecule of this mineral must be exactly the same.

Fourth and finally, a mineral must have a characteristic crystalline structure. The molecules of this mineral must organize themselves into a pattern that regularly repeats in all three dimensions.

Anything that meets those four criteria is a mineral. That is what a mineral is—and it sounds pretty vague and general, as if almost anything could be a mineral. But that set of four criteria doesn't cover glass or plastic. Plastic and glass don't form crystal structures. It doesn't cover nylon or steel. They're not naturally occurring. It doesn't cover dirt, grass, weeds, trees, raccoons, gold fish, or any other organic material. Nor does it cover water, oil, or any gas. They're not solids.

Then what *does* that definition of a mineral cover? Rocks. Most minerals come from the twelve elements that make up almost all the Earth's

FIGURE 4.1 • Elements in the Crust

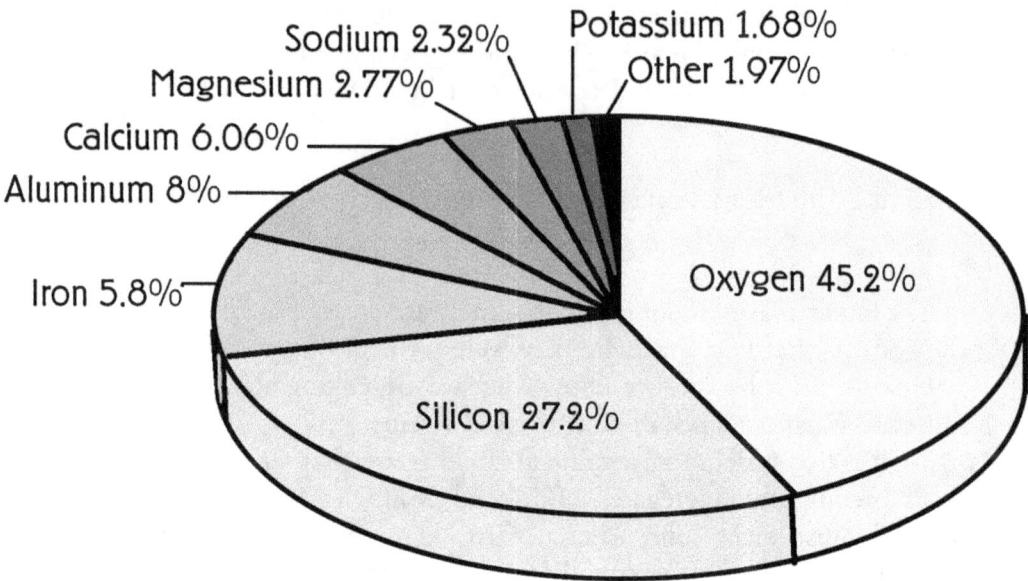

crust. (These elements are shown in Figure 4.1.) As Earth first formed, the elements tended to stratify, to sort themselves. (This was differentiation.) These twelve elements concentrated in the top layers of the Earth and there formed into minerals and into the Earth's solid crust.

Some minerals are commercially valuable. Salt is a mineral (sodium chloride, or—written in its chemical formula—NaCl [Na stands for one atom of sodium, and Cl for one atom of chlorine]). Every molecule of table salt is made up of one atom each of sodium and chlorine. If you study grains of salt under a microscope, you'll find that salt forms into regular cubes. It has a crystalline structure.

Some minerals have brilliant colors and are beautiful to look at. We have named those minerals: *gemstones*. But more important for science, minerals contain in them the keys to the conditions that existed when they were created. Minerals give us a picture of what the Earth was like in some distant past we cannot directly measure.

A mineral, then, is a naturally occurring solid with a fixed chemical formula that forms in crystal structures. But what is a crystal?

Many people think that a crystal is a transparent, geometric object that we hang in windows to refract light, that fortunetellers use, or that new-age hippies use to channel natural power and purity. Some think that *crystal* means the fancy wine glasses that their parents pull out for special occasions. (That kind of crystal is actually regular glass with a bit of lead oxide added during production.)

Many of the "crystals" that people buy at crystal shops are actually made of plastic or glass—they aren't crystals at all. The word *crystal* comes from the Greek word *kryos* meaning "icy cold." The first recognized crystals were clear rock crystals, a colorless form of quartz thought to be ice frozen so hard that it would never melt.

But what does science mean by the word *crystal*? In Earth Science, a crystal is any solid that grows with straight (planar) surfaces and parallel edges. To do that, the molecules of the substance must arrange themselves, layer by layer, into a regular three-dimensional network—a matrix. A skyscraper is very much like a crystal matrix. The building is organized into floors—each one exactly the same size and shape—that are layered in a regular pattern, one floor on top of the other. The building grows with straight sides and parallel edges. If the rooms were the size of molecules, 50-story skyscrapers would be tiny crystal grains.

Salt, sugar, ice, diamond, feldspar (a source of potassium and aluminum), silicon chips for computers, quartz crystals used in communications systems, ruby crystals used in lasers—all are crystals. Crystals tend to break along flat planes or faces. Mica (an electrical resistor used in some electronics) breaks into thin sheets. Feldspar breaks into hexagonal columns. Granite is a rock made up of a mixture of different minerals—all formed as crystals.

What *isn't* a crystal? Plastic and glass aren't crystals because their molecules don't organize themselves into a regular pattern and structure. Wood and other living plants aren't crystals for the same reason. Liquids and gases can't form into crystals.

Crystals are a common structure in nature. Minerals are crystals. Crystals form minerals. Minerals form rocks that form mountains and the very crust we live on. Minerals are Mother Nature's notebook. In minerals she wrote the history of the world. Certain conditions and groups of available elements were required to create specific minerals. The presence of specific groups of minerals in a rock tells researchers what conditions and elements existed when the rock formed.

Fine so far. But where do gems fit in? After all, it's the rubies, emeralds, sapphires, and diamonds we are after! Technically, a gemstone is any mineral that can be cut and polished for a setting in a piece of jewelry. If someone cuts a mineral along the edges and planar surfaces of its crystal structure, polishes it to make it lustrous, and sets it in a piece of jewelry—voilà—it's a gemstone.

Gemologists and geologists use the word *gem* to mean "a rare, hard, expensive, lustrous, durable (long-lasting) mineral crystal structure with brilliant color that has grown large enough to be cut, shaped, and polished as a gemstone."

An important quality of gems is *hardness*, a measure of a gem's ability to resist scratching. Many people think that hardness means that the gem can't be smashed with a hammer. That's not true! Don't test your mother's diamonds by smashing them with a hammer. Diamonds will shatter. But they're almost impossible to scratch because they are amazingly hard. On a ten-point scale for hardness, diamonds are a ten. Topaz is an eight. Glass and the blade of your pocketknife are both 5.5. Fingernails are a 2.5.

The size of the crystal is also important. Most mineral fragments in a rock are far too small to be cut and shaped and used in jewelry. The mineral for amethyst, a common form of quartz, is plentiful. However, most of the time it appears in grain-sized fragments that could never be cut out and used, and thus it is worthless.

Gems are naturally occurring minerals that are found in rocks. Eighty percent of all gems are used in engagement and wedding sets. The world's largest consumers of gems are the United States (45%) and Japan (25%).

How were minerals and gems formed? Not when some supernatural being snaps his or her fingers, but when the elements present in the lithosphere (crust and upper mantle of the Earth) combine to bond into molecules of a specific mineral that then arrange themselves in a fixed, regular crystal matrix. It is actually what the elements and molecules most *want* to do and do most naturally. The myth is wrong—but inventive in its explanation of the origin of precious gems.

> BELIEF: All gems are formed the same way and were formed at one time near the beginning of the world.

The myth said that all gems were formed by being squeezed by a jealous god and were all formed at the same time. Is that true? Is pressure what forms gemstones?

Chemical elements in the Earth want to combine, to bond together. Under certain conditions of temperature and pressure, certain groupings of elements tend to combine in the same way, linking into specific molecules with specific properties and shape. As these molecules of a mineral cool from molten liquid (magma) into a solid, they most commonly and naturally arrange themselves into regular geometric patterns—crystal matrices. That's how minerals form. Atoms automatically bond with other atoms to form molecules. Identical molecules combine to form the crystal matrix of a mineral.

Under the right conditions of temperature and pressure, a few of these minerals form into gemstones. Rocks are jigsaw-puzzle mixtures (aggregates) of various minerals. A rock can have one or more gems buried within it.

There are over 100 natural chemical elements on Earth. However, as shown in Figure 4.1, just nine of these make up over 99% of the crust. The greatest number of minerals are made out of the two most common elements in the crust—silicon and oxygen—followed by combinations of aluminum and oxygen. The minerals that are made of silicon and oxygen are called *silicates*. Topaz, zircon, garnet, and olivine are simple silicates. Tourmaline is a complex silicate.

Quartz is also composed mainly of silicon and oxygen. Different trace additives change the color and clarity of the crystal gems—purple amethyst, yellow citrine. Aluminum and oxygen are the primary elements that make up the group of minerals that includes rubies and sapphires.

Over 100 minerals are commonly used as gemstones. If the mineral is hard enough, if it has a pleasing color, if it can be cut and polished with a lustrous quality—if, in short, it appears beautiful—then it can be used as a gemstone.

A diamond is made up of a single element: carbon. A diamond is still a mineral because, in a diamond, pressure and heat have forced the carbon atoms to form themselves into a fixed crystal matrix.

Diamonds are chemically the same as coal or the graphite used in pencil leads. They are all pure carbon. But diamonds differ in how they were formed. Diamonds form deep in the lithosphere at depths of 100 to 125 miles below the surface and at temperatures of 1,200°C to 1,500°C (2,190°F to 2,730°F). Under those grueling conditions, carbon atoms are forced, over slow millions of years, into a regular crystal matrix and a diamond is born.

No other mineral or gem requires such extremes of pressure and temperature for its creation. If the carbon descended any lower, it would pass back into the upper mantle and melt. If it stayed higher in the crust, it would never be forced to crystallize into a brilliant diamond. Most diamonds formed at this extreme depth will never be lifted near enough to the surface to be discovered—even by the deepest of mine shafts.

The first recorded discovery of a diamond was made in 480 B.C. in India. The word *diamond* comes from the Greek word *adama* meaning "unconquerable." Famed Greek philosopher Plato thought diamonds were a living spirit.

Eighty percent of all diamonds are sold not for gemstones but for industrial uses as cutters and polishers. There are four grades of diamonds.

Gem-quality diamonds are the highest grade and sell for up to $5,000 per carat. Industrial quality diamonds are the third grade and sell for $2 to $8 per carat. The lowest grade are diamonds that either have not completely formed into diamonds and still have some carbon that has not been forced into the crystal matrix or are diamonds that are decomposing back into uncrystallized graphite.

One hundred and fifty million carats of industrial diamonds are purchased and used each year. Most of these are now synthetic. diamonds created in a factory. The weight of gems is measured in *carats* That term dates back to the Middle Ages and the Middle East when one carat equaled the weight of one carob seed. Now science uses a more exact measure. One carat equals one fifth of a gram. One gram equals 0.006 oz. Yes, a carat is a very small amount of weight. But most gems are so small that they are measured not in whole carats, but in *points*. One point equals one one-hundredth of a carat. There are about 2,200 carats in a pound. That's 220,000 points to the pound.

Only three common gems are exceptions to what has been said so far. These three are ordinary gems in that they are solid. They are hard and they are naturally formed. However, these three are created by, and out of, living organisms. They are pearls, coral, and amber.

Pearls are created as a growth within an oyster surrounding some irritant or alien particle. The oyster builds a pearl to protect itself and to isolate its own tissues from the impurity. People do the same thing when they build up scar tissue or a fatty tumor around some grain of alien material that lodges in their bodies. Oysters just happen to create pearls.

The coral we use as a gem is actually the combined skeletal shells of a whole colony of marine organisms also called corals. When the critters die, their thin shells are left behind. Thousands of generations of corals build onto the same giant skeletal structures to produce the great coral fans and the rocky parts of shallow reefs that we call coral reefs. Coral is also unique among gems in its lack of hardness. Coral is the most delicate of all gemstones.

Amber—usually a lustrous deep amber color—is really fossilized tree sap. Fossilization is a metamorphic process that turns the amber into rock just as fossilizing a tree chemically alters the molecules of the tree and turns the tree into stone.

The process of creating minerals and gems is ongoing, as is the process of creating rocks. Every time magma cools and solidifies, every time heat and pressure cause a rock to undergo metamorphic change, new minerals—and perhaps some new gems—are created. Garnets are formed in metamorphic rock, but only when shale (a sedimentary rock) is subjected to high heat and pressure for long periods of time. If the shale doesn't cook long enough or hot enough, it will turn into slate instead of into garnet.

Certainly the process goes both ways. Natural processes destroy minerals and gems as regularly as they create them. Every time a rock that contains gems is subducted back into the mantle, those gems are destroyed. Diamonds become unstable and break down to graphite (loose carbon) once they have been brought to the surface, thus removing the pressure that forced them into a crystal matrix. The process of disintegration takes several million years, but it happens—*is* happening this very minute—to every diamond brought up to the surface of the Earth. Diamonds definitely are not forever! Even the most famous diamonds in England's crown jewels will—someday—be the graphite for someone's pencil.

The belief is mostly wrong. Gems, crystals, and minerals were not all created at one time near the beginning of land. They are continuously being created and destroyed. However, they are all created in the same way. The natural forces and processes of the Earth allow the available elements in the lithosphere to bond into molecules under varying amounts of heat and pressure. Those molecules then arrange themselves into orderly, repetitive crystal structures as magma cools enough for the process to begin. So, in general, all minerals and gems are formed in the same way and pressure *is* a part of that process. However, the specific temperatures, pressures, available elements, and conditions to create each individual mineral and gem vary greatly.

BELIEF: Gems and precious minerals are freak occurrences on this planet.

There are over 3,500 naturally occurring minerals in the crust of our planet. Hundreds of them are commercially valuable, from borax (used in glass, soap, enamel, and antiseptic making) and bauxite (a source of aluminum) to table salt. Minerals are not rare. Just the opposite, they are the normal components of rocks and of the lithosphere of Earth.

There are about 100 minerals with the hardness, luster, beauty, and clarity to make then useful as gemstones. However, it is rare to find a rock that contains a large enough crystal of one of these minerals to cut, shape, and polish that crystal into a gem. Gemstones are valuable, not because that mineral is rare, but because hunks of the mineral big enough to cut and polish are rare.

The rarity of gems, however, doesn't make them unnatural. On the contrary, they are as much a perfectly natural part of the crust as is any other specific mineral formation, including salt, sugar, and ice. Precious gems just happen to be created under less common circumstances and so don't show up as often.

BELIEF: Gems, crystals, and minerals are fundamentally different things.

Many people believe that precious gems are somehow very different than crystals and that both of these are unrelated to the common minerals found in the Earth. As we have seen above, minerals *are* crystals, and with several notable exceptions (opal, pearl, and amber) gems are ordinary minerals.

Minerals are the basic building block of rocks and of the Earth's crust. Crystals are the structural way that the molecules of minerals tend to organize and structure themselves as they solidify. Gems are a few of the many kinds of minerals that we humans find to be particularly alluring and beautiful.

— TOPICS FOR DISCUSSION AND PROJECTS

Here are activities, research topics, and discussion questions you can use to expand upon the key science concepts presented in this chapter.

Research and Discuss. What makes a gem a gem? Do research on this question in the library and online. Also talk to adults. Ask their opinion. Talk to jewelers to see what they think. Why do *you* think gemstones are so expensive and desirable?

An Activity. Survey the gems owned by the families of class members. Make a list showing the total number of each type of gem owned by the collective class families. Which gems are most common? (That is, which appear most often on the list?) Research these gemstones. Find the name and chemical formula for that mineral. What kind of rock does that mineral come from? How is it formed? How is it mined? Where is it found? How are the rough stones taken from the Earth turned into polished gemstones? What is the biggest one ever discovered?

Research and Discuss. Pick one gem and research its history in stories and lore. What purpose did the gem serve in each story? Where does the story come from? How does the gem affect the outcome of the story? From these stories, can you infer what these traditional cultures felt and thought about this particular gemstone?

An Activity. Create your own gem myth. What kind of a gem will your myth be about? Will your story be about finding and hoarding the gem, about creating the gem, or about using the power of the gem? What power? Who owns the gem? Who wants it? What for? What is the point (moral) of your myth? What conflicts arise that involve the gemstone?

Research and Discuss. What is a mineral? What makes a mineral a mineral? Are there combinations of chemicals that help to define a mineral as a mineral? Are there physical properties common to all minerals? Can you find five common household minerals at your home?

Pick one mineral that is commercially mined. What kind of rock is it mined from? Who mines it? What do they do with it? What products are created from this mineral? Write a paper describing both this mineral and its importance to our society.

An Activity. Make a class chart of every mineral used as a gem. Where will you find such a list? Would owners of local jewelry stores be good sources to interview? How many minerals are on your list? Are gems on this list? Are there gems that aren't minerals? Which ones?

Research and Discuss. Are any gemstones manufactured in the lab, or are they all natural? What jewelry stones are manufactured? Why aren't

more manufactured? Make a list of manufactured gemstones and research the manufacturing process for one of them.

SUGGESTED READING FOR STUDENTS

Bown, Deni. *Rocks and Minerals*. New York: DK Publishing, 2002.

Burton, E. *Diamonds*. London: Chilton Books, 1995.

Craig, J. *Resources of the Earth*. Englewood Cliffs, NJ: Prentice Hall, 1998.

Edwards, Ron. *Diamonds and Gemstones*. New York: Crabtree Publishing, 2004.

Flashkids Editors. *Rocks and Minerals*. New York: Flashkids, 2004.

Fuller, Sue. *1001 Facts about Rocks and Minerals*. New York: DK Publishing, 2003.

———. *Rocks and Minerals*. New York: DK Publishing, 2003.

Mercer, Ian. *Gemstones and the Environment*. Westminster, CA: Stargazer Books, 2004.

Neumann, Brent. *Gemstones*. New York: Xlibris Corp., 2004.

Parker, Steve. *Rocks and Minerals*. New York: DK Publishing, 1997.

Ricciuti, Edward. *National Audobon Society First Field Guide to Rocks and Minerals*. New York: National Audobon Society, 1998.

Sorell, Charles. *Rocks and Minerals*. New York: St. Martin's Press, 2001.

Squires, Annie. *Gemstones*. New York: Scholastic Library Publishing, 2002.

Staedter, Tracy. *Rocks and Minerals*. New York: Reader's Digest Books, 2004.

Symes, R. F. *Crystals and Gems*. New York: Dorling Kindersley, 2000.

———. *Eyewitness Rocks and Minerals*. London: Natural History Museum, 2004.

——— SUGGESTED READING FOR TEACHERS

Argenzio, V. *Diamonds Eternal*. New York: David McKay, 1994.

Epstein, E. *The Rise and Fall of Diamonds*. New York: Simon & Schuster, 2001.

Kessler, S. *Mineral Resources*. New York: MacMillian College Press, 1999.

Lutgens, Frederick. *Essentials of Geology*. Englewood Cliffs, NJ: Prentice Hall, 2002.

McGraw-Hill Editors. *McGraw-Hill Dictionary of Geology and Minerology*. New York: McGraw-Hill, 2002.

Murk, Barbara. *Geology: A Self-Teaching Guide*. New York: John Wiley & Sons, 2001.

Press, Frank. *Earth*. New York: W. H. Freeman & Co., 1995.

5   Creating Mountains

—— MYTHS ABOUT CREATING MOUNTAINS

Mountains have always been viewed as places of power, enlightenment, and mystery. Majestic jutting peaks, like jagged teeth, reach toward the sky. They stagger our imagination, lift our hearts, and stir our souls. Mountains are the highest places on Earth, the places closest to the heavens.

Wise men do not seek out valleys that dip below sea level in their search for enlightenment. No. They climb mountains. Mountains are often considered sacred places. Gods live on mountains (Mt. Olympus in Greece, for example). Many cultures worshiped mountains as the homes of powerful gods and spirits. Some believed that the mountains themselves deserved to be worshiped as gods who turned to stone. Often, they made no distinction between the power of the mountain god and the power of the mountain itself.

Moses climbed Mt. Sinai to receive the Ten Commandments. The Hindu gods Shiva and Parvati live on Mt. Kailas. Mountains have traditionally been viewed as pathways between the heavens above and Earth below. Native American shamans climb mountains to acquire visions and revelations. They never sit on the flat prairie grass to do it.

But science is more interested in the *existence* of these stirring mountains than on their emotional and spiritual impact. Why do they exist? Where did they come from? Why isn't the whole world made of smooth plains? Why hasn't gravity dragged these rugged peaks back down to sea level? What force creates these towering backbones of stone looking like the plates of a stegosaur's back?

WONDERS OF THE LAND

Mountains are a major surface feature of the Earth. To understand and study the land requires us to study mountains. Why are they there? What pushed them up so high? Is there rhyme or reason to their location, shape, and length? What can we learn from studying mountains?

Virtually all traditional cultures have needed to explain the existence of mountains and their unique pull on the human soul. In an Apache story, animals built four mounds to reach the upper world. The mounds grew into mighty mountains. In a myth from Nagaland (India), Lijaba created the world. At first he worked slowly and carefully, making broad, even valleys. When he learned that enemies were coming to attack him, he quickly slapped the rest of the land together, not taking the time to smooth it out, leaving mountains and rugged cliffs in his rush.

In a Tibetan myth, the Himalayan Mountains used to be a herd of flying elephants. A displaced god cut off their wings and they crashed in a ragged heap to form the mountains we see today. In a Japanese myth, a giant wanted to fill up the Pacific Ocean with dirt. He grew tired and simply dumped the last shovelful. This shovelful formed islands of Japan—and, especially, Mt. Fuji.

In a Modoc myth from Northern California, Chief of the Sky Spirits grew tired of his home in the Above World and carved a hole in the sky. He pushed rocks, snow, and ice through the hole to form the first great mountain (Mt. Shasta) so that he could climb down and walk around on the Earth. The Kikuyu (Africa) creation myth begins, "When the world was still young, God, the creator, made himself a great mountain as a sign of his wonder and as a place where he could rest from his labors."

The myth that follows explains the creation of mountains in a more whimsical way. Coyote, that famed trickster, could also be an obnoxious pest. Eagle, the chief of all animals, orders the other animals to create mountains for practical, not supernatural or godlike, reasons. Here, it is not the gods but the first animal ancestors on Earth who create the mountains. This myth creates a lighter view of how and why mountains were first formed.

"MOUNTAIN MAKING,"
A MYTH FROM THE MODOC INDIANS OF CALIFORNIA

Back in the Beforetime, in the days after Sun was put into the sky, the animal people could see at last how wide and empty the world was. The plains stretched north, south, east, and west all the way to the sky's edge. In all the world there were no landmarks for the people to enjoy or to guide their travels. All the people were sad and wandered without purpose or plan. Yet they had never known anything else and so did not know how to fix things.

Near the middle of this vast plain sloshed the one lake, named Tulare. On that lake lived all the swimmers and divers among the Beforetime people. Pelicans lived there. So did ducks and geese and mud hens.

The land animals from Jackrabbit to Grizzly Bear, from Jumping Mouse to Eagle, from Coyote to Moose to Jay lived on the wide prairie, wandering where they wanted. Some gathered in small villages. Some drifted from spot to spot.

Now, Coyote, of all the animal people, was filled with delight over his own cleverness. Had not he been the one who tricked Sun into living in the sky? Was his plan not a grand success? Even fussy Crane said so. As Coyote paraded across the prairie, he felt that everyone should bow down and pay homage to his grand cleverness.

But they didn't. Before long, the animal people turned away and suddenly remembered some place else that they had to be when they saw Coyote coming. But the real reason they turned away was that Coyote, besides being so vain, was a terrible snoop and gossip.

With his soft, padded feet Coyote secretly sidled up close enough to overhear secret plans and feelings. And he couldn't wait to spread what he heard far and wide—especially to those who would be hurt the most.

"Did you hear what Muskrat said about Swan?"

"Can you believe how Mouse *really* feels about Jackrabbit? Oh, you haven't heard? Well, let me tell you!"

If Fox told his wife that Skunk's house wasn't particularly tidy, Coyote rushed to tell everyone. With each telling Skunk's house grew dirtier.

"Have you heard that the floor of Skunk's house is littered with mouse bones? It's true. Fox says so."

"Did you hear? Fox says that Skunk's food baskets store more maggots than food."

"Have you heard what Fox saw? Skunk's blankets are so stiff with dirt that he cannot fold them during the daytime. He props them against the wall!"

Soon, happy as a swallow in springtime, Coyote trotted off to tell Skunk that Fox had been spreading vicious lies about him. And then Coyote would howl with glee for days.

Even worse than *that*, Coyote was a meddler. He loved to meddle and couldn't stop himself from meddling even if he had wanted to—which he didn't.

"*That* is no way to shell an acorn!"

"*That* is no way to feather an arrow!"

"*That* roof will never keep out the rain!"

So the other animal people called Coyote "Old Nosey" and "Trouble Maker," and they turned away whenever they could.

But then Coyote turned his tongue's mischief on Eagle, chief of the animal people. Coyote whispered this. He whispered that. He made up this. He invented that—always at Eagle's expense.

"Did you hear that Eagle ate Cottontail's cousin?"

"Wolf told me that Eagle is almost blind in one eye and so lazy that he makes other birds do his hunting for him."

At last Eagle could stand no more. But he could not bring himself to harm Coyote, so he decided to find a place where he could live far away from meddlesome Coyote.

But where?

Then Eagle realized that Coyote was lazy. He would never bother to work hard enough to climb—not up high mountains.

But there were no mountains.

Eagle called all the animals together—all of them except Coyote. Eagle announced, "I am moving away to high mountains."

"What are mountains?" they asked.

"You will help me build them," Eagle announced. "As we build my mountains higher and higher, you will see what mountains are."

Eagle was a good chief. So all of the birds and animal people did as Eagle asked. They dug earth to form deep valleys and filled the dirt into their baskets. They slung these bulging baskets onto their backs and marched east following Eagle, who flew high above.

Where Eagle pointed, the animals dumped their baskets, creating vast mounds and jumbled peaks. Then they returned for more. Weasel, Bear, Caribou, and Mountain Lion worked beside Jackrabbit and Field Mouse.

Higher and higher the jagged mountains rose. Basket by basket, higher and still higher until snow began to fall across the mountaintops, covering them in a lacy blanket of white.

"Enough!" cried Eagle. "Enough!"

Panting animal people paused to look at what they had created—mountains. Towering mountains, jagged mountains, ragged cliffs, and slopes of mountains that seemed to poke the sky.

Baskets that were still full were spread along the western slopes of Eagle's towering mountains. Eagle thanked the people, cried his joy, and rose to the frozen peaks.

You can still see these mountains along the eastern edge of California. They are called the Sierra Mountains. The rolling foothills that stretch west toward the deep Central Valley are where the final baskets were dumped, the leftovers from building Eagle's hideout from Coyote.

THE SCIENCE OF CREATING MOUNTAINS

The following beliefs are either directly stated or strongly implied in the presented myth. Here is what modern science knows about the aspects of mountains explained by each belief.

> **BELIEF: Mountains were formed by the hand of the creator.**

In the myth, the first mountains were created because the head of the animals ordered them to be built. In the myth presented in the chapter on gems and minerals, the gods of the upper and lower regions built the first mountains for their own glory. But what *really* causes mountains to defy gravity and raise up to scrape the sky?

Two things can push up mountains: plate tectonics and volcanoes. But that answer is too general. It doesn't explain what actually happens well enough to make it understandable. Let's look first at plate tectonics. (These are shown in Figure 5.1.)

Plate Tectonics

There are three ways tectonic plates can create enough pressure to push up a few billion tons of rock to create a mountain range. This won't happen by accident. It won't happen just by chance. It takes a tremendous amount of force to shove that much weight thousands of feet higher.

Try carrying 100 pounds of rocks up one flight of stairs. It's work! Now do the math to see what it would be like to create a mountain. You lifted your rock about 9 feet. You'd have to lift it a thousand times as high to create mountains. You lifted 100 pounds of rock. You'd have to lift several billion times as much rock to create a mountain range.

How do tectonic plates create that much energy? There are three ways. First, they can smash together (collide). Second, they can pull apart (separate). Third, the movement of adjacent plates can squeeze one plate so that it ruptures along fault lines and pushes up a huge block of crust (block faults) to make room for the rest of the Earth's crustal plates. Let's look at each case.

FIGURE 5.1 • Forming Mountains

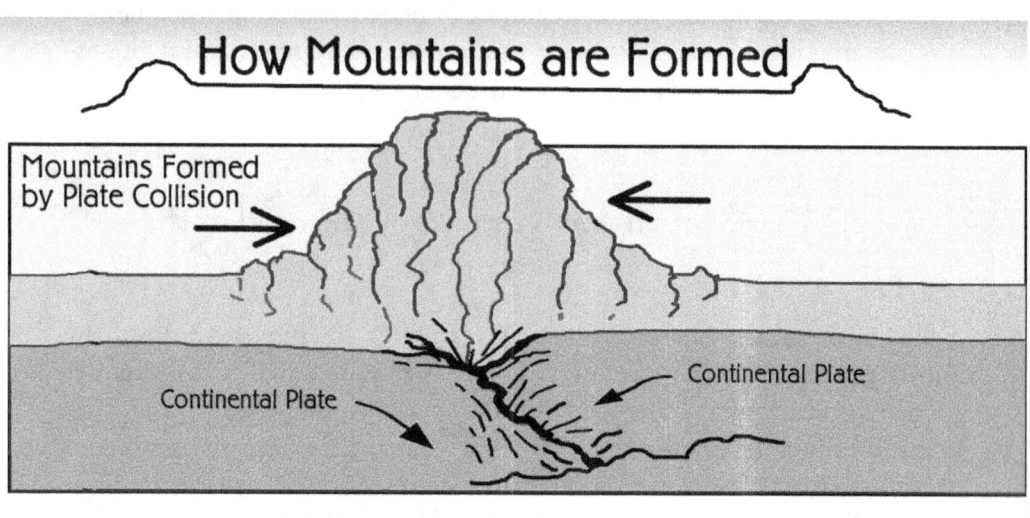
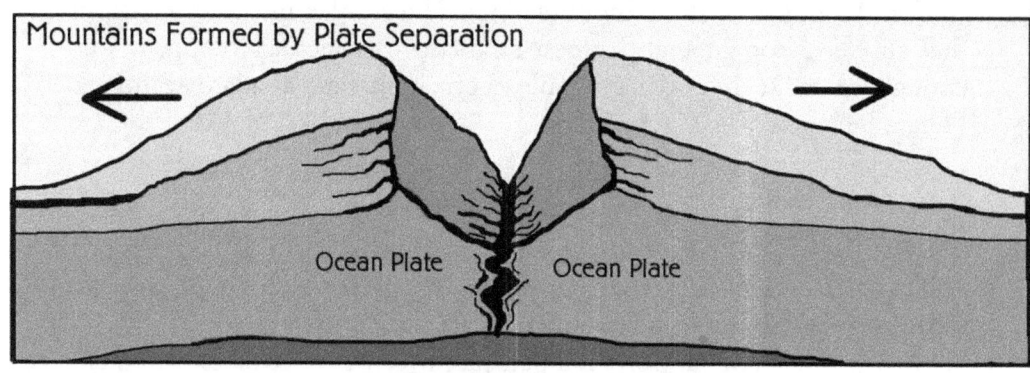
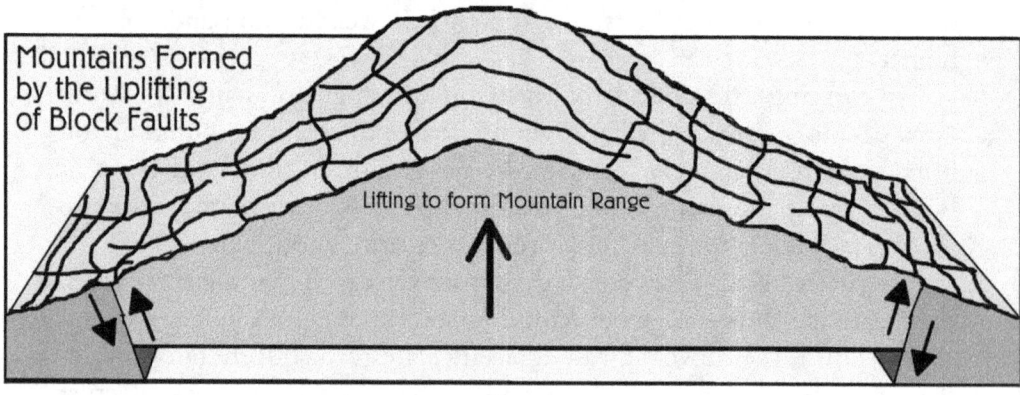

Creating Mountains

Collisions

We have already seen that plates can collide in three kinds of pairings: two continental plates can collide, two oceanic plates can collide, or a continental plate can collide with an oceanic plate. Any plate collision can be viewed as a car wreck. Fenders and bumpers are crumpled. Frames are twisted and squeezed. The fender-bender crumpling of crustal plates creates mountains.

When two oceanic plates collide, the collision and its effects are hidden deep beneath the ocean's waters. At this time there are no places in the world where two oceanic plates are colliding along deeply submerged plate boundaries.

When two oceanic plates collide, a *rift valley* will form along the actual boundary as some plate material is *subducted*. Earthquakes abound. Undersea volcanoes erupt. A mountainous ridge will form along one side of the plate boundary. If the collision continues long enough, that mountain range will build to the surface. Mountaintops will begin to appear as islands.

When an oceanic plate and a continental plate collide, the more dense oceanic plate is subducted. The leading edge of the continental plate is lifted and rides up over the oceanic plate. Earthquakes reverberate through the region as the bottom edge of the continental plate grinds over the oceanic plate. The continental plate scrapes sedimentary material off the oceanic plate and builds a line of new continental land along its boundary with the oceanic plate. The west coast of the United States has added almost 300 miles of new land in this way over the past 40 million years as it collides with, and grinds past, several oceanic plates.

Friction between the two plates will cause the leading edge of the continental plate to buckle and fold as it is lifted over the oceanic plate. A mountain range forms along the length of the border between these two colliding plates. A characteristic of these plate collisions is the formation of a narrow, long mountain range (the Andes in South America or the Sierras in California, for example). This range will be punctuated by teapot (and possibly soufflé) volcanic peaks as the oceanic crust is forced lower in the lithosphere, heats, melts, expands, and begins to push upward as magma. The Pacific Ocean is ringed with mountain ranges and volcanoes created in this way.

When two continental plates collide, it's like a classic, high-speed front-end collision between two full-sized cars. Not just the fender and hood get crumpled. The whole car seems to twist and deform. It's as if two sumo wrestlers slammed into each other, pushing, shoving, twisting, trying to force the other out of the way. Neither wrestler ducks under the other. Neither tries to climb over. They both slam straight into each other and try to muscle the other one out of the way. The plates buckle. This is called a *thrust* fault, or *folded* fault, since the plates are thrust upward by literally being folded back on top of themselves just as would be a rug that you pushed up against a wall.

These collisions don't produce volcanic activity, but they do produce earthquakes and rumpled, massive mountain ranges. The plates fold, fracture, and crumple. Giant rock faces crack and break. Sideslip faults develop as the plates try to slip around each other. The collision creates a large, fat impact area. The Himalayan Mountains' impact area is 1,250 miles by 1,900 miles (2,000 km by 3,000 km). The Indian plate is still crashing north at over 5 centimeters (2 inches) a year. The Himalayan Mountains are not through building yet.

The Swiss Alps were created when the African plate sailed north and collided with Europe. Those plates have now quieted, and that collision appears to be over. The Alps will now slowly weather. In 100 million years the famed Matterhorn Peak will be a rolling, grassy hill. The Appalachian Mountains were formed this way 250 million YAG back when all continents squeezed into a single master land mass called *Pangaea*. At that time the Appalachians probably rose up in 12,000-foot-high jagged peaks.

When continental and oceanic plates collide, they produce long, skinny mountain ranges. When continental plates collide with each other, they produce fatter, more jumbled ranges.

Separation

Mountains can also be formed when two plates pull apart (separate). The Atlantic Ocean's mid-oceanic ridge is such a mountain range. As two plates separate, they leave a thin gap in the crust between them. Magma pushes up through this weakened line in the crust. The lines of mountains thus produced are volcanic mountains.

These mountains never grow excessively tall because the plates on either side of the rift are pulling apart. That force stretches the new volcanic rock, pulling it sideways to become part of the spreading plates. Since much of the lava that would normally build the mountain range vertically is being pulled sideways, the mountains never achieve much height. This is certainly true for the mid-oceanic ridges through the Atlantic and Indian oceans.

Block Faults

There is one other way tectonic forces can push up a mountain range. If a plate is being squeezed from both sides, it will buckle somewhere in the middle.

Try it with a rug. Lay the rug on the floor and have two people push from opposites sides of the rug. Soon it will buckle. One section will be lifted up. The carpet will bend back on itself in an S shape. The same thing happens to plates. Stress builds up in rock layers of the plate as pressure squeezes in from plates on either side. Faults develop. The rock cracks, fractures, and rips apart. One section (block) of the crust breaks loose and is literally lifted up to make room for the rest of the plate. The edges of the lifted block usually buckle and fold back on themselves. This usually happens to large areas we often call *plateaus*. Sometimes a plateau lifts smoothly with little buckling to become a level high mountain plateau—until weathering forces begin to carve into it. Often, block faulting is accompanied by thrust faults. Part of the lifted block crumples and twists as it is wrenched upward. Then a mountain range forms.

The Tibet plateau (1,000 by 2,000 miles) has been lifted 5,000 feet by the India-Eurasia plate collision over the past 40 million years. The Colorado plateau was lifted in this way. As it also buckled and folded, the Rockie Mountains came into being.

That's how tectonic forces in the Earth's crust create mountain ranges by moving crustal plates around on the Earth's surface. There are two other ways the mountains we see can be created. The first is by volcanoes.

Volcanoes

We have taken an entire chapter to describe volcanoes and volcanic action. What volcanoes create with their flows of lava is giant mountains. Some of the most photographed and revered mountains in the world are volcanic mountains. Some of these mountains sit over hot spots. Some sit along the boundaries of plate collisions where an oceanic plate is being subducted.

Examples include Mt. Fuji in Japan, Mt. Shasta in California, Mt. St. Helens in Washington, the Three Sisters, Mt. Hood and Crater Lake in Oregon, Mt. Kilimanjaro in Kenya, Mt. Pinatubo in the Philippines, El Chichón, Popocatepeti and Pico de Orizaba in Mexico, Mt. Vesuvius in

Italy, Mauna Loa and Mauna Kea in Hawaii. These and many more famous mountains are volcanoes. Volcanoes create mountains.

Erosion

Tectonic forces and volcanoes can build up mountains. However, there is one other way individual mountains can be created. The forces of erosion, including water, wind, gravity, and glaciers, can wear down the land surrounding a mountain peak leaving some denser rock exposed and looking very much like a mountain. This usually happens when a dense, igneous rock plug forms in a lava tube, feeder pipe, or magma chamber (and when there isn't enough gas present in the magma to force a soufflé-type explosion). If that plug is big enough and if it is surrounded by soft, easily eroded sedimentary layers, then weathering and 50 million years or so can leave the plug standing hundreds—and even thousands—of feet above the surrounding plain.

Two excellent examples of this kind of mountain exist in the western United States: Ship Rock in northwestern New Mexico and Devil's Tower in Wyoming.

The belief is wrong. There are perfectly natural explanations for every mountain and mountain range on Earth. Tectonic and volcanic forces push mountains up. Weathering tears them down. Any existing mountain is the result of the war between these two sets of forces. You might wonder if making mountains is really that simple. If so, why are mountains all jagged and so complex? Rock in the crustal plates is brittle. It shatters and fractures as it folds and lifts. It breaks and cracks. These tectonic forces act on the rock over millions of years. Weathering attacks the exposed rock. It all makes for ragged, complex structure. But the forces that drive it all are relatively simple and easy to master.

BELIEF: Mountains and mountain ranges are unchanging and have always been as they are now.

The myth implied that once Eagle completed construction of the Sierra Mountains, they have sat unchanged from that time in the distant past to the present. Have they? Do mountains change or, once they are created, do they stay the same for millions of years?

As we have seen, mountains are battlegrounds for great, slow-acting armies. In one army, tectonic and volcanic forces push mountains. In the

Creating Mountains

other army, gravity combines with the weathering forces to pull them back down. Both armies have existed and fought over mountains for over 4 billion years.

The Himalayan Mountains were rolling hills 70 million years ago. They are a young range today and only began to look like mountains 65 million years ago. They will likely grow taller as India continues to push north, crumpling the edge of the Eurasian plate. The Sierra Mountains are also new—not more than 50 million years old and still growing as plate collisions along the Pacific coast continue.

A new island in the Hawaiian chain is being built as the Pacific plate moves west-northwest and pulls the Island of Hawaii off that well-established hot spot. The new island mountain is already 13,000 feet tall and only a few hundred feet from breaking above the surface of the Pacific Ocean.

The Andes Mountains may continue to grow as the oceanic Nasca plate (in the eastern Pacific Ocean bordering Chili) continues to be subducted under the South American plate. Or perhaps the plates may change their direction and speed and push up mountains somewhere else, create new rift valleys, and new seas and oceans.

Weathering begins as soon as mountains exist. Water, wind, ice, glaciers, earthquakes, and a host of living organisms attack all exposed rock and erode it back to a smooth level plain. (The last five chapters of this book examine the forces that erode and tear down the land.) Two hundred million years ago the Appalachians were as tall and jagged as the Alps. That's what 200 million years of weathering can do.

Mountains are thrust up over millions of years. It takes millions more to wear them back down. In 80 million years the Rockies will look like the Appalachian do now. Who can guess what new mountain ranges will have been born and, during that same 80 million years, rise with snow-swept crowns toward the heavens.

Mountains are ongoing masterworks in progress. The history and struggles of our planet are written in the mountain strata of rock. Ancient mountains wrinkle the land and then weather to stubs that are rewarped and refolded as new crustal plates collide. Sediment piles up, miles thick, and becomes new sedimentary rock. As plates shift, the land dips below sea level and now accumulates oceanic sediment. The plate is lifted again, pushed up and refolded into new mountains. Land strata again are tortured, fractured, and twisted. Layers of land sediment mix with layers of marine sediment. The layers appear confusing and meaningless. It takes years of study and practice to be able to make sense of the rock layers you find on an exposed hillside.

If tectonic forces suddenly stopped and the crust's plates ceased their movement, weathering forces would make the world as round and smooth as a Ping-Pong ball in short order (a few million years). But tectonic forces are still alive and active on our planet. All we know for sure is that the world of the future will look different than the present world looks.

The belief is wrong. Mountains never stay the same. The changes, while they go on every day, just happen too slowly for us speedy humans to notice.

BELIEF: Valleys were created by a creator and are unchanging.

In many creation myths, valleys are created by Eagle dipping his wings low over the new land. Some myths say that a creator carefully shaped and smoothed broad valleys for use by humans.

This chapter focuses on the tectonic forces that create the great features of our landscape. So we must separate valleys and canyons from "basins." The erosive force of water and glaciers creates valleys and canyons. They will be discussed later in Chapters 6 and 8. Here we will look at *basins*.

A basin is a large depressed area created by tectonic forces. There are two ways tectonic forces can create a basin. The first is when part or all of a plate sinks. Something happens deep underground to allow the surface layers to settle lower. This process is called *subsidence*. Tectonic plate movement could thin the crust, so the surface settles lower. Large magma chambers under the plate might cool rapidly and condense. Then the surface layers *subside* to fill in the gap. If the water table dropped rapidly, lowering groundwater levels, the surface can subside to fill in the vacant spaces that had been filled with water.

If subsidence happens over a large area and if the surface drops hundreds—or even thousands—of feet, then a basin is created.

The second way a basin can be created is through *continental extension*. A single continental plate can begin to split in two, to pull apart (to *extend* itself), forming a wide rift valley between the two parts. This happened to the North American plate some 40 million YAG. Slowly pull a piece of taffy apart and the middle stretches, thins, and sags. The same thing happens to the Earth's crustal plates. If the extension continues, the rift valley eventually dips below sea level and becomes a new sea. If the process stops, the rift valley becomes a depressed basin within the continent. That's what happened in North America. The continental stretching stopped 5 million years after it started, leaving a basin behind in the upper Mississippi River valley. Over the years, that basin has filled in with several thousand feet of sediment. Still, the basin reminds us that it could start again with occasional rumbling earthquakes through Missouri and the surrounding states.

Our planet is restless and is forever changing. Just as mountains are forever being pushed higher, basins dip lower. Just as the forces of erosion tear down mountains, they fill up basins, depositing countless tons of sediment in every depression to bring it back to smooth ground level. Earth's continents are not so solid and static after all—always shifting, subsiding, lifting, thrusting, buckling, moving, turning. Just like the planet, itself, they act as if they were very much alive.

WONDERS OF THE LAND

— TOPICS FOR DISCUSSION AND PROJECTS

Here are activities, research topics, and discussion questions you can use to expand upon the key science concepts presented in this chapter.

Research and Discuss. Let's compare old and new mountains. Research to find the oldest and youngest mountain or mountain range. Now research those two to compare their shape, size, features, and history.

An Activity. Let's use carpets (area rugs, runners, or throw rugs) to see how plate collisions create mountains. For this experiment, you will need three pieces of carpet, each at least 4 feet wide. Two should be deep-pile, thick carpet. One should be thin, dense, indoor-outdoor carpet.

Lay the two thick carpets side by side. One person sits on each side and both slowly push their carpet into the other. The carpets crumple along their boundary. They scrunch up and jam into each other. This is a collision between two continental plates.

Replace one carpet with the indoor-outdoor carpet and repeat the experiment. Did the thicker carpet ride up over the thin one? The thin carpet was subducted. This is like a collision between a continental plate and an oceanic plate.

Finally, lay just one of the thick carpets on the floor and let two people push on it, one from each side. The carpet will buckle in the middle. One section of the carpet pops up into the air. This is a block fault. Some of the carpet is shoved higher to make room for the rest of the carpet in the ever-shrinking space below.

Research and Discuss. We don't have a choice. We have mountains. They exist in our world. Some people view mountains as obstacles to travel. Others view them as things of beauty. Think for a while about the advantages and disadvantages of having mountains. Make a list of as many pluses and minuses as you can to having mountains. Remember to consider mountains' effects on atmosphere, water, people, plants, and the planet. Decide if you think having mountains is a net plus or a minus. Write a page justifying your conclusion.

An Activity. Let's see how much energy it takes to push up a mountain. Carry 100 pounds of rocks up one flight of stairs. Make as many trips as you need. It's work! Now do the math to see what it would be like to create a mountain. You lifted your rock about 9 feet. You'd have to lift it a thousand times as high to create mountains. You lifted 100 pounds of rock. You'd have to lift several billion times as much rock to create a mountain range. How does the Earth create that much energy?

An Activity. Create a chart of different mountain ranges with the following five columns: age, height 1, height 2, length, and width. Height 1 is the height of the range's tallest peak. Height 2 is the average of the range's four tallest peaks. You can measure length and width using a good atlas. Height information you should be able to find on the Internet. Research each of your mountain ranges to find an estimated age.

Compare the age and height columns for each range. Are the older ranges lower? They should be, since they have been exposed to more weathering. Now look at the length and width columns. Does the range's shape tell you what kind of plate collision formed the range? Collisions between two continental plates produce wider mountain ranges than do collisions between one continental and one oceanic plate. These collisions produce long, skinny ranges.

An Activity. Create your own myth about a mountain or mountain range. How did it come to be? Why is it the way it is? Why is there (or isn't there not) snow on the top? What happened to cause its creation? Who did it? Why? How will the end of your myth explain the current state of this mountain?

SUGGESTED READING FOR STUDENTS

Bailey, Donna. *Mountains*. New York: Steck-Vaughn, 2000.

Bevan, Finn. *Mighty Mountains*. Chicago: Children's Press, 1997.

Bromwell, Martyn. *Mountains*. New York: Franklin Watts, 2000.

Claybourne, Anna. *Mountains*. New York: Smart Apple Media, 2004.

Crewe, Sabrina. *Hills and Mountains*. New York: Scholastic Library Publishing, 1997.

Cumming, David. *Mountains*. New York: Steck-Vaughn, 2000.

Fowler, Allan. *They Could Still Be Mountains*. New York: Scholastic, 1999.

Ganeri, Anita. *Mountains*. New York: Gareth Stevens, 2003.

Gregory, K. J. *Earth's Natural Forces*. Oxford: Andromeda, 2000.

Locker, Thomas. *Mountain Dance*. San Diego, CA: Harcourt, 2001.

Rotter, Charles. *Mountains: Towering Sentinels*. Lawrenceburg, IN: The Creative Company, 2003.

Simon, Seymour. *Mountains*. New York: William Morrow, 1997.

Staub, Frank. *America's Mountains*. New York: Mondo Publishing, 2003.

Taylor, Barbara. *Mountains and Volcanoes*. New York: Houghton Mifflin, 2002.

Tidmarsh, Celia. *Mountains*. New York: Thomson Gale, 2004.

─── SUGGESTED READING FOR TEACHERS

Farndon, John. *How the Earth Works*. New York: Reader's Digest Books, 1999.

Harris, Stephen. *Fire Mountains of the West*. Missoula, MT: Mountain Press, 1999.

Martin, H. *Intracontinental Fold Belts*. New York: Springer-Verlag, 1993.

Price, Martin. *Mountains: Geology, Natural History and Ecosystems*. Minneapolis, MN: Voyager Press, 2002.

Tabor, R. *Geology of the North Cascades: A Mountain Mosaic*. San Diego, CA: Mountaineers Books, 2002.

II FORCES THAT CHANGE THE LAND

6 Water

MYTHS ABOUT HOW WATER SHAPES THE LAND

Water means life. Without water we, along with the plants and animals we depend on, all die. Water covers 70% of Earth's surface. Water is the creator of life, but it is also the destroyer. Drownings, flooding, tsunamis, and drought (a lack of water) claim thousands of lives each year. That makes water the perfect subject for myths.

Water seeks low ground, always flowing downhill, rushing, tumbling, roaring to get lower toward sea level. Streams, rivers, and creeks swirl, gurgle, tumble, and flow across the landscape. These waterways are always tucked along the bottom of gullies, valleys, and canyons. Waterways are never found riding a ridgeline or marching across the crest of a hill.

Most origin myths begin with water (oceans) and the heavens already in existence. From these, some being forms land and creates life. Literally hundreds of creation myths begin by saying that in the beginning the world was all water.

In myths, water usually affects the land (once land exists) only as a flood. Myths from hundreds of traditional cultures talk about the great flood that scoured the landscape, wiped out early evil or unjust civilizations, and gave humanity a second chance. Even landlocked cultures in arid regions—the Sioux and Arapaho tribes, for example—have myths of a great flood that covers the Earth and kills almost all living beings.

The biblical flood of Noah is one of the few floods that can be traced to a specific geologic cause and event. Most exist in mythology even though there is little evidence that they ever happened in physical reality.

Water is also the source of fog and mist—creepy earthly shrouds that seem to invite mystery, supernatural events, or the arrival of evil. The action of water, especially acidic waters, creates caves and caverns. These empty spaces in the Earth's mass have always been viewed as dark and mysterious places. Caverns are doorways to the underworld and to the land beyond death. To many people it seemed wrong and unsettling that solid Earth should have such holes and gaps, as if caves represented a mistake or the work of a demon.

Certainly, water deeply affects—even controls—life. But does water affect the land itself? Earth Scientists study the land, not the life upon the land and certainly not the marine environment. Does water alter land? Is our land different because of the action of water or the presence of water? Does a study of the land require a study of water and the water cycle?

A few creation myths try to explain the *origin* of the oceans and of water. Virtually none, however, focuses on the *effect* of water on the land, on how water changes the land. Water creation stories typically rely on the mischief, greed, or misdeeds of a character to trigger catastrophic events that create the sea in a great flood. In one especially inventive story from Thailand, villagers decide to build bigger and bigger kites to win a kite-flying tournament. A clever man, helped by a gang of children, builds a kite bigger than houses, bigger than fields, bigger than valleys. A great storm blows in and lifts this enormous kite. The man and the children try to hold on, clutching at trees, grass, rocks, and even the ground itself. But the storm lifts the kite high into the sky, pulling people and a great chunk of the Earth with it. The hole left behind forms the Bay of Siam. The bay fills with water that bubbles up from below, and the water spills over to create the oceans. The chunk of Earth flies up to become the moon. The kite sails even higher to become a constellation of stars in the twinkling night sky.

In a myth of the Tiano people of the Caribbean Islands, a famous hunter is killed by a hurricane. His magical bow is placed in a calabash and, when his people are in desperate need, this calabash splashes out fresh fish. Greedy boys break the calabash, and out pour all the waters of the oceans and seas. In a Venezuelan myth, the sea is trapped in a greedy pelican's egg. The pelican wanted to hoard all the fish for itself. A curious and mischievous boy cracked open the egg and out spilled the ocean to cover everything except the mountaintops that became islands.

In a Yurok myth, Thunder and Earthquake are worried that, without water, the people will not have enough to eat and will not be able to live. Earthquake stomps off to find water. He sinks the land as he goes, and that allows the ocean to flood in.

The following myth from the Hawaiian island of Kauai focuses on the intervention of magical folk. In Ireland they are called leprechauns. In Hawaii they are the *Menehune*. This story's theme is that magic can move mountains, create new canyons, and divert river flows. But can a stream itself accomplish any of those daunting tasks?

"THE GIFT OF THE *MENEHUNE*," A MYTH FROM KAUA'I, HAWAII

More years ago than we can count, thousands of little people—elves called *Menehune*—lived in the Hawaiian Islands. *Menehune* only venture from their hiding places at night, and even then you can only see glimpses of these tiny men in the very corner of your eye.

On the Island of Kauai, there lived a noble and much loved chief named Pi. He should have been happy. Life was good and his people were happy.

But Pi worried. He worried that some day something terrible would happen and his people would expect him to fix it. Pi wasn't at all sure that he could.

Soon enough, there came a terrible time when rain did not come to their valley. The plants withered. The pigs grew thin and became little more than skin and bones. The beautiful fishponds shrank to cracked mud. All the fish died.

The people were hungry and frightfully thirsty and they turned to Pi and demanded that he save them.

Pi called the tribal wise men together for a council. "What can we do?" Pi asked.

One suggested, "The Waimea River still flows through its canyon across the island. Perhaps we could build a dam to stop it and cut a canal through the mountains to make it flow through our valley."

Pi shook his head. "It would take years to complete such a massive project. We would all starve or die of thirst long before the canal was built."

"We could move to another valley that still has a river," suggested another.

"I have also thought of this," Pi answered. "But we would have to fight another tribe to take over their valley and many would be killed."

Pi paced across the woven mats of the floor of the council hut. "There must be another way..."

Pi sat and brooded on a tall rock overlooking his withered valley. He felt lonely and afraid. The brightly colored headdress and feathered cloak that marked him as chief felt unusually heavy.

A flash of color swirled on the rock beside him. A tiny man whose headdress and cloak were miniature matches of Pi's stood with hands on hips. The top of his red and yellow helmet only reached as high as Pi's knee.

"I am the chief of the *Menehune*," he said proudly. "I have come to help you."

Pi almost laughed. "How can anyone as small as you help me?"

"Size has nothing to do with it," snapped the tiny chief.

"I meant no offense," said Pi. "My people are troubled. We have no water. If we could make the Waimea River dig its way through the mountains and flow down our valley, then the grass would grow to feed our pigs. The fishponds would be full. Taro would grow in the fields. We would have water to drink. But it would take my best men ten years to dig the channel. How could one as small as you help?"

"You humans are so stupid," laughed the tiny chief. "My people are better workers than your. We can do it in a single night."

The *Menehune* are known to be pranksters, and Pi grew suspicious. Still he said, "If you could really do that, I would give you anything you want."

"Done and agreed!" said the *Menehune*. "I have but two conditions and you'll have your water before sunrise tomorrow."

Pi drew back, fearing the worst. "And the two conditions?"

"First, all of your people must stay in their houses with their doors shut and their windows covered. If anyone peeks, we shall vanish."

Pi nodded. That was easy enough. "And the second condition?"

"On the next full moon you will prepare a feast of fish for my men. There must be enough food for all of them."

"That's all?" stammered Pi, "Done and agreed!" They solemnly bowed to seal the bargain and the *Menehune* vanished.

That afternoon Pi ordered all of his people to a meeting. He said, "I have been visited by the chief of the *Menehune*."

The people gasped and groaned, thinking a devilish trick would heap new calamity upon them.

Pi held up his hands for quiet. "He promised to cut through the mountain and build a gorge that will divert the Waimea River to flow into our valley—tonight."

The people laughed at how ridiculous Pi's statement sounded. Again Pi sternly held up his hands. "I do not know if they can do such a wonderful thing, but no harm can come from letting them try. There are only two conditions."

Again the people groaned, but Pi shouted over them. "First, no one must watch. Stay inside tonight with your doors shut and your windows covered. Anyone who peeks will be severely punished. Second, on the next full moon we must feed the *Menehune* workers. Now go to your houses."

Everyone stayed shut inside that night listening to the distant sounds of picks and shovels, of chisels being hammered, of rocks rumbling down the hillside and being tumbled into place.

As soon as the sun rose, Pi's people rushed outside. Water already trickled down their valley. At first it all soaked into the parched earth, but soon there was a steady, strong flow. It gurgled over stones and swirled around bends, singing the bubbling river song that had not been heard in the valley for months.

By midday the river flowed bank to bank and the fishponds began to fill. Pi and two elders hiked up the canyon and found a deep and lovely gorge cut through the mountains looking as spectacular and natural as even the best work of nature. It looked as if the Waimea had always flowed through this deep mountain cut and down into Pi's valley. He could not believe that the *Menehune* had done this wondrous work in just one night.

Pi sat alone, marveling at the glory of his new river, when he sensed a flutter of feathers as if a brightly colored bird had flown from the treetops. The chief of the *Menehune* appeared beside him.

"You kept your first condition," smiled the chief. "No one peeked."

Gesturing to the flowing river, Pi blurted, "This is wondrous and wonderful. How could you have moved mountains—in just one night?"

The chief smiled and shrugged. "My men are better workers than you mere humans." He eagerly rubbed his hands together. "And now the second condition."

Pi thought for a moment. "Dinner. Of course."

"A *feast* of fish," the *Menehune* chief corrected.

Pi nodded. "Gladly. Tell me how many workers there were so we can prepare enough."

The chief cocked his head and began to count on his fingers. "Twelve thousand—give or take a couple." And he disappeared.

Pi was dumbstruck. How could his small village ever prepare enough food to feed twelve thousand hard-working *Menehune*? Pi suddenly knew he would fail and the Menehune would strike great calamity upon them.

Pi trembled as he raced down the mountain and called an emergency council meeting, where he repeated his impossible problem.

The wise men wrinkled their brows as they pondered. But a young nephew of Pi's who overheard began to laugh. "You have answered your own question uncle. The *Menehune* are tiny men and can each be fed with one tiny fish.

Pi beamed. "One shrimp per *Menehune* will be plenty! We can do *that*."

By the day of the full moon the tribe's fishermen had caught a mountain of shrimp in their nets. Others kept great fires burning on the beach to heat the water that would cook the shrimp. The rest of the tribe busily wrapped each shrimp in a dark-green broadleaf and tied them to the branches of the trees near Pi's house.

As the full moon rose, it shone on twelve thousand tiny packages gently swinging from tree branches. By morning every package was empty. Nervously Pi checked. The river still flowed and gurgled. The *Menehune* were satisfied.

To this very day the river still bubbles and sings over the rocks. And to this very day the mountain that the *Menehune* had to cut in order to make a channel for the river is called Shrimp Mountain to honor the day that the *Menehune* saved Pi's tribe.

——— THE SCIENCE OF HOW WATER SHAPES THE LAND

The following beliefs are either directly stated or strongly implied in the presented myth. Here is what modern science knows about the aspects of water's effect on the land explained by each belief.

BELIEF: Water was created before the land existed.

So which came first? The chicken or the egg? The sea or the land? In the story presented in Chapter 1, the ocean existed and the land was created only after a woman fell through the sky.

Five billion YAG—give or take several hundred million—hot gases and space dust began to condense into a planet—the Earth—as they spun around a glowing, pulsing star—the Sun. Over the next billion years that hot, molten mass cooled so that its crust hardened and solidified into solid rock. But the planet was not quiet. Volcanoes ripped the crust apart. Molten lava and gases boiled across the land. An atmosphere of gases began to form above the planet. Water vapor, spewed into the sky from the volcanoes and vent gases, filled that atmosphere and formed into thick clouds.

It began to rain. For centuries and eons as the volcanoes blasted steam and glowing lava into the air, the clouds poured down torrents of rain.

The rain gathered into lakes and rivers that tumbled toward the lowest lands, filling those to become the oceans.

Three hundred and fifty million cubic miles of water now exist on Earth. Virtually all of it existed billions of years past when the oceans first formed. Water cycles through oceans, clouds, rivers, dinosaurs, trees, evaporation, polar ice caps, and humans and goes back to the oceans.

That is science's best estimate of how the land and oceans formed. What does it mean? First, land existed before the oceans were made. Second, it took millions (probably hundreds of millions) of years to form the oceans. Third, water is neither created nor destroyed. It cycles and recycles through the Earth. The water you drink today is really billions of years old. It might have been lapped up by a wooly mammoth, a diplodocus (a dinosaur), or a saber tooth tiger. It might have been sucked out of the Earth by a prehistoric redwood tree. It might have been locked for a million years into the ice structure of an ice age glacier. Two hundred thousand YAG an early human might have looked at his reflection in a pool that held one of the water drops you drink today.

There is still some water below the crust of the Earth. It reaches the oceans and atmosphere when volcanoes erupt and when undersea vents pour forth their fiery steam and gas. The belief is wrong. Land existed before the oceans.

It is also important to look at where Earth's water is. Ninety-seven percent of our 350 million cubic miles of water sloshes in the oceans. That means that 340 out of our total 350 million cubic miles of water is saltwater. Only 3% of Earth's water is freshwater. Of that tiny portion, two thirds is locked up in the polar ice caps.

That leaves only 1% of all of Earth's water (3.5 million cubic miles) as freshwater for us to drink, to cook with, to bathe in, to grow crops with, to wash cars and clothes with, to generate power with, and to water our lawns with. However, much of the world's unfrozen freshwater is not available for our use. Over half of all freshwater is locked up either as buried groundwater or as water vapor in the atmosphere.

The world has 350 million cubic miles of water. All humans, plants, and animals on this planet try to get by using the 1.6 million cubic miles of available surface freshwater! Freshwater is truly a precious and scarce resource.

The Water Cycle

So, where is that freshwater? Where does it go? How does it move? There is a cycle that water flows through. Of course, it is called *the water cycle*. Water flows continuously and endlessly through this cycle, as shown on Figure 6.1.

Let's begin with *evaporation*. Water exposed to air will evaporate—change from liquid water into gaseous water vapor. Most evaporation happens from the oceans because that's where most of the water is. Evaporation also happens from lakes, streams, swimming pools, and glasses of water. You exhale small amounts of water vapor with every breath. Water evaporates off your skin to cool you. Plants give off water vapor through the pores of their leaves.

All this evaporated water rises into the atmosphere. When the air cools, this water forms into clouds and then into droplets that fall as rain and snow. That's called *precipitation*. Water evaporates *up* and precipitates *down*.

When water lands on the surface, it will do one of two things: percolate down into the ground or run off along the surface of the ground. If water percolates into the ground, it either will be absorbed by plants (to be released into the air again as evaporation) or will enter into some

FIGURE 6.1 • The Water Cycle

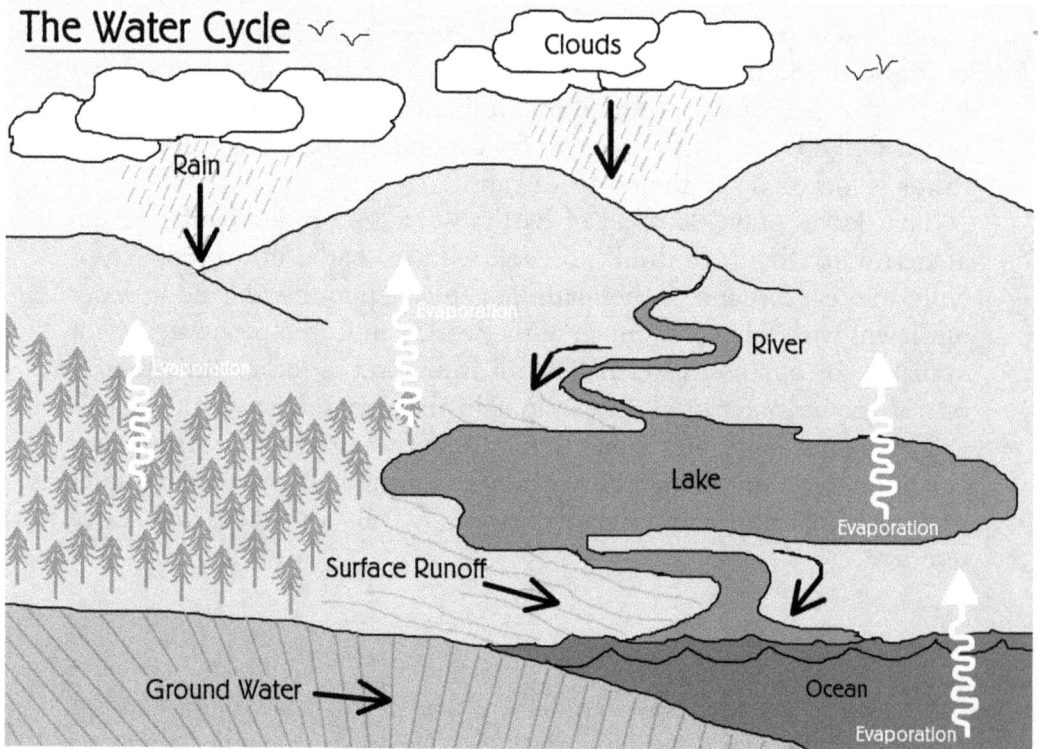

groundwater system. Groundwater either will emerge onto the surface as a spring, will feed into a lake, or will eventually flow into the ocean. Surface runoff flows into creeks, streams, rivers, lakes, and—if it doesn't evaporate along the way—eventually back into the ocean.

That is the water cycle. Water is constantly flowing between oceans, atmosphere, surface, and subsurface (underground). Along the way drops, molecules, and gulps of water regularly pass through plants, animals, and humans as well as our factories and farms.

BELIEF: Water just flows past and doesn't change the land.

Does water change the land, or does it just pass by as it flows through its endless cycle? The truth is that water is the most powerful erosive force on Earth. Running water can move mountains. Water does so much to alter the land that we must divide our discussion of water into separate parts.

Rain

If you have ever stood under a heavy rain, you know that raindrops can hit hard enough to hurt. Each drop is like a tiny jackhammer. One drop does virtually no damage. But 10,000—or a million—striking the same spot on the same rock over the years can do real damage to the rock. Rock grains and flakes chip off to be carried away by wind and flowing water. Weak spots and joints in the rock erode and turn into wide cracks and fissures.

Over the centuries, rain physically beats on, and wears down, rock. However, there's more. Rainwater is naturally slightly acidic. It chemically eats away at rock surfaces while physically pounding on them. In a process called *chemical weathering*. Look at the headstones in an old graveyard. They will show you what rain can do to rock. In polluted air, airborne sulfur dioxide (a pollution product of burning fossil fuels in combustion engines) mixes with rainwater as it falls. Now you get *acid rain*, a much more potent acid that eats quickly through many sedimentary rocks—especially limestone and sandstone.

Rainwater seeps into tiny cracks, pores, joints, and crevices in exposed rock, mostly along planes and edges of the crystal structure of minerals in the rock. There water actually dissolves some chemicals and minerals, leeching them out of the rock. The cracks and crevices widen, making room for roots to tear the rock apart.

As the rainwater filters down through rich soil and humus, it picks up carbonic acid (the stuff that makes soda pop fizz and bubble), another mild acid. These acids help the water etch channels and paths deep through bedrock layers below.

Rainwater will also wash away all unprotected soil, carrying it into the nearest creek or stream to be deposited miles away. We humans need the rain, but it is the most damaging weathering force on Earth for rock and soil.

Rain can also cause more sudden and violent changes to the land. When rainwater saturates the soil and rocks in a hillside, it is easier for the rocks and dirt to slide. The result is mudslides and landslides. Whole sections of a hill or mountain slide downhill like an avalanche, leaving bare, ugly scars on the land above. Hundreds of tons of dirt and rock move lower down the mountain as a result.

Ice

When water freezes, it expands. When water trapped in a rock crack or crevice freezes, it tries to push the rock apart to create the room it needs to freeze into ice. Freezing water exerts the same force on a rock as would a mile-high column of ice. That's a lot of pressure!

Over the course of a single winter, the water molecules trapped in rock crevices might freeze, thaw, and then refreeze dozens of times. Each time the water freezes, it pushes the crack a little wider—letting in more water to push even harder on the rock with the next freeze. Water drops that repeatedly freeze and thaw shatter countless rocks each year.

The sun's heat can do the same thing, especially in the desert, where temperatures can vary 50 degrees or more from day to night. The daytime sun heats the outside of a rock. As is true for all matter, the parts that heat try to expand. But some minerals in the rock heat faster than others. The *inside* of the rock stays much cooler that the outside. Some parts expand. Some don't. This creates great stress between the different layers and sections of the rock and pulls at the bonds that hold the rock together. Over and over again, day after day, the joints and edges between layers of the rock are stressed until the bonds begin to weaken and break down. The rock cracks and separates.

Waves

Eventually all rainwater reaches the ocean. There the wind whips it into waves. Along the shoreline, these waves pound the coastal rocks and shore. If raindrops are like tiny jackhammers, then waves are like giant wrecking balls. An 18-foot-high storm wave can pick up and throw a 10-ton boulder. Every wave—big or small—hammers on coastal rocks. In many places coastal bluffs are eroded as much as 3 feet a year by the pounding waves.

Waves and coastal currents move millions of tons of sand every day—moving it both along the shoreline and, periodically, onto the beach or back offshore into underwater sandbars.

Streams

Raindrops roll into tiny rills that gather into puddles that feed into gullies and streams that flow into rivers. Every one of those flowing bodies of water erodes the banks (sides) and bed (bottom) of its channel.

Such erosion is called *scouring*. Running water with suspended particles of sand and grit in it is like sandpaper scraping across the streambed. Streams constantly dig and gouge at their banks and bed, ripping out dirt and small flakes of rock and carrying them away downstream. Streams and rivers move amazing amounts of material out of mountains and down onto flatland this way.

Streams carry particles in three ways. First, some minerals actually dissolve in water (like table salt) and are carried as part of the water flow (called *dissolved load*). Some small particles of sand, grit, silt, and dirt are suspended in the current (called *suspended load*). Bigger rocks too big to be picked up are rolled along the stream's bottom by the current (called *bed load*).

An example will help. Fill a large glass two thirds full of water. Add a teaspoon of salt and stir the water. The salt disappears. It has dissolved and chemically bonded with the water. It is now dissolved load. Wherever the water flows, the salt will flow with it.

Now add a spoonful of sand and stir the water again. As long as the water keeps moving, it will carry the sand particles. But you can still see the sand. It is still sand. It hasn't dissolved or changed form. Sand is suspended load. As the water slows, the sand will drop to the bottom of the glass. The salt is dissolved and will not drop to the bottom even when the water completely stops moving.

Now add a few marbles and stir again. The sand rises back into the water and is again carried in suspension. The marbles stay on the bottom. But they do roll some with the water current. They are bed load.

If you stirred the water really fast, the marbles would actually lift into the water column and become suspended load. As water flows faster, it can carry bigger rocks as suspended load. High up in mountains, the slopes are steep and streams roar by at high speeds. They can tear away and carry large rocks down the mountain and quickly erode deep canyons in the mountainside. Lower down in the foothills, the slope becomes more gradual. The river's speed slows. Larger grains and pebbles drift to the bottom. By the time the stream becomes a sluggish river meandering across lowland plains, it can carry only the finest grains of silt and mud.

Rivers act like sorting machines. They gouge as much rock as possible from the tops of mountains and then drop the biggest rocks first while still far upstream. Silts and mud are carried the farthest downstream. Sand and gravel are dropped in the middle.

How much can a stream carry? It depends on how big the river is and on how fast it flows. The Amazon is the world's biggest river—over 5 miles wide at its mouth. It carries as much sediment into the ocean as every other river in the world combined. You can see the muddy brown plume of its waters stretch 50 miles into the Atlantic Ocean.

Waterfalls are a part of a river system that erode the land very quickly. The power of the stream's water rushing over the falls quickly erodes the top lip and front face of the streambed at the falls. As the rock at the waterfall erodes, the waterfall itself inches farther upstream. In effect, waterfalls walk upstream. Soon the falls will have moved hundreds of feet back upstream. Horseshoe Falls on the Canadian side of Niagara Falls, for examples, moves upstream at a rate of over 5 feet every year! In 20 years the falls move 100 feet. Repeat visitors actually notice the change. The falls have moved 7.1 miles in the last 12,300 years.

As rivers near the ocean and slow to a crawl, they tend to drop almost all of the material they have dutifully carried down from distant mountains. They are like a continuous line of giant dump trucks pouring sand, silt, and dirt around the river's mouth—all day, every day. All this new material extends the land out into a wide fan shape called a delta. The Mississippi River is a good example. The river used to end close to New Orleans. But the river delta now extends another 80 miles downstream. That delta dirt used to be part of hills and mountains spread from Montana to Missouri to Pennsylvania. An aerial photograph of the Nile River in Egypt shows a giant and classic fan shape to its delta.

In desert areas the rivers that flow out of mountains during the infrequent heavy rains rarely reach the ocean. Once the river reaches the flat desert floor, the water is absorbed into the dry ground. The river disappears and drops all the material it carried down from the high mountains into wide fans at the foot of the canyons leading out of the mountains. These fans are called *alluvial fans*. Some of them are huge. The California cities of San Bernadino and Riverside are built on a single 30-mile-wide alluvial fan.

Groundwater

Underground rivers flow under most of the land of the continental plates. These rivers are *groundwater*, or water flowing through the ground. If you drill a well, you'll eventually hit water. That's groundwater. Some of these groundwater systems are hundreds of miles wide. Most percolate slowly through the rock, advancing only a few feet each day. Some flow much faster and have carved out underground tunnels and caverns to flow through.

Groundwater systems are moving rivers. In all the ways that rivers scour and erode their streambeds, groundwater erodes the rock it flows through. However, most groundwater flows are very slow and so don't erode their streambeds nearly as fast as surface streams do. It is the acids that groundwater has picked up, especially carbonic acid, that do the real damage to rock. Carbonic acid dissolves rock—especially sedimentary rock, and most especially limestone and sandstone. This is how most caves and caverns are created.

Flooding

Periodically rivers overflow their banks and spread out to cover wide areas on both sides. The speed of river water increases. Erosion along the riverbanks increases dramatically. Often a river actually changes its course during a flood and carves a whole new channel.

Floods do terrible damage to human homes, stores, and communities, but they are actually good for the open land of the floodplain. Floods deposit rich new soil over the flooded area. The floodplain is a part of a river system. It's the land on either side of a river's channel that is periodically covered by floodwater.

The belief is wrong. Water is the most powerful and effective erosional force on Earth. Not only is water a powerful weathering force, it has so many ways it can attack the land—rain, streams and rivers, flooding, slides, waterfalls, groundwater, scouring, and chemical erosion. No wonder water reshapes the land so dramatically. The land we know would look very different were it not for rain and moving water.

BELIEF: Water flows through existing canyons.
(Canyons were formed first.)

In the story, the *Menehune* had to build a canyon before the water could flow through the mountains and reach Pi's valley. Canyons exist and then water flows through. Is that true?

Moving water (rivers) creates canyons and valleys. A stream flowing across a flat plain will erode its banks and bed, washing away some of that material. Soon the streambed is lower than the surrounding ground. But streams never stop their work. They continuously scour and erode their channel. The river cuts deeper and deeper into the land. However, this means that its banks grow higher and higher.

Soon the banks grow too high and too steep to be stable. Mudslides and landslides collapse part of the bank down into the river channel—where the river dutifully carries the material away downstream. Rainwater running down the steep sides of the river valley washes away the soil, making the growing valley wider and less steep.

Over time, the river continues to dig deeper. Rainwater and slides make the valley wider and its slope less steep. Soon you have a narrow canyon if the sides are a hard rock that resists weathering, and so it remain steep. If the sides erode more easily, the process creates a rolling river valley.

Amazingly, rivers can cut their way straight through mountains and ridgelines. The Delaware Water Gap is such a cut through part of the Appalachian Mountains. So are the Cumberland Gap and the Wiamea River Valley on the island of Kauai.

Canyons are steeper. Valleys are broader and have more gentle slopes. However, both are V shaped. At the bottom of the V lies the river—ever digging the bottom of the V deeper and deeper. The shape and steepness of the sides depends on how much rain falls on them (the more rain that falls, the more the sides are eroded and the gentler the slope) and on the hardness of the rock that makes up the valley or canyon sides.

How deep can a river go? The Grand Canyon is 1 mile deep and, at places, 15 miles wide. The Colca River Canyon in Peru is twice as deep—just over 2 miles from rim to river level!

The belief is wrong. Water creates valleys. Streams and rivers carve out and sculpt canyons and valleys.

BELIEF: Caves and caverns were formed when the land was formed. Caves don't grow and change but are now as they always have been.

Caves and caverns are spooky places with narrow twisting passages and perpetual darkness. Tom Sawyer and Becky Thatcher were terrified of a cave in Mark Twain's book. Caverns are hidden places deep in the bowels of the Earth. They seem to be access routes to the demons underground. They seem like mistakes, gaps that the Earth forgot to fill with solid rock. Why do these strange things exist? How did they come to be?

Caves and caverns are created by water. A cave is a hole in the ground with an opening to the outside. So, technically, most caverns are caves. But the word *caverns* usually refers to large underground chambers with connecting passages and wiggleways. Cavern systems often extend for many miles and contain dozens of chambers. Not all caverns connect to the surface. Many undiscovered caverns still lie deep within the Earth's crust.

Caves are created by physical erosion. Waves pound the coast and scoop out caves that extend back into coastal bluffs. The same happens at river waterlines along steep hillsides. Cave development can be sped up by chemical erosion of rock layers that weakens the rock and makes it easier for waves and currents to wash it away and lengthen the cave.

Caverns are created by chemical erosion. Period. Water plus carbonic acid (picked up as the water down through soil and humus) plus a dash of sulfuric acid (acid rain) equals erosion of soft limestone, gypsum, chalk, and other sedimentary rock layers. These acids dissolve the rock along seams, joints, and weak spots opening up a network of tunnels and chambers.

Large horizontal chambers usually form between two layers of harder rock as acids in groundwater eat away the softer rock between them. The tallest chambers are often created when the thin rock layers between a series of smaller vertically stacked chambers collapse. Groundwater carries away the rubble, leaving a glorious, cathedral-tall cavern behind.

Groundwater builds these cavern systems in one other way. The level of the groundwater in the rocks rises and falls over time—sometimes by hundreds of feet. The top of the groundwater flow in any given spot is called the *water table*. When the water table is high, acid-ladened groundwater eats away at soft sedimentary rock layers. A thousand years later, the water table might drop 100 feet lower. As it slowly drops, it carries the rock sediment with it and leaves empty caverns behind where there used to be solid rock. Now actual streams flow through the chambers and passageways, rushing to reach to the water table below.

Water drips from chamber ceilings and dribbles down chamber walls. The water table might rise and fall hundreds of times over a million-year period. By that time, the complex cavern systems that we enjoy, and that brave spelunkers try to map, have been created.

You can watch this process in action. Visit any of the major caverns in the world. Feel the chamber walls. Many will feel damp. Some will have thin films of water flowing over them. Taste the water. It will have a mineral taste. Those minerals are from the rocks that are being dissolved above and carried down to the water table. Look for stalactites and stalagmites. (Stalactites hang from the ceiling and hold "tight." Stalagmites rise up from the floor with all their "mite.")

Dribbles of water run down each stalactite and drip down to the top of a stalagmite below. These features are made out of minerals and bits of limestone carried from somewhere above and deposited here by the passing water. Stalactites and stalagmites used to be rock in some rock layer above that is being hollowed out by water trickling down toward the water table. Flowing sheets of water down cavern walls often form hanging deposits that look like draperies (called *draperies*), flowing curtains of deposited limestone. Water acts as a sculptor's tool inside a cavern.

Caves and caverns exist in every country on Earth. They exist in every state and along all coastlines. These caverns often develop thriving and unique ecosystems—ecosystems so different from what we are used to seeing on open land that they deserve special study. Villa Luz Cavern in southern Mexico is a good example.

The air in many of the chambers of this 5-mile-long cavern system is saturated with deadly hydrogen sulfide and hydrogen fluoride acid. The walls drip with a watery sludge stronger than battery acid, as corrosive as the strongest lab acids. Pools of mud on the floor are so acidic, one touch could raise ugly blisters and burn your skin. Without specialized protection and breathing systems no human could survive in many of the rooms and chambers for more than a few seconds.

This toxic nightmare should kill every living organism. Yet the cavern teams with life. Creatures—even unique whole species—have adapted to this toxic environment that would kill a human in moments. Spiders, microbes on walls and floors, tarantulas, albino turtles, blind fish comfortable in the perpetual blackness of the cave, and a dozen other species live quite happily in acid that would dissolve your flesh and bones. No one yet knows how these creatures adapted to this acidic environment and how they survive. While the creatures live quite happily, the rock walls and floors of the cavern continue to erode at a rapid rate as the acidic water dissolves the rock.

Caves and caverns have a significant effect on the rock structure of the crustal plates, but rarely do they directly affect the surface of the land. Rarely, but not never.

Some 4,700 YAG, the city of Ubar on the Arabian Peninsula was a major trading center. Caravans crossed the desert from all directions to reach this ancient trading Mecca. Then Ubar vanished. The whole city disappeared.

By the dawn of modern times, most scientists and historians thought that Ubar was a myth, that there never had been such a place. Some still searched across the desert for traces of Ubar, but they were laughed at by serious scientists.

In the late 1990s, satellite infrared images where taken of that region of the Arabian Peninsula. They showed faint lines through the desert that converged at a single spot. Researchers discovered that crushed desert sand reflects heat and light slightly differently than does regular sand. Ancient camel trails contained packed, crushed sand, ground down by countless passing camels. The faint lines were ancient camel trails.

Using Global Positioning System (GPS) satellite locators, archeologists raced to the spot where the ancient trails converged. Nothing was there but blowing sand. They began to dig. Several hundred feet down, they found the remains of Ubar.

Unbeknownst to the builders, Ubar had been built on sand that sat directly above a large limestone cavern. The cavern roof collapsed, plunging the entire city to the cavern floor 100 feet below. Desert sand flowed in to fill the hole. In a matter of days Ubar was buried beneath 100 feet of sand and every trace of the city was gone. It must have been quite a shock to the next caravan to find that Ubar had disappeared!

The belief is again wrong. Water creates caves and caverns. As we have seen, water is responsible for more of the actual shape and contour of the land we live on than any other force.

 ## — TOPICS FOR DISCUSSION AND PROJECTS

Here are activities, research topics, and discussion questions you can use to expand upon the key science concepts presented in this chapter.

Research and Discuss. We have all heard of the water cycle—evaporation, precipitation, surface flow, ground flow. Research the elements of this cycle. How does evaporation happen? Why does water evaporate? Why does water vapor in the air form clouds? Why are clouds at the height that they are? Why are clouds shaped the way they are? How can so much rain (water is heavy) come out of a cloud that has almost no weight at all and is so light that it floats in the air? How does water flow through the ground? Why doesn't it keep flowing down deeper? Write a one-page paper that describes just one small part of the water cycle in great detail.

An Activity. Do a demonstration experiment to create a graphic image of how much water exists on Earth and how much of it is fresh water. You will need a good garden hose, a 5-gallon bucket, a tablespoon, a teaspoon, several shallow cups, and a 1-gallon container for this demonstration.

First, turn on the hose to simulate the first rains pouring water down on a new and barren Earth. Time how long it takes your hose to pour 4 gallons of water into the bucket. A hose with average pressure can flow at about 4 gallons per minute. If your hose poured water continuously every minute of every day at that same rate, how long would it take your hose to produce the 350 million cubic miles of water that exist on Earth?

Answer: a long time. One hundred and twenty-five trillion years to be exact, or 7,500 times longer than the universe has existed. If you used *a million* hoses, each pouring water at 4 gallons per minute, it would take them "only" 125 million years to produce the Earth's supply of water. That's a lot of water!

Now let's pretend that 1 gallon of water represents the Earth's entire supply of water. (Fill the 1-gallon jug with water for this demonstration.) If that 1 gallon represents all water on Earth, how would you divide it to represent Earth's saltwater and freshwater? Remove *2 tablespoons* of water from your 1-gallon jug and pour them into a shallow cup. The water still in the jug represents the Earth's supply of saltwater. Those 2 tablespoons represent all the Earth's fresh water.

However, two thirds of the Earth's fresh water is trapped in polar ice caps. How much is left for all human, plant, and animal uses on Earth—the amount in all rivers, lakes, streams, and groundwater aquifers? Lift 2 *teaspoons* of water out of the cup and place these few drops in a sec-

ond cup. That tiny amount represents all the fresh water we and all other land-based life forms ever see or use. All the rest of Earth's water either is locked in polar ice caps or is salty seawater.

Does that give you a sense of how big the oceans are? Does it make you think of how precious the planet's tiny freshwater supply is? Explain and defend your beliefs in a persuasive essay.

Research and Discuss. When you turn the faucet, freshwater comes out. Where does it come from? Research you water supply from your tap back to its original source. Research what happens to the water along this route. Draw a model of this route showing everything that happens to the water between source and your tap.

An Activity. Let's model all three ways that a river can carry material. Fill a large glass two thirds full of water. Add a teaspoon of salt and stir the water. The salt disappears. It has dissolved and chemically bonded with the water. It is now dissolved load. Wherever the water flows, the salt will flow with it.

Now add a spoonful of sand and stir the water again. As long as the water keeps moving, it will carry most of the sand particles. But you can still see the sand. It is still sand. It hasn't dissolved or changed form. Sand is suspended load. As the water slows, the sand will drop to the bottom of the glass. The salt is dissolved and will not drop to the bottom even when the water completely stops moving.

Now add a few marbles and stir again. The sand rises back into the water and is again carried in suspension. The marbles stay on the bottom. But they do roll some with the water current. They are bed load.

If you stirred the water very fast, the marbles would actually lift into the water column and become suspended load. As water flows faster, it can carry bigger rocks as suspended load. Would you expect a tumbling mountain stream to carry bigger particles than the sluggish Mississippi River as it flows past Louisiana? Which would you expect to carry more total material? Why?

An Activity. Let's measure one stream's suspended load. Go to a local stream with a large glass jar that has a screw-on lid. Either wade, boat, or swim to near the center of the stream with your jar. Guess at the height of the stream at this point and try to collect your water sample from near the vertical midpoint of this height. (It is not important to be exact.) To collect your sample, start with the jar lid screwed on. Don't unscrew it until you have positioned the jar at the collection point, facing upstream. Unscrew the lid, fill the jar, and rescrew the lid before bringing it back up to the surface.

Once you get the jar to shore, shake it vigorously to stir up all sedi-

ment. Then watch as the sediment settles. Try to note the size of the biggest grains (the ones that settle first). Note how long it takes for the finest particles to finally settle to the bottom. Let the jar sit overnight and carefully pour off most of the water without losing any sediment. Shake up what's left and pour it through a coffee filter. Be sure to get all the sediment out of the jar. Let the filter dry for a day before weighting the sediment that was carried in your jar of water. (Remember to subtract the weight of the filter.)

Finally, do the math to estimate how much sediment a mile of your stream carries. Estimate the height and width of your stream and calculate its cross section area (height × width). Calculate the size of your jar (πr^2 if it's round; length times width if it's a rectangle). Divide the stream cross section by your jar's cross section to find out how many times larger the stream is than your jar. This is the number of jars you'd need in order to fill up the stream across that one spot with jars. Let's call this number "A."

We're almost there. Measure the height of your jar in inches and divide that number into 63,360 (the number of inches in a mile). This is the number of jars you'd have to line up in a row to be a mile long. Let's call this number "B."

Multiply A times B and that number times the weight of the sediment you collected in your jar. That number is your estimate of the total weight of the suspended load carried in just 1 mile of your stream. Now imagine how many miles of streams exist in the world and how much material they erode from mountains and carry toward the oceans every second of every day!

Research and Discuss. What's the difference between a *canyon* and a *valley*? Research both terms and decide what *you* think marks the real difference between the two. Then write an essay both explaining your view of the difference and justifying using that criteria (whatever it is) as the "official" difference between a valley and a canyon.

SUGGESTED READING FOR STUDENTS

Cole, Joanna. *The Magic School Bus Wet All Over.* New York: Scholastic, 1998.

Curry, Don. *The Water Cycle.* Mankato, MN: Capstone Press, 1999.

De Weese, Robert. *Land and Water.* New York: Evan-Moor Educational Publishers, 2000.

Downs, Sandra. *Shaping the Earth: Erosion.* Brookfield, CT: Twenty-First Century Books, 2001.

Gareri, Anita. *Crumbling Earth*. Chicago: Raintree Publishers, 2004.

Gifford, Clive. *Weathering and Erosion*. New York: Smart Apple Media, 2005.

Harmon, Rebecca. *Water Cycle*. Portsmouth, NH: Heinemann, 2005.

Locker, Thomas. *Water Dance*. San Diego, CA: Harcourt, 2002.

McKinney, Barbara. *A Drop around the World*. Spokane, WA: Dawn Books, 1998.

Nelson, Robin. *Water Cycle*. New York: Lerner Publishing Group, 2003.

Olien, Rebecca. *Erosion*. Mankato, MN: Capstone Press, 2001.

Patent, Dorothy Hinshaw. *Shaping the Earth*. New York: Clarion Books, 2001.

Rowe, Julian. *Water*. New York: Franklin Watts, 2001.

Spilsbury, Louise. *Disappearing Mountain and Other Earth Mysteries*. Chicago: Raintree Publishers, 2005.

Winner, Cherie. *Erosion*. New York: Lerner Publishing Group, 1999.

SUGGESTED READING FOR TEACHERS

Boardman, John. *Soil Erosion by Water.* New York: Springer-Verlag, 1998.

Downs, Sandra. *Shaping the World: Erosion.* New York: Lerner Publishing Group, 2000.

Julien, Pierre. *Erosion and Sedimentation.* New York: Cambridge University Press, 1998.

Schullery, Paul. *America's National Parks: The Spectacular Forces That Shaped Our Treasured Lands.* New York: DK Publishing, 2001.

Troeh, Frederick. *Soil and Water Conservation.* New York: Pearson Educational, 1998.

Wilcox, Charlotte. *The Water Cycle.* Mankato, MN: Capstone Press, 2000.

7 Wind

MYTHS ABOUT HOW WIND SHAPES THE LAND

Wind is a multifaceted resident of Earth. It blows both good and bad. It is essential and pleasant, and yet it is also deadly destructive. Wind brings a gentle summer breeze to cool us. Wind blows in needed summer rains to grow crops. For thousands of years wind in our sails was how people and cargo moved across seas and oceans. But this same capricious wind drives fierce storms that destroy and kill—hurricanes, tornadoes, and cyclones. The same wind that gently flies kites also snaps trees in half and crushes houses.

Winds drive the deserts sands and propel massive sandstorms that bury whole cities. Howling winds drove the dust storms that crippled the American Midwest during the Dust Bowl. The word *desert* comes from the Egyptian word *deshret* meaning "the red lands." The word implies that deserts are dangerous, evil, places of marauders and death. The desert is a land of mirages—visions—as if the gods were toying with human travelers. Deserts are rolling seas of lifeless, shifting sand. Deserts are the home of the wind.

But wind is also breath. Our breathing in and breathing out is a form of wind. Wind is the breath of life. In many myths, it is the wind god who blew (breathed) life into the first people.

Wind is invisible, swirling through our world like a bodiless trickster on a whim. But wind has a voice. It can be heard—bellowing, moaning, and howling as it blows past. Invisible voices are things of the gods.

Humans have always been in awe of the wind. We can feel it and hear it, but we can't see or touch it. We use it and depend on it, but we have no idea where it comes from, why it blows, or where it's in such a rush to get to.

No wonder traditional cultures have had a difficult time describing and understanding the wind. What are mere mortals to make of such a phenomenon? Wind seems to relate to many other factors and forces of the Earth but seems to answer to none. People have always believed that wind has no master and can do whatever it wants to do.

Is this true? Is wind an independent force on Earth? Are there rules (natural laws) it must follow? Does wind have a place in a study of the land? Wind is obviously important to understanding weather. Wind affects sailors. Wind affects human comfort. But is wind relevant to Earth Science? Does wind affect the land itself?

Most cultures have tried to explain the wind in their mythologies. In many myths, winds from different directions were assumed to be different gods, each with his or her own personality. This explains why some winds are friendly and some angry, raging, and deadly. Some cultures believed that wizards or sorcerers brewed the winds and flung them at humans for revenge and spite, for pity and kindness, or for favor and friendship—depending on their mood at that moment. Many myths propose that winds were evil demigods (forces) held in prison by true gods. But those pesky winds regularly escaped—just a little—to blow in all their wrath and power across the land.

The Nenets of Siberia talk about Kotura, Lord of the Winds. In their myths, young women must be sent to him as sacrifices and must pass difficult tests in order to win his leniency for their people. If these women don't satisfy Kotura, he will blow fierce winds to torment and disable the tribe. That concept is shared by many other myths.

A number of cultures have myths about the Son of the Wind. Several African tales are typical of this group. The Son of the Wind is a boy who likes to play with real boys and is kind and polite—until someone speaks his name. He then falls to the ground kicking and flailing and hurls giant, unstoppable wind balls that roar across the Earth.

The myth that follows is typical of myths that honor wind above other natural forces (most often sun and water). The same story (with slight shifts of characters) appears in cultures from Russia to Malawi in Africa and from Mexico down the Americas to Chili. This version comes from elements common to myths across many of the eastern republics of the former Soviet Union.

"Sun, Water, and Wind,"
A Myth from Russia

One day, Sun, Water, and Wind came down to Earth and strolled along the roads near Drenberg (Eastern Russia). The day was pleasant. Birds chirped, and the three travelers sang and joked as they walked.

Soon they came upon a simple peasant who was walking the other way. "Greetings, oh great sir," the peasant hailed with a deep bow. "May God's blessings be upon you. Long may you live and longer may you prosper. May all good things come to you and yours now and forever more. May all your kin be blessed for all their lives." Again he bowed and continued on his way.

"What a good and decent fellow," beamed Sun. "He certainly has learned how to offer a proper greeting. I am touched and flattered that he greeted me so respectfully."

Water bristled, sloshing his head from side to side. "What makes you think the peasant was greeting you? He said 'great sir,' and that surely means that he was addressing me."

"You soggy fool," laughed Sun. "Of course it was me he greeted so politely. I warm the man and make his crops grow." Sun shrugged and chuckled. "Of course, I can also burn his crops, wither his fields, and destroy his well-being. The peasant owes me everything and fears me above all else. Of course he pledged greetings to *me*."

"You bag of hot gas," laughed Water. "He can go much longer without you than without me. Water is life. Life only occurs where I grace it with my flowing presence. It is me the peasant fears and worships with his greeting."

Water and Sun both raised fists and slowly circled as if to fight. Both snarled and spat.

But before the first fist flew, Wind said, "I'm afraid you're both wrong and I can prove it."

"How?" demanded Sun.

"Simple. We'll ask the peasant."

Sun, Water, and Wind raced back down the road after the peasant. And asked, "Good sir. You gave a gracious and proper greeting, but it seemed that you addressed it to only one of us. Which one was it?"

"Why, the wind," replied the peasant without a moment's hesitation.

Sun reddened with anger. "Insolent fool! I'll teach this peasant to insult me. I blast him with my heat. I'll burn him and his crops to a blackened crisp!"

Wind shook his head and smiled. "No you won't. I'll fan the peasant with a cooling breeze. I'll blow clouds over him to block your rays from burning his crops. As long as I blow, you'll not harm him."

Water boiled and foamed. "Stupid man. Without my good graces, you die! I'll drown you under raging flood waters for this!"

"You can do nothing of the kind," laughed Wind. "I'll simply blow your clouds away and keep you from dumping your torrential rains on his valley."

"Then I'll dry up his valley and laugh when he withers and dies of thirst."

"No, again," answered Wind. "Even a simple peasant knows that when I blow my storm winds, I can blow water-soaked clouds over this valley to meet all his needs for water."

Sun bristled, "He is just an ignorant peasant. Come with me over the hills to a better place and I will show you people who properly worship the Sun God—*me*!"

Wind replied, "And I will make them regret that folly."

They traveled across the hills to a lush land of waving grass and vast herds of animals. Sparkling temples were crowned with images of the sun. Sun crossed his radiant arms and sneered. "You see. Here are enlightened people."

Wind's cheeks puffed out and began to blow across these fertile fields, hot and dry. Sun tried to stop him, but could not. Water tried to reach the quickly parched lands, but could not. The people wailed and dropped to their knees, begging for salvation. Even as their crops and animals and neighbors withered and died, they prayed to the Sun God, who stood helplessly in the road and could do nothing without the help of Wind.

Wind blew until the crops blackened, until the rivers all dried to dust, until the ground cracked and turned to dust and sand. And still Wind blew. Vast clouds of sand swept across the now-dead land covering all living things with hot death, turning the land into desolate desert.

Sun and Water both bowed their heads in defeat and departed back to the sky. You can still see that parched land, now turned to the desolate Red and Black Deserts (Central Asia) by Wind's ravaging. The few people who scrape out a living there now offer reverent and thankful greeting to all three forces—Sun, Water, and Wind. But especially they praised the wind. For it is the wind that carries in springtime each year and chases out the cold of winter. It is the summer wind that cools them and nudges in the gentle summer rains. And yet, when Wind is angry, death and destruction surely follow.

THE SCIENCE OF HOW WIND SHAPES THE LAND

The following beliefs are either directly stated or strongly implied in the presented myth. Here is what modern science knows about the aspects of wind's effect on the land explained by each belief.

BELIEF: Wind is created by a god. Wind *is* a god.

In the story, wind seemed all-powerful. It seemed able to blow wherever it wanted to blow, anytime it wanted to. Can it? Does the wind control clouds and rain? Does it act independently of the sun?

The answer is no, yes, and no. Winds don't blow just because they want to. Winds are created by natural forces. In this case it is the Sun's heat and the spinning of the Earth.

The Sun heats the Earth. But more of the Sun's heat pours down onto the tropics (near the equator) than on the upper latitudes and polar regions. Heat rises from the tropical oceans and heats the tropical air. As air heats, it expands and rises.

This moist, hot air rises high over the tropics, into the upper atmosphere and drifts outward toward the mid-latitudes (20° to 40° North and South latitude). As this hot air rises and drifts at high altitude out toward the mid-latitudes, it cools. Cool air can't hold as much water vapor. As this air cools, clouds form and begin to rain. This rain is heaviest over the tropics where the air holds the most moisture and tapers off as the air is wrung dry and moves toward the mid-latitudes. When this air reaches the mid-latitudes, it descends as cool air. As it descends, it begins to warm up again. As it warms, it can hold more moisture and, so, stops raining.

As hot air rises over the tropics, cooler air from the mid-latitudes is pulled at a low altitude toward the tropics to replace the hot air that rose. The now cool, dry air, which originally rose over the tropics as hot air, descends over the mid-latitudes to replace the air that just flowed toward the equator.

In this way, the Sun's heat creates circulation patterns in the atmosphere, as shown in Figure 7.1. In the Northern Hemisphere, air warms and rises over the tropics, flows north at high altitude and descends at mid-latitude (20° to 40° North). There, as cool air, it begins

WONDERS OF THE LAND

FIGURE 7.1 • Global Air Currents

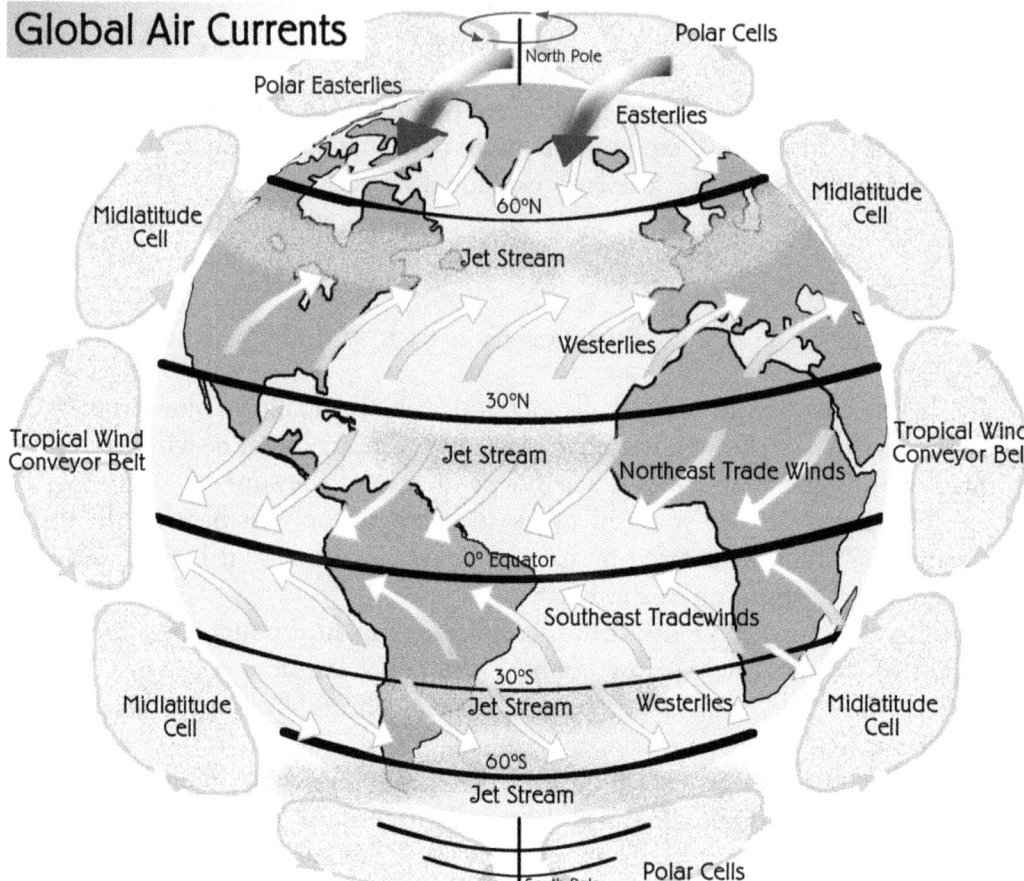

the return flow south at low altitude toward the equator. In the Southern Hemisphere, the same thing happens—only the directions are reversed.

This is like a conveyor belt of wind (known as the *tropical wind conveyor belt*). In this conveyor belt, most rain falls near the tropics as the rising air first begins to cool. By the time the air reaches mid-latitude and descends, little or no rain falls. Virtually all of the world's non-polar deserts are located in this mid-latitude band (between 20° and 40° either North or South latitude). The Gobi, Sahara, Sonoran, Death Valley, Kalahari, Namib, West Australian, and Chilean deserts are all in these bands and *not* near the equator, where it is the hottest, because of the tropical wind conveyor belt.

The Earth also spins. Spin a glass ball (or heavy rubber ball) in a pan of water. As the ball turns, it tugs at the water molecules right next to it, so the water nearest to the ball will spin fastest. The water farther away will spin slower (if it spins at all). The planet does the same thing with the atmosphere around it. The air nearest to the Earth is pulled along faster in the direction of Earth's spin while the air higher up feels less of a pull and so moves slower. This sets up wind currents *around* the world. The jet stream is one of these around-the-globe winds. You can see this effect in the wind directions shown in Figure 7.1.

Combine these two phenomena and add in one more factor and you have the world's major wind patterns. What's that other element? Weather systems. High and low pressure systems form and drift around the world. They grow and become stronger. They grow weaker and fade. Air flows from high pressure to low. Every time two of these systems are near each other, wind blows from the high-pressure system to the low-pressure one.

Winds caused by solar heating and the Earth's rotation are steady winds. They blow predictably all year long. Sailors invented names for each of these winds and for the calm patches where these winds don't usually blow. They planned their sailing routes to follow theses major winds.

Winds created by weather systems change every day, however, as the high- and low-pressure systems move. They cause the local winds to vary and shift direction from moment to moment.

These three forces create and control the winds. The Sun is one of the major forces fueling and driving the winds, and so, in a sense, the Sun creates and controls our winds.

BELIEF: Wind is more important than rain or sun in determining weather and landforms.

The story claimed that the wind is definitely more important than Sun or water. Is it?

Water, wind, and the sun's heat are three of the weathering forces that erode soil and rock and reshape the landscape. Of these, water is the most powerful—when it rains. But it can only rain when the wind blows moisture-laden clouds over that particular patch of land. Thus the story was correct. Wind controls rain.

Wind is also a powerful weathering force in its own right. Wind picks up tiny particles of sand, dust, and grit and hurls them at exposed rocks.

It's just like the sandblasting that painters use to blast all loose paint off a building before they slap on a fresh coat of paint. Actually, it *is* sandblasting, since sandblasting is just sand carried by a strong wind (wind created by a machine in this case).

Wind tends to smooth and round exposed rock, wearing away any corners and points. Wind does the most damage to rock and soil in regions of pour soil and in sandy areas—deserts. These are the areas where the wind can scoop up the most particles and where the lack of vegetation gives the wind easy, direct access to hammer against exposed soil and rock.

Wind-ravaged areas of the Southwest offer magnificent examples of the power of wind erosion. Sculpted rocks and rounded cliffs look as if an artist made them. The wind seems to "polish," round, and smooth the surface of exposed rocks.

The bigger the area a wind blows over and the stronger it blows, the more rock and dirt material it will actually carry. The faster (stronger) the wind, the bigger the individual grains and rocks it will carry. As is true for streams, winds carry *suspended loads* and *ground loads*. Suspended loads are the particles of dust, sand, and grit that are actually carried in the wind. Ground load are those larger rocks and grains that are bounced and rolled along the ground by the wind.

Most winds can lift grains of sand and gravel no more than 3 feet off the ground. These particles swirl up into the wind, sail forward a bit, and then fall. Then they're lifted again, and then fall again. It's as if they "hopped" along with the wind.

Even mighty sandstorms are only *sand* storms for the bottom 3 or 4 feet. Above that they are really *dust* storms. This accounts for "pedestal rocks." These are rocks that look like fat, teetering rock mushrooms balanced on skinny stems. The bottom 3 feet have been sculpted into a narrow pedestal. They have been sandblasted by the wind. The top part of the rock has been spared the effects of sandblasting erosion because sand particles can be lifted by the wind. The top part has been "*dust*" blasted—not nearly as effective at eroding rock.

You can also see this effect on desert telephone poles and road signs. The bottom 3 feet will be badly eroded by wind-borne sand. Above that the pole will show little sign of wear.

While winds can't lift sand and gravel far off the ground, winds *can* lift dust, ash, and silt particles high into the atmosphere. Winds carry dust and ash 1,400 miles from Australia to New Zealand. Dust from China regularly falls on Japan. Dust from Africa's Sahara Desert falls on some of the Caribbean Islands.

In a May 1935, wind storm, during the American Dust Bowl days, the wind carried so much dust east from the prairie farm belt from Texas to the Dakotas that midday in New York City, 1,850 miles away, looked like twilight. Those same winds dumped enough dirt and grit on the decks of ships 300 miles out to sea that crews had to sweep and shovel it up. Wind can carry dust from a large, explosive volcanic eruption around the world.

Stronger winds can pick up and carry larger particles. A 100-mile-an-hour wind in a hurricane can blast a piece of straw straight through wood siding or bury it in a tree trunk as if the straw were a bullet. It can rip up trees and carry large planks of wood as if they were made of balsa wood.

The strongest winds on Earth are the roaring winds that circle inside a tornado. These winds can top 200 mph. At those speeds, tiny wind-driven particles could tear skin and muscle off your skeleton—if you could somehow stand still and not be blown away. These storm winds radically change the local landscape.

Does wind erosion change the land? You bet! During the Dust Bowl, ground level was lowered 3 feet in just a few years by the howling winds. Over just 600 years (a lightning-fast blink in geologic time) wind blew enough sand off the beaches of several of the California Channel Islands to smother and kill an entire oak forest, leaving behind only rolling sand dunes and the bleached trunks of dead trees.

Wind actually causes less erosional change than does water. Still, wind is a powerful weathering force, and it is the dominant weathering force in deserts where little rain falls.

BELIEF: Wind creates deserts.

In the story, the wind blew clouds away and created a desert. Does the wind do that? In a word, yes.

A desert is defined as an arid region that receives less than 10 inches of rain per year. Deserts are places of bleached bones, circling vultures, burning heat, and not a cloud in sight—because prevailing winds push them all away. Deserts are wastelands of sparse vegetation.

Twenty-five percent of all land outside the polar regions is desert: the Sahara Desert (at 3.9 million square miles the biggest of the world's deserts), Death Valley, Arizona's Sonoran Desert, the Africa's Kalahari (Arabic for "always dry"), the Gobi Desert in China, the Mexican and Baja

FIGURE 7.2 • The World's Deserts

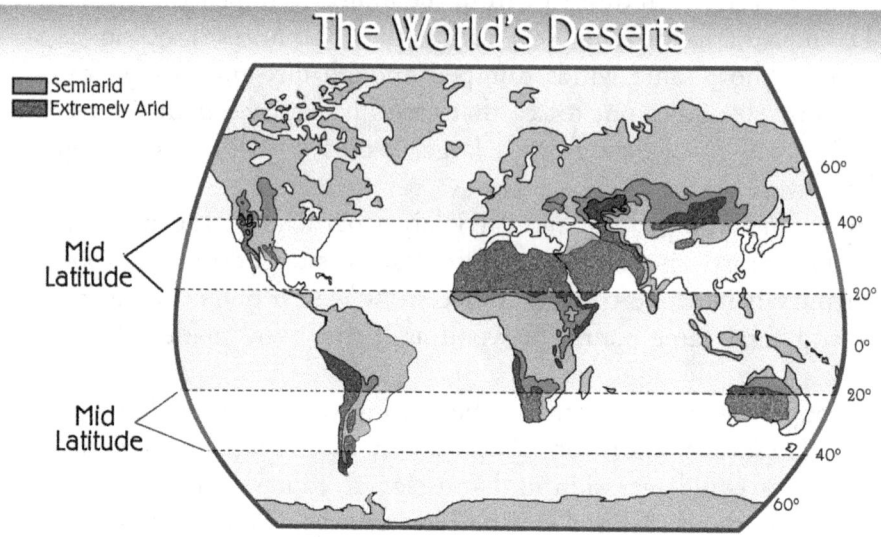

deserts, and the Atacama Desert in northern Chili. (The Atacama is the world's driest desert. It often stretches over a decade between measurable precipitation.) Scorching deserts seem to be *everywhere*. But are they?

To find the world's deserts look between 20° to 40° latitude both north and south of the equator. In those bands lie all of the world's non-polar deserts (see Figure 7.2). Why here? It's that tropical wind conveyor belt again. Warm air rises over the tropics, and its moisture is wrung out before it cools and descends as dry air into the mid-latitudes. Those areas (20° to 40° North and South latitude) get less rain.

But not all the land in these mid-latitudes is desert. *Besides* a location in the mid-latitude bands, what else is needed to create a desert?

There are a number of specific conditions that can create a desert. Any one of them is enough in the mid-latitude belt to reduce rain below 10 inches a year.

Deserts can form in the shadow of mountain ranges. Air rises to get over the mountains. As it rises, it cools and drops its moisture as rain on the windward side of the mountains. As the air crosses the peaks and descends on the mountain's lee side, it warms and can again hold more water vapor. It stops raining. The clouds evaporate. The deserts in eastern Oregon, in Nevada, and in Africa (the Kalahari Desert) are examples of shadow deserts. So are the desert-dry leeward sides of most of the Hawaiian Islands.

Deserts are often located right along the ocean shore where cold ocean currents flow near the shore. You'd think these would be lush areas, being right next to the ocean. But cold ocean currents chill the air above them. Cold air won't absorb much water vapor. As the air flows on shore and warms, it becomes dry air that can't form a cloud. The Atacama Desert in Chili and the Namib Desert in Namibia, Africa, are examples of this type of coastal desert.

There are some deserts that get little rain because the air that flows over them has already blown across a large continental land mass. Air picks up moisture when it blows over a warm ocean or tropical area. Air loses moisture through precipitation (rain) when it cools and when it flows over land. By the time air has blown across 1,000 miles of land, it's pretty dry. If it doesn't then pass over a body of water to soak up evaporating water vapor, it won't be able to rain over the next land area it crosses. That's exactly what happens to the air masses that reach the China-Mongolian border where the Gobi Desert lies. It is also what happens to the air that reaches North Africa and the Sahara Desert.

Some spots in the world sit under semipermanent atmospheric areas of high pressure. High-pressure weather systems are fair weather systems. Clear skies and warm temperatures abound. High-pressure systems are perfect for a weekend trip to the beach. But when high pressure becomes a permanent condition, it creates a desert. The Mexican deserts and the Baja Desert have been created this way.

Finally, the polar regions are mostly desert. Yes, I know. They're cold and covered with blowing snow. But they are still deserts. They have sparse vegetation and less than 10 inches of precipitation a year. That makes them deserts.

Some deserts are flat and long, stretched out over miles of rolling sand dunes and barren stretches of dirt, flat as a tabletop. The Sahara, the West Australian Desert, and the Kalahari are like that. Some deserts feature steep-walled mountains (mostly volcanic) separated by narrow basins (called *interior basins*, since no water ever gets out) that contain dry lakebeds. The Nevada Desert and Death Valley are shaped like this.

Desert Winds

Winds are often stronger over deserts than over areas of lush vegetation. Deserts heat faster and hotter than other areas during the day. Sand reflects most of its heat up into the atmosphere. Air over deserts heats quickly and rises—hot and dry—by midday. Strong winds then howl as air rushes in to replace the air that has risen. At night, deserts cool faster than areas with thick vegetation. The desert air also cools quickly and rushes back again—but now blowing in the opposite direction from the afternoon.

All wind erodes. It picks up and moves uncovered dirt and sand. It chips away (sandblasts) at exposed rocks. (Even in a very sandy desert—like the Sahara or the Arabian Peninsula—sand covers only 35% of the land. Dirt and rock cover the rest.) There is little vegetation in a desert to protect dirt and rock from the effects of the wind.

The ultimate desert wind is a sandstorm. Sandstorms can blot out the sun and completely change the landscape in a few hours. However, sandstorms are only *sand* storms for the bottom 3 or 4 feet. Above that they are really *dust* storms.

By blowing desert sand and dust beyond the edge of the desert, desert winds expand deserts, burying vegetation at the edge of the desert under mounds of sand and dry dirt, gobbling acre after acre as they march across the land. Deserts often advance slowly—only a few hundred feet a year. But when conditions are right, a desert can race forward many miles in a single year. Overfarming and overgrazing destroyed the natural ground cover along the southern flank of the Sahara Desert. As a result, that desert has spread 217 miles (350 km) south over just the last 20 years.

Sand Dunes

Think of deserts and most people think of sand dunes (even though sand covers only one third of even the sandiest deserts).

All the sand in every sand dune used to be part of a rock. Most of it came from somewhere in a mountain. Sand that is carried in streams winds up in the ocean, often piled up on the beach. Sand carried by wind often finds its way to sand dunes.

What the wind picketh up and taketh away, it must giveth back—usually by piling the sand into a sand dune. An area covered with sand dunes has the same rolling look as the ocean. Individual sand dunes resemble individual ocean waves.

Sand dunes feature a gentle, gradual slope on the upwind side (the side the wind blows *from*). The downwind side is always much steeper and is called the *slip face* (see Figure 7.3). As sand builds up on the upwind side of the dune, the crest grows higher and the slip face grows steeper. Eventually, the slip face grows too steep. A sand avalanche oc-

FIGURE 7.3 • The Shape of Sand Dunes

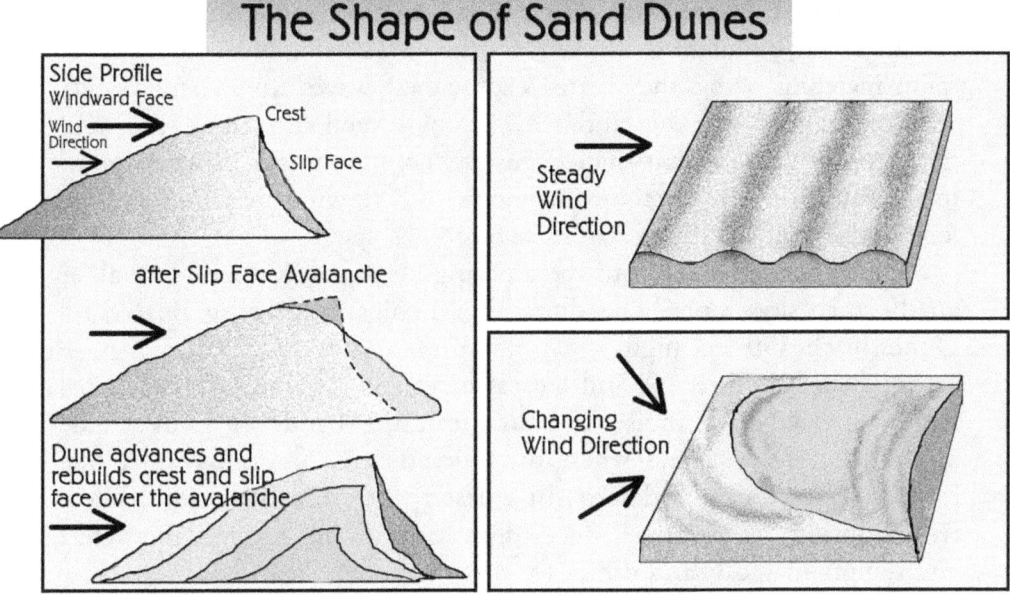

curs. The dune's crest and slip face slide forward (they "*slip*"), tumbling down the slope. This avalanche advances the mass of the dune in the direction the wind is blowing. Now the wind dutifully begins to rebuild the dune, adding sand to the upwind side, building the crest higher, making the slip face steeper again.

Over and over through the day, through the year, and through the centuries this process repeats itself. Each time, the dune edges forward. Sand dunes can advance 100 feet in a year this way. In a short 1,000 years, wind can blow a single sand dune across an entire desert. Wind drives waves in the ocean. On land, wind creates and moves sand dunes (desert waves).

It's hard to stop an advancing sand dune—or a sea of advancing sand dunes. You might as well try to stop the wind. Fences and walls won't stop them. Trees won't stop them. When sand dunes advance, all you can do is get out of the way.

The shape of an individual sand dune is a function of the strength of the winds that created it and the number of directions from which the wind blows over the course of a year. In the beginning, each new dune needs an anchor to start the dune, something for the first grains of sand to catch against. It can be as small as a small bush or even one deeply rooted blade of grass. Wind piles up sand around that anchor and begins a dune. Once a dune has formed, it can roll away from its anchor and still maintain its size and shape.

In some deserts, the wind always blows from the same direction. That produces long undulating ridgelines for dunes. They look like orderly wave trains marching across the ocean—except these waves are frozen in sand.

If the wind is variable and blows from several directions, the sand tends to form in crescent-shaped dunes where both ends curve to point in the direction the average wind blows. Where wind direction and velocity varies widely, dunes can look more like stars.

Sand dunes can pile up to the amazing height of 700 feet—as tall as an 80-story skyscraper. The dunes in Michigan's Sleeping Bear Sand Dunes reach 450 feet high.

The belief is correct. Wind creates deserts in two ways. First, global wind patterns drive moisture away from the bands of mid-latitude around the globe. That's where most deserts are. Second, wind blows hard and long through deserts. In a desert, the wind is the most effective sculpting, weathering, and erosion force. Wind extends the desert and sculpts magical sand dunes for us to enjoy.

BELIEF: Wind changes the land.

We have seen that wind can use sand to destroy vegetation and turn productive pastureland into barren desert. Wind can shift clouds and rain patterns to change both the vegetation of an area and also the amount of water erosion it suffers. Wind will sculpt and sandblast exposed rock, changing its appearance and shape. Wind can move massive amounts of material (in the form of sand, silt, and dust) over long distances. Wind can create deserts and pile up towering sand dunes.

Wind often combines with rain to increase the effective erosion by raindrops. Rain that is lashed by strong wind will hammer harder against exposed rock and will penetrate farther into rock cracks than it will without the help of wind.

Extreme winds instantly alter the landscape. Hurricanes destroy property and vegetation. They can cause massive erosion of coastal areas, creating or removing beaches and beach sand. Tornadoes (the world's strongest winds) destroy, and then pick up and carry away, anything in their path—including topsoil and small rocks they glide over.

Desertification, the process of turning non-desert land into desert, is driven by the wind. However, that process has been aided and sped up by human overgrazing and overfarming. Over the past 100 years, almost

10% of the land of the American Southwest has become new desert. That's an area equal to the size of the original thirteen colonies.

The Indus River region of eastern Pakistan and Northwest India is now called the Rajputana Desert. Four thousand years ago it was the site of a great and advanced agricultural civilization with lush fields as far as the eye could see. Those fields disappeared during a 100-year period as their agricultural land collapsed and turned to desert. They overfarmed and overgrazed their land and turned rich soil into barren dirt.

That opened the door for the wind. Winds blew hard and long. Dust storms began to billow over the region as more and more land was stripped of its vegetation and as the winds had more and more exposed dirt to lift into the sky. Up to 5 tons of dust hung in the air over every square mile of land. As each wind died, the dust settled covering everything. Within a century the whole region was uninhabitable desert.

The belief is correct. Wind is a powerful weathering force that can change both the shape and placement of rock and soil across the Earth's surface.

— TOPICS FOR DISCUSSION AND PROJECTS

Here are activities, research topics, and discussion questions you can use to expand upon the key science concepts presented in this chapter.

Research and Discuss. Research deserts. Shade in all the deserts you can find on a world map. Research the location, size, annual rainfall, and terrain features of each. Is each desert growing or shrinking? If they are growing, can you find the cause? Has human action in the area made it easier for the desert to expand?

An Activity. Let's model the suspended load that wind can carry. You will need a good table fan, a 12-foot-long piece from a roll of white butcher paper, and a supply of coarse-grained sand, fine-grained sand, and dust (or silt). Do this activity outside to avoid a big cleanup effort at the end.

Put your fan on the ground, pointing straight ahead (if it is an adjustable fan) and lay the butcher paper out in front of it. Mark the paper in 1-foot increments so that you are marking distance from the fan. Turn the fan on low. Gently drop a hand full of coarse-grained sand just in front of the fan. Don't hold your hand up high. Hold it just above and just in front of the fan as you slowly drop the sand. Once you have released all the sand, count to 3 and turn off the fan. See how far downwind the fan's wind has carried these sand particles by seeing where they land on the butcher paper. On the butcher paper, mark the farthest, nearest, and "average" distance these grains were carried in the wind. Did all the coarse sand land on the butcher paper? What percentage (approximately) did?

Brush the butcher paper clean and repeat the experiment using fine-grained sand. Repeat again using dust or silt. Did any of the dust or silt land on the butcher paper, or was it all carried higher up into the air? What does this experiment tell you about wind's ability to carry particles? What do you think will happen if you repeat the experiment with the fan on high? Try it to see if your prediction was correct.

Research and Discuss. Research wind in your area. How often does it blow? From which directions? Talk to a local weatherperson for this information. What you'll find is called a *wind rose*, a chart of the direction and frequency of winds blowing from every direction over the course of a year. Which of these winds do you think are caused by weather systems and which are caused by the prevailing air currents that surround the globe? What makes you think that?

An Activity. Imagine being in a raging, blinding sandstorm. Which desert would you be in? Why are you there? What are you doing when

the storm hits? Write a page describing what you'd hear, feel, and see and what you'll do during the storm. Include a description of how the sandstorm affects the landscape where you are. Conduct the background research you need for this story at the library and online.

An Activity. Let's make a sand dune. For this outdoors activity you will need two fans and lots of sand. Place the two fans side by side, both pointing straight ahead. Spread sand in a thick, even layer in a large area in front of the fans and turn the fans on low. The sand blows, it may form ripples, but does it form into a sand dune? Probably not. Sand dunes need an anchor. If your fans didn't move much sand, try upping the fans' speed one notch.

Place a small block of wood in the sand, repile and smooth the sand and repeat. Watch around the block. Does a sand dune start to form? Let it develop. Make sketches of the upwind and downwind faces. Does the dune look like a long wave on the ocean? That's typically what happens when the wind always blows from one direction.

Spread the fans apart so that their edges are 2 feet from each other and turn them inward, each at a 45° angle. Resmooth the sand and turn the fans on. See if the shape of your sand dune changes to a crescent shape.

An Activity. Make a map showing the major wind currents of the Northern and Southern Hemispheres. Which way does the Earth turn? Mark that direction with a red arrow on your map. Why do the major air currents flow west to east if the Earth turns from east to west? Hint: Which turns faster, Earth or atmosphere? (See discussion on page 133.) If you were standing on the Earth (as you are), which way would the air *appear* to move? This is like being on a slowly moving train that passes a stationary train. To you, the stationary train *appears* to be moving because *relative to you*, it is.

SUGGESTED READING FOR STUDENTS

Downs, Sandra. *Shaping the Earth: Erosion*. Brookfield, CT: Twenty-First Century Books, 2001.

Gallant, Roy. *Sand on the Move*. New York: Franklin Watts, 1997.

Gareri, Anita. *Crumbling Earth*. Chicago: Raintree Publishers, 2004.

Gibbons, Gail. *Deserts*. New York: Holiday House, 1999.

Gifford, Clive. *Weathering and Erosion*. New York: Smart Apple Media, 2005.

Hogan, Paula. *Expanding Deserts*. New York: Gareth Stevens, 2001.

McLeish, Ewan. *Spreading Deserts*. Chicago: Raintree Publishers, 2000.

Olien, Rebecca. *Erosion*. Mankato, MN: Capstone Press, 2001.

Patent, Dorothy Hinshaw. *Shaping the Earth*. New York: Clarion Books, 2001.

Prager, Ellen. *Sand*. Washington, DC: National Geographic Society, 2000.

Rowe, Julian. *Water*. New York: Franklin Watts, 2001.

Rozario, Paul. *Spreading Deserts*. Chicago: Raintree Publishers, 2004.

Spilsbury, Louise. *Disappearing Mountain and Other Earth Mysteries*. Chicago: Raintree Publishers, 2005.

Stille, Darlene. *Deserts*. New York: Scholastic Library Publishing, 2000.

Watson, Jane. *Deserts of the World*. New York: Penguin Books, 1998.

Winner, Cherie. *Erosion*. New York: Lerner Publishing Group, 1999.

SUGGESTED WEB SITES

Discovery Science. www.discovery.com/area/history/dustbowl/dustbowl1.1.html

Field Guides. www.fieldguides.com/desert/desert.htm

—— SUGGESTED READING FOR TEACHERS

Bonnifield, M. *The Dust Bowl*. Albuquerque, NM: University of New Mexico Press, 1999.

Bryson, R. *Climates of Hunger*. Madison, WI: University of Wisconsin Press, 1997.

Geist, Helmut. *Causes and Progression of Desertification*. Aldershot, England: Ashgate Publishing, 2004.

Greely, R. *Wind as a Geologic Process*. Cambridge, MA: Cambridge University Press, 2000.

Hollon, W. *The Great American Desert: Then and Now*. 3rd ed. New York: Oxford Univesity Press, 1996.

Hurt, R. *The Dust Bowl*. Chicago: Nelson House, 2001.

Jaeger, E. *The North American Deserts*. Stanford, CA: Stanford University Press, 1995.

Schullery, Paul. *America's National Parks: The Spectacular Forces That Shaped Our Treasured Lands*. New York: DK Publishing, 2001.

8 Glaciers

—— MYTHS ABOUT HOW GLACIERS SHAPE THE LAND

Glaciers seem like alien and foreboding landscapes to most humans—cold, powerful, immense. These frozen rivers of ice, towering masses of cracked and tortured snow, and massive ice cliffs that rise above the sea are certainly dramatic, even breathtaking. Glaciers have been called "eaters of hills" by several Alaskan tribes. They are also deadly dangerous. Glaciers mercilessly grind their way to the sea, crushing, scouring everything in their path. Hidden crevasses, like carefully laid traps, lie in wait for the unwary hiker.

Glaciers groan and creek almost as if they were in pain, almost as if they were calling out to lure the innocent into their deadly web. They roar and growl. They creep and flow—but too slowly for humans to notice.

Humans have always eyed glaciers with suspicion, believing them to be sinister and cruel. The Athapaskan and Tlingit tribes (two Native Alaskan tribes) believe that glaciers listen, pay attention, and respond to human behavior. They believe that glaciers make moral judgments and punish infractions. Stories about glaciers come primarily from the polar regions—Iceland, Norway, Alaska, New Zealand, and Tierra del Fuego (South America)—even though glaciers covered much of North America and Europe during the last ice age. Glaciers never represent good or hope. Universally we regard them as instruments of misfortune and ill, of danger and woe.

But glaciers have carved out some of the world's greatest spectacles for us to see and appreciate. Yosemite Valley in California and the Matterhorn Mountain in Switzerland (the model for Disney's Matterhorn ride) were both created by glaciers.

Glowing white to eerie blue guardians of the frozen wasteland at the poles, glaciers and the giant icebergs they produce gave rise to legends of floating islands and lands that appear and then mysteriously disappear.

But are glaciers of any significance to a study of Earth Science? Are they such rare occurrences that they don't deserve serious attention? What can we learn of the land and its history from studying these frozen fringes of the Earth? In general, do glaciers affect the land?

Few myths try to explain the origin of glaciers or try to explain their existence. In myths, glaciers usually occur when a chill or frozen god of winter overpowers other (warmer) gods and storms south. This god is always described as being resentful and fierce, determined to wreck havoc as he plows toward warmer continents. Glaciers are associated with these evil spirits, sea demons, or wicked goblins—all intent on tormenting poor humans with their frozen creations. In an Icelandic myth, Imir the Creator is a frost giant. Glaciers are his evil servants as he tries to invade the warmer lands to the south. He is blocked and stopped by the god Odin.

The other option used in myths to explain the existence of glaciers is grief. In a New Zealand myth, glaciers are formed from a young girl's tears when she cried long and hard after her lover slipped and fell to his death off a high mountain ledge.

The myth that follows comes from the southern tip of South America and blames the existence of glaciers, not on some evil god, but on the whims of a "touchy," sensitive bird, the ibis, considered the harbinger of spring and the happy end to long, bitter winters.

"The Touchy Ibis,"
A Myth from the Yamana People of
Tierra del Fuego

Once in the old days, as spring drew near after a long winter of howling winds, a man looked out of his lodge and saw an ibis flying by overhead. The ibis circled and landed on a bare rock outcropping just a little ways from the man's house.

Joyously the man cried out to the other lodges, "An ibis has just flown over my house and landed on the rocks. Come see!"

The other people heard him and rushed out of their lodges shouting loudly, "Spring has returned. The ibises are flying!" They leapt and danced on the frozen ground and made a great and happy noise. More people flocked in from more distant lodges. As each new person approached, the crowd cheered, "Spring is here! The ibises are flying. Look!"

And that new person would leap and cheer and dance with the others.

But ibises are sensitive birds and easily offended. An ibis must be treated with proper respect. When that ibis heard the commotion made by those men, women, and children, she became irritated. When they carried on and on with their raucous laughing and dancing, the ibis became highly provoked.

Still the people would not stop, and the ibis's anger grew icy cold and she knew she had to teach these people a lesson. In her rage, she summoned forth a massive snowstorm with raging winds, bitter frost, and much ice that slashed at a person's exposed skin. Snow fell thick and hard, building into mounds. The snow blew into giant drifts and would not stop.

For hours and then for days it snowed without letup. People were trapped inside their lodges. Their canoes were buried deep beneath the snow. They couldn't go out to find food. Everyone grew hungry and weak. And still it snowed.

It turned bitter cold. Lakes and rivers froze. Even the oceans were covered with a thick layer of ice. People began to die from starvation and exposure to the cold. The snow fell blizzard thick so that people couldn't even go out to gather firewood. More and more people died. The wind howled and moaned, swirling around people's lodges, and almost drove them mad.

Finally the snow ended and the world was covered with thick white snow. The sun came out and reflected off the packed snow so fiercely that it blinded the people who looked. The snow was so thick it mounded even up over the mountaintops.

The sun took pity on the starving people and poured down its heat onto the snow to melt it. Soon wide rivers flowed from the bases of the shrinking layers of ice. People could hunt for food and wood. Deaths stopped.

The sun burned the snow back away from the valleys and hills and coast so that summer plants could grow and blossom and so that the people could get to their canoes to fish. But still thick rivers of ice clung to the high valleys and tall peaks. The sun was not strong enough to melt them. Those thick ice rivers can still be seen, reaching even down to the sea.

Since that terrible storm, the Yamana people have treated every ibis with respect and reverence. When an ibis approaches their lodges, the people smile but keep still. They make no noise. They hush up the little children and keep them from shouting. They smile and nod and cheer "Spring is here!" only deep inside their own heads. For every time one of the people disturbs an ibis, the ice rivers groan and creek and begin to grow and threaten the people with another terrible storm.

—— THE SCIENCE OF HOW GLACIERS SHAPE THE LAND

The following beliefs are either directly stated or strongly implied in the presented myth. Here is what modern science knows about glaciers' effects on the land explained by each belief.

BELIEF: Glaciers are rare and are created by outside forces.

What *Is* a Glacier?

Glaciers are not layers of ice, slabs of ice, or sheets of ice, thick or thin. A glacier is a *river* of ice. The ice in glaciers moves—as does the water in a river. Glacier ice, however, moves slower than a lazy snail. Glaciers are long blocks of ice formed on land that flow downhill because of their immense weight.

There are two types of glaciers—big and monstrously huge. The monstrously huge type are called *continental glaciers*. Continental glaciers are gigantic sheets of ice the size of continents. Picture pancake batter being slowly poured onto a hot griddle. The batter spreads out in all directions. The more batter that is poured into the middle, the more it spreads toward the edges of the griddle. That's what continental glaciers do. As more and more snow falls on top of them, they spread out in all directions, covering everything, shoving obstacles (such as mountains) out of their way so they can expand ever outward toward the sea.

There are now only two of these glaciers. One covers most of Greenland. The other covers Antarctica. It is almost impossible to imagine how big the Antarctic glacier is. In many places it is over 8,000 feet thick.

That's over 1.5 miles of ice stacked straight up! That one glacier is as big as all forty-eight contiguous states of the U.S. mainland. If it were plopped down over the United States, it would cover everything except Alaska and Hawaii and would have plenty of glacier left over to spread out over large sections of Mexico and Canada.

Ninety-nine percent of all the ice in glaciers is piled inside the two continental glaciers. Two thirds of all the world's freshwater is locked into just those two glaciers! Take all the water in all the lakes, rivers, ponds, pools, streams, creeks, marshes, reservoirs, pipes, water bottles, plants, and people in the world. Add in all the water in the atmosphere and all the water flowing underground. Combine every drop of available freshwater in the world, and you'd still have to double it to match the amount of water in just those two glaciers.

They're *big!*

Only two continental glaciers exist now, but during the ice ages, continental glaciers covered North America, Europe, and Asia. (There have been many ice ages. The last one ended 10,000 YAG.)

The other kind of glacier is *valley glaciers*, sometimes called *alpine glaciers*. These are the rivers of ice we all picture when we think of glaciers. There are around 200,000 valley glaciers in the world. All of them are gigantic—hundreds of feet high and miles long. Yet, cumulatively, they contain only 1% of all glacier ice. Valley glaciers can form and begin to move in hundreds of years. Continental glaciers probably take tens of thousands of years to form—but no one is sure because humans weren't keeping detailed written records when the last continental glaciers formed beginning about 90,000 YAG.

A typical valley glacier is 600 feet high at its deepest point. (That's the same as sixty school buses stacked on top of each other. It's like a 60-story skyscraper.) A good rule of thumb is that a glacier is about half as deep as it is wide. That means that the average glacier is a quarter of a mile wide. A *river* flowing 600 feet deep and a quarter of a mile wide would qualify as one of the world's major rivers. Those dimensions characterize just an *average* glacier.

Some valley glaciers are giants that can dwarf any object humans have ever built. The deepest valley glaciers are around 4,000 feet thick. That's four times the height of the Empire State Building in New York City, three times the height of the world's tallest building. That's tall enough almost to fill up the Grand Canyon! Some glaciers stretch out over 200 miles long.

Some valley glaciers were created during the recent mini–ice age (A.D. 1400–1700). Some have probably existed for millions of years.

Glaciers also glow with an eerie blue light instead of the white color we expect to see in snow and ice. When light passes through water (or ice), the water absorbs the red, yellow, and green parts of the color spectrum. It doesn't absorb blue light. That's why the ocean looks blue. The light reflected back out of the ocean has lost all the parts of its color spectrum except for blue.

Air pockets in snowflakes reflect light before water molecules have a chance to absorb any light, so snow looks white. But the air has been squeezed out of glacier ice. Glacier ice, like the ocean, absorbs all but the blue light from the sunlight that strikes it.

Glaciers are not freak occurrences on Earth. There may not be a glacier near where you live now. But there likely has been. And if there was, the land around you was shaped and molded by that glacier.

Some common terms are used to describe glaciers. It will be useful for you to be familiar with a few of them. (Figure 8.1 shows a typical valley glacier and locates these features for you.)

Face. The lower end of a glacier always forms a vertical cliff of ice. That front edge of a glacier is called its *face*. Cruise ships that tour Glacier Bay in Alaska show passengers the face of several glaciers—cliffs of eerie-blue ice rising hundreds of feet above the water level.

Source. The *source* of a glacier (sometimes called its "*head*") is the top end of the glacier. This is the end of the glacier highest up the mountain. It is the place where the most snow falls and the least summer evaporation and melting occurs. It is where the glacier accumulates new ice that then begins to flow down the length of the glacier toward the bottom end. A glacier flows down a valley from its source.

Crevasse. Vertical cracks and crevices called *crevasses* crisscross the surface of a glacier, making a hike on a glacier a deadly dangerous outing. Some crevasses are 100 feet deep. Many are hidden beneath a thin sheet of ice and snow waiting, like bear traps beneath a layer of scattered leaves, for the foot of an unwary hiker to crash through.

Terminus. The end of a bus line is at the terminal. The end of a glacier is at its *terminus*. It is the bottom end of the glacier, as far downhill as the glacier ever gets. A glacier's face never reaches past the terminus (it may be away from the terminus if the glacier shrinks [or retreats]). Sometimes a glacier's terminus is high up a mountain valley (true for most nonpolar glaciers). Sometimes the glacier reaches all the way to the ocean, and the terminus is in the sea.

Moraine. Glaciers pick up and carry enormous amounts of rock and dirt—debris. When the glacier ice melts, it dumps this load of debris. Hills, ridges, and mounds of this debris are called *moraines*. The

FIGURE 8.1 • Valley Glaciers

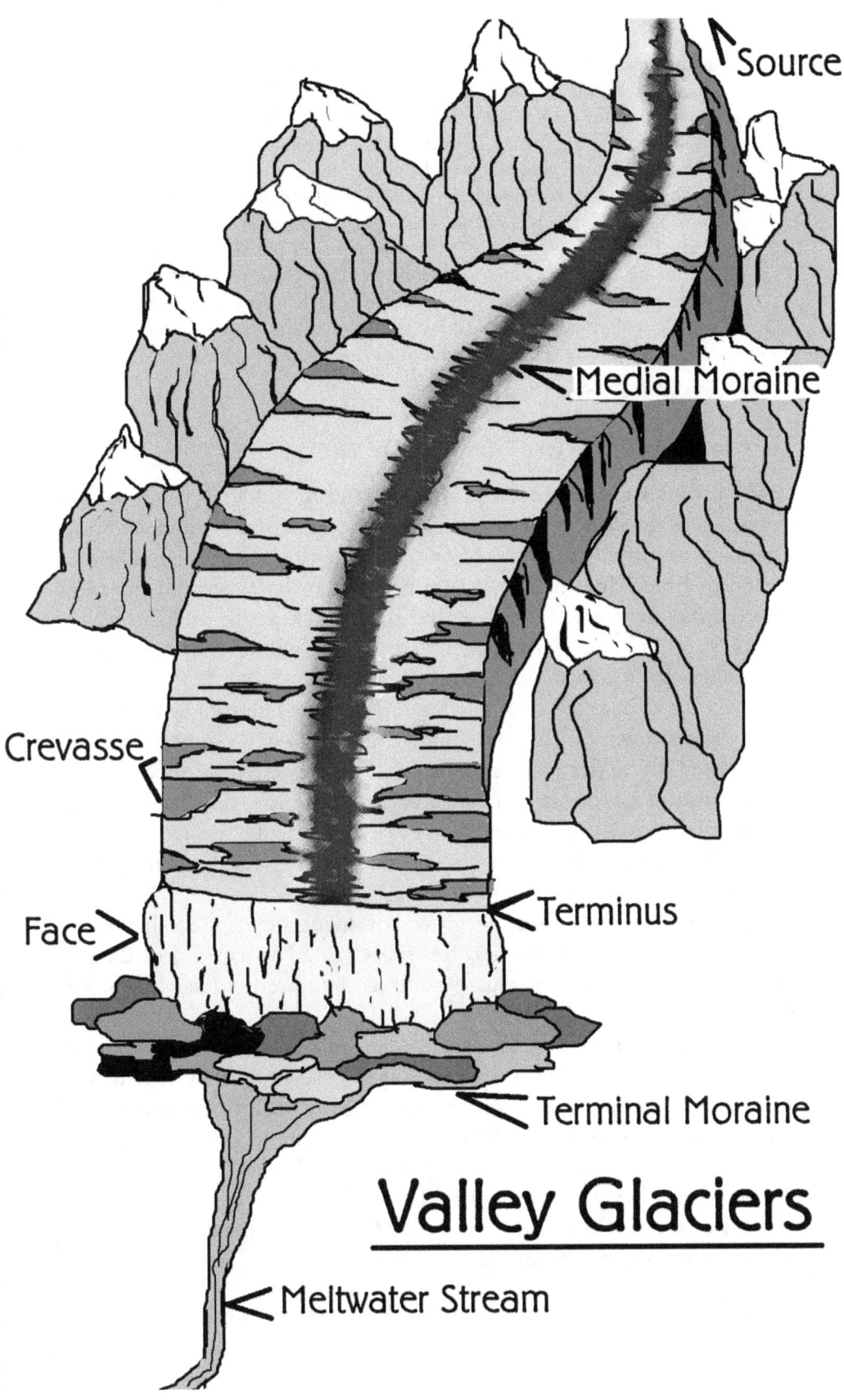

biggest and most important moraine is at the terminus (the *terminal moraine*). Think of a glacier as being like a debris conveyor belt. Rocks and dirt are scraped off valley floors and sides higher up the mountain and are carried downhill to the terminus. There the glacier ice melts and dumps the rocks in a moraine.

Some terminal moraines reach 1,000 feet tall and dam up lakes behind them. Moraines, however, are any gathering of the rock, dirt, and debris carried by a glacier. Besides terminal moraines, glaciers commonly have *side moraines* (debris piled up along the sides and edges of a glacier) and *center moraines* (lines of debris—usually looking like a black skunk's stripe down the length of the glacier—carried by glacial ice that is now locked into the middle of the glacial flow).

How to Grow a Glacier

What causes glaciers to form, to grow, and to suddenly begin to flow down a valley? Glaciers form when, over a long period of time, snow accumulation in the winter exceeds summer melting. How long is "a long period of time"? It depends. If summer heat melts almost all the snow that fell that year, it may take several thousand years to build to glacier thickness. If summers are suddenly mild and winters harsh, a glacier could form in just *hundreds* of years.

Year after year, snow piles deeper and deeper. The weight of the top snow presses down on the snow underneath. Slowly the bottom snow is compressed. Over the years, snowflakes are compressed into ice, squeezing out almost all the air that forms so much of each snowflake. The ice is squeezed into a rigid crystal structure. Eventually the ice sheet has grown so thick and heavy that it begins to move, heeding the pull of gravity. *Now* you have a glacier.

The glacier will continue to grow, advancing down the valley a few inches every day, a few hundred feet every year. The top end of the glacier stays anchored to the source point as the lower end slowly spreads down the mountainside or valley.

Every year more snow piles onto the top of the glacier, thickening it. As the ice slides downhill, it spreads out to cover the valley, side to side (just as a river would). As it advances, the glacier sculpts the bottom and sides of the valley as it goes. When two glaciers meet, they merge, flowing down together as a single megaglacier.

Eventually, the glacier stops its advance. Why? Because the air grows warmer as the glacier descends to lower and lower altitudes. The rate at which the glacier's face and leading sections melt and evaporate increases.

At some point, the glacier will melt as fast as its glacial ice advances downhill. The glacier's advance stops. It's the sun's heat and warm air that stops a glacier. Ice *in* the glacier will continue to flow downhill. But it melts as fast as it advances so that the glacier itself doesn't advance.

The only other thing that can stop a glacier is the ocean. When a glacier reaches the ocean, water melts the glacier's face. Water will melt ice faster than air can (just as 50°F water chills your body faster than 50°F air can). In addition, great slabs of the glacier break off and crash into the ocean as icebergs. This is called *calving*.

Snow—especially high up near the source—builds the glacier, pushes the glacier downhill, and makes it advance. Melting, evaporation, and calving—mostly near the terminus—stop the glacier's advance and try to make it retreat back uphill. Often, glaciers advance a few feet in the winter, when the lower altitude air grows cold, and then retreat in the summer as the air warms and the glacier's face melts faster than new ice can advance to take its place. When a glacier retreats, its ice doesn't flow back up hill. The ice simply melts faster than it can be replaced by the steady, 20-inches-a-day forward creep of the glacier.

Many think that the ice in glaciers must be bitter cold and many degrees below zero. This is not true. Glacier ice is only a few degrees below freezing. That's why the bottom edge of a glacier tends to melt. The tremendous pressure of the glacier pushing down and the friction with the rocks below create heat—enough heat to melt ice. The bottom of the glacier is often a film of water. As the bottom edge melts, it lubricates the glacier and promote its advance downhill. Still, it takes a lot of heat energy to melt ice. In fact, it takes eighty times as much heat to turn 32°F *ice* into 32°F *water* (that is, to melt it) as it does to raise that same amount of water 1°F. That's why glaciers melt so slowly.

The process becomes a balancing act—a dance. In years with more snow than melting and evaporation, the glacier steps forward, advancing farther downhill. In years with lighter snowfall and warm temperatures, the glacier steps backward, retreating up the valley 10 or 20 feet.

During long periods of average weather, a glacier's terminus stays more or less in the same place. Each season and year it will advance a few feet or retreat a few feet. But without a long-term warming or cooling trend, it will stay more or less in the same place. When this happens, all the rocks and debris carried downhill by the glacier are dumped just ahead of this terminus in a great—and ever growing—terminal moraine that can become a major ridgeline across a valley's landscape.

Ice Ages

We are in a warm period now, between periods of major glaciation. But in the past, huge ice sheets covered much of the land of Earth. These periods are called *ice ages*. During ice ages, glaciers are the most important tool for sculpting the land of Earth.

An ice age is defined as a period when the Earth is cold enough for more than 386,000 square miles (1 million square kilometers) of glaciers to form to a depth of more than 1 mile on nonpolar continents. How often do ice ages happen? More often than you might think.

The last mini–ice age started in A.D. 1400 and lasted until A.D. 1700—only 300 YAG. Ice covered northern Canada. Glaciers advanced all over the Northern Hemisphere. New glaciers formed and spread. But 300 years is not nearly long enough for large ice sheets to form across continents.

Earth's first ice age began about 2.5 billion YAG and lasted many millions—even hundreds of millions—of years. The last ice age lasted about 1 million years with ten repeated periods of warming and cooling. Glaciers advanced, melted, and advanced again (about once every 100,000 years). No one is sure if that ice age is over. It might have ended and the world is warming out of it, or we could just be in a warmer period between glacial advances.

The last major glacial period ended about 10,000 YAG—not so very long ago. A giant continental glacier covered 6.2 million square miles of North America. It reached as far south as St. Louis, Missouri. New Hampshire was covered with 8,000 feet of ice. Glaciers covered over one-third of all land. The places where two-thirds of the world's population now lives, and where two-thirds of our food is grown, were under thousands of feet of ice.

Sea level dropped 500 feet because so much of Earth's water was locked into glaciers. Land extended 50 or more miles farther out to sea than it does now. You could walk from France to England. San Francisco Bay was dry land. So was Long Island Sound.

What Causes an Ice Age?

No one knows what causes an ice age. Scientists know a number of factors that *could* be the cause. But they cannot tell which one—or ones—is the most important trigger. Our weather records only date back a few hundred years. Unfortunately, that is not nearly long enough to understand ice ages that come and go over millions of years.

Here are the six factors most often mentioned as possible causes for ice ages. The first three relate to Earth's orbit around the sun. Only the sixth factor relates to human behavior.

Orbital Eccentricity. Earth's orbit around the Sun is not a perfect circle. Neither is it always the same. The shape of our planet's orbit changes a little bit each year. This change is called *orbital eccentricity*. Sometimes the orbit is more circular. Sometimes it's a bit more elongated. The orbital pattern repeats every 100,000 years.

The orbit's shape doesn't have to change very much to make a big difference in Earth's temperature. During periods when Earth's annual orbit is more elongated, there will be seasons each year when the Earth is the farthest away from the Sun that it ever can be. That extra distance could be enough to trigger an ice age that will last for a few thousand years until the shape of the obit changes.

Precession. In every year, no matter how elongated or circular the orbit is, there will be some day when the Earth is at its closest to the Sun, and some day when Earth is farthest from the Sun. In some years, the Earth is closer to the Sun during our winter, and those will be mild winters.

In other years, Earth will reach the point when it is farthest from the Sun during the middle of winter in the Northern Hemisphere. Those should be the coldest winters and might be enough to trigger an ice age. It takes 23,000 years for our planet to complete this cycle. This phase is called *precession* and means that once every 23,000 years Earth is as far as possible from the Sun during the middle of our winter.

Wobble. We know that the Earth is tilted on its axis. The North and South poles don't point straight up and down. That's what creates summer and winter in the first place. As the Earth makes its annual lap around the Sun, sometimes the axis is tilted so that the Northern Hemisphere points more directly at the Sun (summer), and sometimes it points away from the Sun (winter). But the amount of that tilt doesn't stay the same. Our planet slowly *wobbles* on its axis like a spinning top that wobbles. Sometimes Earth is tilted more over on its side. Sometimes it stands straighter up and down. When the planet wobbles farther over on its side, the seasons will be more extreme. It takes 41,000 years for our planet to progress through its cycle of tilt angles and get back to where it started.

It is possible that none of these orbital factors individually could bring on an ice age, but it is quite possible that all three, acting together, could. If, when Earth is tipped farthest over on its axis, winter happened to occur when the Earth was also farthest from the Sun during an extremely elongated orbit, *then* the Northern Hemisphere would for many years experience long and bitter cold winters. That could equal an ice age.

Continental Drift. Some think that ice ages are more likely when tectonic forces have pushed the continents closer to the polar regions. After all, the tropics never suffer through glacial ice sheets. According to this view, when the continents have been shoved north and south away from the equator (so that most of the land is closer to the poles), can an ice age happen.

Gulf Stream. The Gulf Stream is an ocean current that flows from southern Florida north along the east coast of America and across to northern Europe. The tropical (warm) water in this current carries tremendous amounts of heat into the North Atlantic Ocean. However, there have been periods in the past when the Gulf Stream reversed directions. Instead of carrying tropical heat north, it carried Arctic cold south. These reversals seem to coincide with past ice ages. Some scientists think that a reversal of the Gulf Stream is the trigger that *starts* an ice age.

Carbon Dioxide. Carbon dioxide is the famous greenhouse gas. It traps heat in the atmosphere just as the glass roof of a greenhouse does. A reduction in atmospheric carbon dioxide as the planet's first plants began to draw carbon dioxide from the atmosphere probably caused the first great ice age on Earth 2.5 billion YAG. We are in a period when the carbon dioxide content in the atmosphere is increasing rapidly. Much of this increase is the result of the burning of fossil fuels—a human activity. Increased atmospheric carbon dioxide causes global warming. But in an odd twist of fate, many scientists believe that rapid global warming could, as it causes the Greenland continental glacier to melt, disrupt the flow of the Gulf Stream, reverse its direction, and actually bring on an ice age.

No one knows for sure which of these factors is the most important in triggering the devastation of an ice age. Once started, however, most scientists agree, ice ages come on with frightening speed. Ice reflects more heat than land does. Once an ice sheet starts to form, it reflects more heat back out into space, dropping Earth's temperature even more and promoting faster glacial expansion.

Only time—tens of thousands of years of time—will tell for sure what causes ice ages and whether or not we are due for another. What we do know is that when glaciers advance, they become a major factor in reshaping and reforming the land of Earth, as described next.

BELIEF: Glaciers don't affect the land.

Our Earth is a planet of fire and ice. Volcanoes (fire) build the crust. Ice (glaciers) pushes the crust around and reshapes it. Glaciers are giant bulldozers. They gouge, scour, dig, rip, and scrape. They polish rocks and smash rocks. They gouge out valleys, create new lakes, and redirect rivers. In Yosemite Valley, California, for example, a famous glacial valley, the advancing glacier ran into a large dome of dense, solid igneous rock. It was a classic battle between an unmovable object and an unstoppable force. The glacier won, splitting the giant dome of rock in two. The glacier pulverized the half that fell into the valley and carried it away. The half that the glacier left is now called Half Dome, a perfect 3,000-foot-high half dome of granite and one of the most photographed rocks in the world.

Glaciers are nonstop workers who put busy beavers and industrious ants to shame. Glaciers are on the job 24/7 ripping out and scraping off dirt and rocks, carrying them down a mountainside or valley, and dumping them at the bottom. Glaciers are like garbage trucks. They scoop up all loose Earth debris and move massive amounts of dirt and rock into dumps (moraines).

How do glaciers do all this scraping? Stick your tongue against a frozen pipe. It sticks. In the same way, rocks stick to the bottom and sides of flowing glaciers. Once attached to a glacier, these rocks act like coarse sandpaper, scraping away more material from the lands they flow past.

Glaciers routinely gouge away whole sides of a mountain. The famed Matterhorn Mountain in the Swiss Alps is a good example. Glaciers created the sharp, knife-edge ridgelines defining the slopes of this mountain, as well as those of many others. When glaciers form on two sides of a mountain, they each gouge out the rock on their side. What is left is the narrow ridgeline between the two source points of the glaciers.

While rivers cut valleys in a deep V shape, glaciers bulldoze valleys into a wide U shape. Glacial valleys have flat bottoms, often with broad meadows and meandering rivers that carry the melted water from the retreating glacier.

Evidence of the amount of reshaping work done by glaciers can be found in their moraines, the dumping grounds for the rock and debris the glaciers have excavated along their downhill journey. The terminal moraine is the best place to look. But also look for the dark stripes down the middle and edges of glaciers. These are center and side moraines—thick lines of material scraped off a valley's sides and being carried toward the terminal moraine.

Center moraines were once side moraines, scraping thick layers of dirt and rock from a valley's side. When that valley merges with another valley that has its own glacier, the two glaciers merge. Side moraines mash together like merging lanes of traffic on a busy freeway and combine to form a single, thick center moraine.

Terminal moraines for a small glacier can still be hundreds of feet thick. Many have formed thick walls that cross a valley like a dam and back up large lakes of glacier melt water behind them. Some terminal moraines have grown to be over 1,000 feet high.

The belief is wrong. Glaciers are critically important to life on this planet and to reshaping the land of our continents.

Even during this period of minimal glaciation, twice as much freshwater sits in glaciers as in all other sources. During heavy ice ages, over one-third of all Earth's water can be locked into mountainous continental glaciers.

Past glaciers are responsible for much of the large-scale shaping and reshaping of this planet's land. Only 10% of all land is now covered by glaciers. But glaciers during past ice ages shaped the surface features and contours of 75% of all land.

Glaciers scraped out all the fjords (narrow inlets to the sea with steep cliff walls) in Norway, New Zealand, Canada, Iceland, and Chili. (Chili has the deepest fjord in the world. Half a mile across, the fjord is 4,226 feet deep.) Fjords are really partially submerged, U-shaped glacial valleys. Glaciers gouged out the Great Lakes. The state of Minnesota is covered 1,000 feet thick with glacial debris (probably the world's largest terminal moraine). The last ice age scattered a thick layer of rich debris over much of the midwestern farming belt.

The Missouri River used to flow north until the last ice age resculpted the land so that the river had to reverse course and flow south in order to flow downhill.

As the vast North American continental glacier melted 14,000 YAG, it formed Lake Bonneville, in what is now Utah. Towering terminal moraines formed the two sides of the valley that held this vast lake. (Great Salt Lake is the tiny remnant of Lake Bonneville.) Lake Bonneville stood over 1,000 feet deep and stretched several hundred miles from end to end. When the north ridge surrounding Lake Bonneville broke and collapsed, it released the greatest flood in North American history. A 300-foot-high wall of water raced at over 75 mph across the countryside. The lake drained for weeks, leaving Great Salt Lake like a puddle compared to the giant lake that had been.

On mountain after mountain, and in place after place, glaciers have been the defining hand that sculpted the shape of the land we see today.

BELIEF: Glaciers happen only in the polar regions.

Around half the world's 200,000 valley glaciers are in Alaska. Both remaining continental glaciers are in polar regions (Greenland and Antarctica). Glaciers currently cover 3% of Alaska. At the peak of the last ice age 90% of Alaska was covered in ice.

Thus, it is true that *most* glaciers and almost all the total glacial ice are in polar regions. However, glaciers can be found in seven of the lower forty-eight states (California, Wyoming, Colorado, Idaho, Oregon, Washington, and Montana). Glaciers exist on all continents except Australia.

At this time all nonpolar glaciers have retreated to elevations of above 6,000 feet in the mountains. Even with those temperature restrictions, the nonpolar world houses over 10,000 glaciers for us to admire.

Currently all the glaciers that reach the ocean are in polar regions. Thus, all icebergs begin their long floating voyages in polar waters, since they are calved from glaciers and ice sheets. Tens of thousands of icebergs form every year and slowly drift from their polar birthing grounds toward shipping lanes. Such an iceberg sank the unsinkable *Titanic* in 1912.

Icebergs are deceptively small above water. Eighty-seven point five percent of an iceberg rides underwater. What you see above the surface is only one-eighth of the total iceberg. Often icebergs jut out sharply to the sides just below the waterline. Icebergs also tend to be much larger than most people imagine. The biggest iceberg ever recorded broke off the Antarctic Ross Ice Shelf in 1987. This monster stretched over 100 miles long and 30 miles wide. It covered 2,412 square miles—almost the same size as the whole state of Delaware and over 50% bigger than the state of Rhode Island. That one iceberg held enough water to supply all the needs of everyone in the city of Los Angeles for 675 years!

BELIEF: The ice in glaciers is ancient and has been locked in the glacier for millions of years.

As we have seen, glaciers move. The ice in them flows slowly downhill, just as the water in a river flows downhill toward the ocean. It takes just over three weeks for a drop of water to swim the length of the Mississippi River from head waters to the Gulf of Mexico. But the Mississippi River itself has existed for many thousands of years.

In the same way, glaciers can exist for eons. But each particle of ice in them flows down the glacier until it either melts or evaporates. Ice in an average valley glacier moves 20 inches each day, or about 600 feet each year (about the length of fifteen school buses parked end to end in front of a school). It takes the average ice particle a little over 9 years to travel downhill 1 mile. Since few glaciers are more then 20 miles long, it is rare to find a particle of ice in a valley glacier that is 200 years old.

The oldest ice in each glacier will be found at its face. This is the ice that has made the entire journey from source to terminus and is about to melt and return to liquid form. Valley glacier ice is young.

Continental glacier ice is another story. Because these glaciers are so vast, ice can last in the glacier much longer before it reaches the terminus and either calves or melts. The oldest continental glacier ice is estimated to be around 250,000 years old.

How Glaciers Move

The age of valley glacier ice is, however, difficult to estimate because glaciers move in several different ways. Not all of a glacier moves at the same speed. Friction against the ground holds the bottom edge of a glacier back. It moves more slowly than do the middle and top parts of a glacier above it. The same is true for the side edges. They scrape against the rock lining a valley's walls. That slows them down in their journey. As the middle and top of a glacier inch ahead of the bottom layer and sides, the ice column deforms. Like saltwater taffy being pulled on a stretching machine, the ice in glaciers pulls and changes shape as it advances. This is where much of the noise that a glacier makes comes from. The glacier groans, pops, and snaps as ice continually breaks to allow different parts to move at different speeds and then refreezes into its new structure.

Occasionally a glacier will surge ahead for a short period of days or weeks at a speed up to twenty times normal. This is called *surging*. Surging glaciers have been clocked at speeds of 600 feet in a single day! That's a year's worth of movement in just 24 hours.

Why do glaciers suddenly surge? It happens in the summer, and usually only to the thinner, leading portions of the glacier. Summer warmth can melt a thick layer at the bottom of the glacier. This layer of water (up to several inches thick) acts as a lubricant for the glacier just as a thin film of water lubricates a plastic Slip 'n Slide you hook to a hose and slide along in the yard.

Suddenly friction is greatly reduced. The glacier's bottom stops dragging along the ground and slips and slides downhill. Once that layer of water drains away, the surge ends.

Surging glaciers can race forward to block rivers, valleys, or roads. In a matter of days a surging glacier can seal off the routes for migrating salmon and caribou. They can dam streams and form new lakes.

Not all of a glacier surges during a surge period. Just some sections do—usually just the lowest sections where it is the warmest and where the bottom of the glacier will be subjected to the greatest amount of melting. As some parts surge, the rest of the glacier is stretched, pulled, and deformed. The result is more cracking, groaning, creaking, and popping from the glacier. The noise of surging glaciers keeps nearby campers awake at night.

Crevasses

The different kinds of movements all force glacier ice to crack and split. Every time the glacier reaches an obstacle, it must bend and deform as it climbs over or around the obstacle and continues on its journey. Each time the glacier reaches a natural bend in the valley it is following, the glacier must crack and split in order to make the turn. In a glacier, these cracks and splits, you will recall, are called *crevasses*.

Try it. Get a block of ice to see if you can make just the front part of the block turn even a slight bend without having the back part turn with it. The ice refuses to do it. It would take a great amount of force to make just part of the ice turn. That force would have to split the ice.

Each turn and each hump in the valley floor forces the glacier's ice to break into new crevasses. Each time the middle inches too far ahead of the glacier's edges and bottom, the ice has to split to allow different parts to move at different speeds.

The surface of a glacier is laced with a crisscrossing network of crevasses. Crevasses can be as deep as 100 feet and as wide as 15 feet. Some stretch for 100 yards. Most are much shorter and smaller. These crevasses allow the glacier to flex—a critical ability if the glacier is to maneuver over and around obstacles and bending valley walls.

TOPICS FOR DISCUSSION AND PROJECTS

Here are activities, research topics, and discussion questions you can use to expand upon the key science concepts presented in this chapter.

Research and Discuss. Research ice ages. How many have thee been? Is there a cycle to ice ages? Is there a pattern to when and how often they happen? Research the causes for an ice age. What did you find as the most probable causes? Why do ice ages end? Why does an ice age not continue forever once the world is covered in thick continental glaciers?

An Activity. Try to compact snow into clear, solid ice—something every glacier does. You try to do this when you make a snowball. How close can you come? In order to succeed, you'll have to squeeze the air to of the snow and form the ice crystals into a repeating matrix structure. That will change the color from white to clear. (If you made a *big* block of ice—3 or 4 feet thick—it would begin to look bluish.) Why couldn't you do it with your own hands and strength? How does a glacier do it? How much pressure and time would you need in order to turn your snow into ice?

Research and Discuss. The Gulf Stream was mentioned in relation to ice ages. Research this important ocean current. What path does it follow? Research the *North Atlantic gyre*. The Gulf Stream is a part of this great gyre. How much heat does the Gulf Stream carry north? Search for information about reversals of this famous current. How often has it happened? When was the last reversal? What happens when the Gulf Stream flows north to south instead of south to north?

An Activity. Let's model glacier movement and the effect of that movement on the landscape it passes through. For this activity you will build a model glacier and a landscape for it to flow through. Refer to any of these three sites that each contains good directions for this activity: www.ktca.org/newtons/15/glaciers.html; www.lpb.org/glaciers; www.nps.gov/akso/Parkwise/teachers/nature/KEFJ_Glaciers/activties/ImpactofGlaciersonLandscape.

An Activity. Let's look at how pressure can melt ice. For this activity you'll need a block of ice (freeze a half-gallon milk carton full of water), about 4 feet of wire, and two 5-pound weights. Put towels on the edges of two tables and lay the block of ice between them so that the middle of the ice hangs over empty air. Tie one weight to each end of the wire and lay the wire across the middle of the ice so that one weight hangs down on either side. Watch what happens and record your results.

Did the wire cut through the ice? How long did it take? Would it have

been faster if you had used heavier weights? Why or why not? Did the ice split in two? Why or why not? If the pressure of the wire melts the ice right below it, the area right above the wire has no pressure on it. Is that why the ice refroze?

An Activity. Icebergs are fascinating things. Let's make an iceberg and see how it floats in water. Put some water mixed with a little food dye (use any color you like) in a plastic bag, tie it tight with a rubber band, and freeze it solid in the freezer. Remove the plastic bag and place your iceberg in a bowl of water. Try to measure how much of the iceberg is above the water line and how much lies below. Seven-eighths (87.5%) of the ice should be below the water line. Watch your iceberg melt. Does it melt faster above or below the waterline? Why?

Put several large ice cubes in a glass and fill the glass with water as full as possible. What do you think will happen as the ice melts? Why? Water expands as it freezes and contracts as it melts. That's why ice floats.

Research and Discuss. Research a modern glacier. Pick one of the glaciers *not* in a polar region. See how much information you can find on the history of the glacier. How big is it? How old? Is it shrinking or growing? Research its effect on the surrounding landscape. Now pick a glacier in Alaska to see if you can find more information about that glacier. Compare the information you were able to find on these two glaciers.

SUGGESTED READING FOR STUDENTS

Bender, Lionel. *Glacier*. New York: Franklin Watts, 1998.

Bramwell, Martyn. *Glaciers and Icecaps*. New York: Franklin Watts, 1996.

Brimner, Larry. *Glaciers*. New York: Scholastic Library Publishing, 2000.

Carruthers, Margaret. *Glaciers*. New York: Franklin Watts, 2005.

Charlton, W. *Ice Ages*. Alexandria, VA: Time-Life Books, 1998.

Fowler, Allan. *Icebegs, Ice Caps, and Glaciers*. New York: Scholastic Library, 1997.

Gallant, Roy. *Glaciers*. New York: Scholastic Library Publishing, 1999.

George, Michael. *Glaciers*. Lawrenceberg, IN: The Creative Company, 2001.

———. *Glaciers: Rivers of Ice*. Lawrenceberg, IN: The Creative Company, 2004.

Llewellyn, Claire. *Glaciers*. Portsmouth, NH: Heinemann Library, 2002.

Mattern, Joanne. *Antarctic: World's Biggest Glacier*. Ontario, Canada: PowerKids Press, 2003.

Matthews, William. *Glaciers and the Ice Age*. New York: Harvey House, 1994.

Radlauer, Ruth. *The Power of Ice*. Chicago: Children's Press, 1995.

Simon, Seymour. *Icebergs and Glaciers*. New York: William Morrow & Co., 1997.

Wiley, Sally. *Blue Ice in Motion: The Story of Alaska's Glaciers*. Anchorage, AK: Alaska Natural History Association, 1999.

SUGGESTED WEB SITES

http://tqjunior.advanced.org/3876/glaciers.html

http://www.ak.usgs.gov/glaciology/FAO.htm

http://www.glaciers.rice.edu/land/5_icemovement.html

http://www.npht.sbg.ac.at/npht

SUGGESTED READING FOR TEACHERS

Benn, Douglas. *Glaciers and Glaciation.* Cambridge, England: Edward Arnold Publishing, 1998.

Elias, Scott. *The Ice Age History of Alaskan National Parks.* Washington, DC: Smithsonian Institute, 1997.

Fagan, Brian. *Little Ice Age: How Climate Made History, 1300–1850.* Philadelphia, PA: Basic Books, 2001.

Hambrey, M. *Glaciers.* New York: Oxford University Press, 1999.

Macdougall, Doug. *Frozen Earth.* Berkeley: University of California Press, 2004.

Sharp, R. *Living Ice: Understanding Glaciers.* New York: Oxford University Press, 2000.

9 Earthquakes

MYTHS ABOUT HOW EARTHQUAKES SHAPE THE LAND

To humans, earthquakes have always been terrifying, invisible, unpredictable, and unimaginably destructive displays of nature's power. You jerk awake but aren't sure why. The bedside clock jiggles. You hear a growing rumble, like a passing eighteen-wheeler, and a deep growl that sounds as if the Earth had turned into a mad dog about to attack. Then the floor and walls creak and groan. Lamps sway and rattle. The sound grows to rolling thunder. Cupboards fly open. Plates and glasses crash. Pictures tumble off wall. Windows shatter. Broken glass explodes across the room. Your heart races as you stagger out of bed as the room lurches around you like the deck of a ship caught in a violent storm. That's an earthquake.

Most earthquakes are so small they can't be felt. Some, however, are big enough to flatten whole cities. A giant earthquake, in part, destroyed the fabled land of Atlantis. Earthquakes arrive with no warning other than an ominous sound like the rumbling voice of an angry god. Earthquakes have always terrified people. Traditional cultures needed to assign responsibility for these acts of wanton chaos and destruction. They needed to know who to appease in order to prevent—or at least to minimize—them.

Humans have always viewed earthquakes as something going wrong with the planet. Earthquakes seemed to say that the Earth was both capable of, and intent on, ripping itself apart. This meant that either the Earth itself was alive (some pictured the Earth as a giant tortoise on whose hard shell we live), or that some hidden entity was powerful enough to rattle the Earth. In either case, that entity was certainly capable of destroying puny humans and was elevated to the status of a god.

Are earthquakes significant for scientific study of the Earth? What can be studied in an event that is so unpredictable? What can we learn about the structure and processes of the Earth from the shaking and rumbling of its crust? Certainly earthquakes are major events. Certainly they terrify humans. But do they mean anything for Earth Science?

Before cultures had modern scientific tools and techniques, all they could use as the basis for their explanation of frightening earthquakes were their beliefs. These beliefs usually involved all-powerful deities and were usually expressed in the form of myths.

In India, earthquakes were explained as the burrowing of a giant mole. In many lands it was the stamping of a giant or dragon. In a Maori (New Zealand) myth, Ruau-moko, the youngest child of the sky god, Rangi, and the Earth goddess, Papa, was never born but remained trapped inside Papa's womb. His wiggling and kicking, as he is trying to be born, is what causes the Earth to rumble and shake.

Some Asian tribes blame Shie-Ou, an evil god imprisoned in the Earth by the sun god. Several Japanese myths blame the wiggling of a giant catfish. The Greek scientist Aristotle attributed earthquakes to wind trying to escape from underground caves. Greek myths, however, blamed the giant Typhon (the god for whom Typhoons were named). Many myths say that earthquakes happen when the giant who holds the Earth shifts his position and moves the Earth from shoulder to shoulder. In Timor, when an earthquake happens people shout to this god, "Don't drop the Earth!"

The myth presented here takes a different view of earthquakes. A cousin to the Chicken Little story, but with a nice twist at the end, this Indian myth acknowledges the nature of earthquakes and focuses on demystifying earthquakes and on ways to understand their effects—both on the land and on living creatures.

"The Lion's Earthquake," A Myth from India

Once, long ago, there stood a palm grove studded with *bel* trees (an Indian tree sometimes called the woodapple tree) lying close by the western sea. There a rabbit lived all alone under a small palm shrub at the foot of one of the towering *bel* trees. One day, after bringing his dinner back underneath the palm shrub, the rabbit thought, "If an earthquake came along right now and swallowed up the earth, if the earth should shake and rumble and fall to pieces, then what would become of *me?*"

At that very moment, a ripe *bel* fruit fell onto the little palm shrub rattling and shaking its wide palm leaves. Terrified, the rabbit sprang straight into the air, convinced that an earthquake had struck and that the Earth was falling to pieces. He fled wildly away whimpering in fright without ever glancing back.

Another rabbit saw him racing along, scared to death, and asked, "Why are you running away looking so terrified?"

The first rabbit pointed back over his shoulder and cried, "Earthquake! The earth is falling to pieces back there!"

So the second rabbit fled with him. In the same way they saw a third and a fourth until there were hundreds of rabbits all scampering for their lives in a tight bunch down the path.

Then a deer saw them and asked why they ran in fright. At the cry, "Earthquake!" the deer joined the stampede. Then came a boar and a buffalo and a gazelle and a rhinoceros and a tiger and a pair of elephants.

Each animal asked and was told the same thing. "Earthquake! The earth is falling to pieces back there!" And, suddenly as terrified as all the others, each new animal bellowed its fright and joined the stampede.

A mighty lion saw the thundering herd and asked, "What is this? Why do you run?"

When he was told the story by one of the elephants, the lion thought, "I did not feel any earthquake. I have not seen or herd the earth falling to pieces. Surely, any earthquake big enough to be worth running from would want to be felt by a lion above all other beasts."

He almost laughed out his scorn. But he thought, "They are truly terrified. If I say there was no earthquake, they will not believe me. I must invent a story they will accept if I am to save their lives."

And the lion said, "I can stop the earth from falling to pieces if I see the exact place where it started."

The elephants shrugged, "We only heard about it from the tiger."

The tiger said, "I heard about it from the rhinoceros."

The rhinoceros said, "Ask the gazelle."

The gazelle: "Ask the buffalo."

The buffalo: "The boar."

The boar: "The deer."

The deer pointed at the rabbits. "*They* told me."

All the rabbits pointed at the one lone rabbit. "*He* is the one who started it."

The one lone rabbit nervously nodded. "It's all true! We must run! I was sitting all alone under a small palm shrub at the foot of one of the towering *bel* trees in the palm grove lying close by the western sea about to eat my dinner when there was a great crash and the leaves began to shake and that was when I knew that a mighty earthquake was ripping the earth apart."

The lion thought, "No doubt a ripe *bel* fruit fell onto the palm bush leaves." But knowing that the crowd of frightened animals needed more, he said, "This sounds serious. Show me the place and I will stop the earthquake and save the earth."

Trembling with fright the rabbit lead the lion back to the palm grove lying close by the western sea and pointed to his palm bush. "There," the rabbit whispered.

The lion nodded, "Now run and rejoin the others. I will stop the earthquake and tell you when it is safe to return."

As soon as the rabbit was out of sight, the lion used his long claws to rip and rent the ground, leaving long jagged gashes across the Earth. He pushed over trees and threw giant boulders into the stream to alter its flow.

Then he chuckled to himself and walked back to the other animals. "I have fought with the earthquake and made it stop. Come and see for yourselves."

All the animals marched back to the palm grove studded with tall *bel* trees lying close by the western sea and shuddered to see the earthquake's terrible destruction. Gazing at this devastated landscape, each was convinced that the Earth had been about to rip itself apart. Then they turned and gazed in awe and respect at the mighty lion who had stopped an earthquake and saved the Earth. They chanted praises and bowed down, and from that day to this, every animal in the jungle and on the plain has acknowledged that the lion is king.

—— THE SCIENCE OF HOW EARTHQUAKES SHAPE THE LAND

The following beliefs are either directly stated or strongly implied in the presented myth. Here is what modern science knows about the aspects of earthquakes explained by each belief.

BELIEF: Earthquakes are caused by angry gods.

What *Is* an Earthquake?

First, what exactly is an earthquake? Earthquakes are a shaking and trembling of the ground. That's true. But when an eighteen-wheeler rumbles past your house, or when a heard of buffalo thunders through the backyard, the ground shakes and trembles. Dishes clatter and tinkle in the cupboard. We don't call those earthquakes.

An earthquake is caused not by a disturbance *on* the ground, but by a disturbance deep *in* the ground. An earthquake is a release of pressure along the border between two plates of the Earth's crust. It is a shifting, a movement by the plates that make up the crust. Earthquakes are created by rock plates deep underground grinding against each other as the two plates collide.

Plates in the Earth's crust don't glide easily past each other. Their movement is jerky, not smooth like well-oiled pistons. They are not lubricated and greased surfaces that slide frictionlessly past other plates. The plates want to move and slide. But their edges are made of rough rock. Rocks catch on other rocks and halt the plate's progress. As these huge plates inch forward, pressure builds up in those rocks along the plate boundary that have jammed into, and stuck against, rocks in the other plate.

Eventually the pressure is too great. The stuck rocks shatter. That section of the plate snaps forward like a released rubber band. The explosion of shattering rock and the forward lurch by part of a crustal plate sends out shock waves. Those shock waves physically shake the ground. That's an earthquake.

What Cause Earthquakes?

If that's what earthquakes *are*, what causes them? Not angry gods. Plate tectonics is the culprit. The crust of the Earth is broken into seven major and a dozen smaller chunks called *plates*. Those plates float on top of the semiliquid mantle below. Atlas is pictured carrying the world on his shoulders. Actually the mantle carries the crustal plates on its shoulders.

The Earth's plates move independently, like skaters on a frozen pond. But while the skaters all agree to go in the same general direction around the pond so that they won't bump into each other, the Earth's crustal plates have made no such agreement. They act more like bumper cars at the county fair midway, intentionally crashing and slamming into each other just for the fun of it.

The motion of our crustal plates and the forces in the mantle underneath that drive them are called *plate tectonics*. Plate tectonics moves these massive plates around on the surface of the Earth. Some 70 million years ago there was no Atlantic Ocean. North America and Europe were joined together. And 100 million years ago, India was an island out in the ocean, moving north, but had not crashed into Asia. The plates may move only a few inches each year, but that adds up to 1,000 miles in a million years—a short period in geologic time.

Sometimes the plates pull apart. More often, they either try to grind past each other or smash head on. Those are the times that the rocks at the edge of one plate are mashed against rocks in the other plate. Those are the times that these rocks seem to be crushed in a vice until they can no longer take the strain and shatter. Then the plates lurch forward—and send out the shock waves that we call an earthquake.

Here's where our bumper car analogy breaks down. There's a lot of open space between bumper cars. Not so with plates. They cover the Earth—the entire Earth. There are seams—boundaries—between plates, but no open spaces where no crust exists and where plates would be free to maneuver. When one plates moves, as during an earthquake, it affects all the other surrounding plates. Earthquakes relieve tension between plates in the area where the earthquake happened. However, relieving tension in one spot just transfers that tension to another spot. The boundaries of Earth's plates form a spiderweb across the surface of our planet. An Earthquake along one thread of that web vibrates and twinges them all.

An earthquake in Turkey might shift tension along plate boundaries to a spot between two plates near Indonesia and speed up an earthquake there. An earthquake in Japan could shift plate tension to a spot in Alaska and set up a big earthquake there. In early June 2005 a moderate earthquake (7.4 on the Richter scale) rumbled 80 miles off the coast of Eureka in Northern California. A week later, a trembler shook Southern California, 800 miles to the south. The two were linked. Relieving tension along the plate border in Northern California shifted tension south along that plate boundary to another weak spot 800 miles away.

Where Are Earthquakes?

Earthquakes occur along fault lines. Fault lines are weak spots in the Earth's surface where rocks are splitting and shattering as two plates collide. They are lines along the Earth's surface that mark the division between plates. However, rocks shatter, crumble, and split in complex ways. There won't be a single, neat fault line marking the boundary between two plates, but a region with dozens—or hundreds—of more or less parallel, individual fault lines.

Some fault lines, like the San Andreas fault line in California, are long and well marked. Most are shorter and less well known. (The maze of known fault lines through California is shown on Figure 9.1.) Most fault lines occur along the boundary between two colliding plates. But not all.

FIGURE 9.1 • California Fault Lines

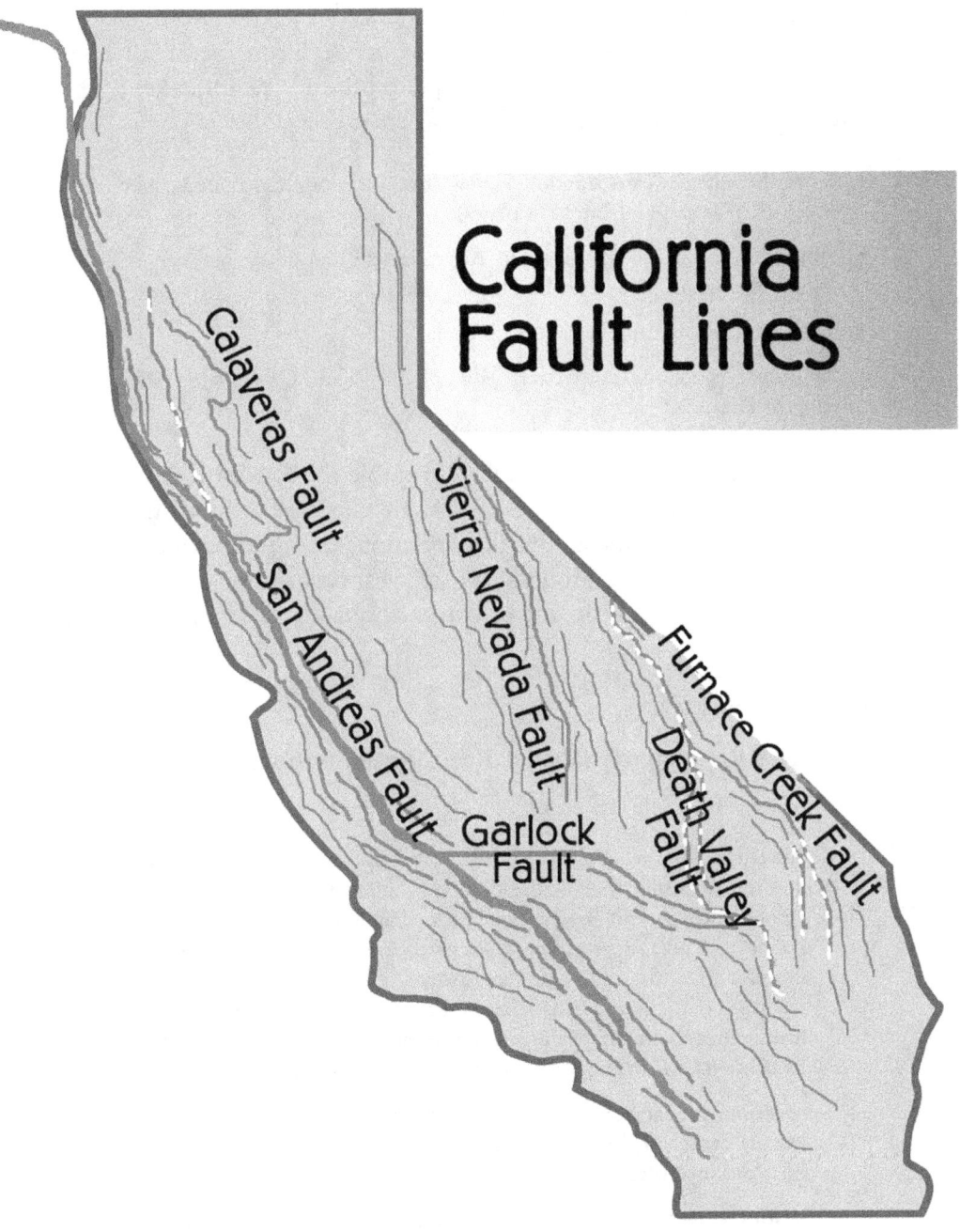

Some fault lines—the New Madrid fault line through Missouri, for example—lie in the middle of a plate and mark weak areas and places where the rock layers have, like scars, split and reformed under past pressure.

Most fault lines occur along plate boundaries. In past chapters we have looked at the kinds of collisions that can occur between plates. Head-on collisions and glancing—sideswipe—blows between continental plates or between a continental and an oceanic plate produce earthquakes.

The four most active earthquake areas span the globe:

- From the Alps east to Istanbul, Turkey (the line along the boundary between the African and Eurasian plates).
- From the Himalayas southeast to Australia (the boundary between the Indian-Australian plate and the Eurasian plate).
- The San Andreas Fault system (California).
- Southeast Asia along the western edge of the Pacific Ocean (the Pacific Ring of Fire).

Every year over 1 million earthquakes rumble the Earth (their locations are shown on Figure 9.2). Of these, 90% are clustered around the Pacific Ocean's Ring of Fire. Almost 99% of all earthquakes are too weak to be felt on the surface. On average, around 800 each year create some damage somewhere in the world, but only one or two earthquakes cause major damage.

Earthquake Terms

There are some commonly used earthquake terms that are useful to know.

Epicenter. An earthquake's epicenter is the spot on the surface of the ground that is directly above the location of an earthquake. Earthquakes happen underground. That's where rocks shatter and slip. Some are as shallow as a mile or two under the surface. Some are as deep as 50 or 60 miles under the surface. Often earthquake reports list the epicenter and depth of the earthquake—that is, they identify the spot on the map directly over the center of the earthquake event and indicate how deep the center of the earthquake actually was below that spot.

Location. An earthquake's location is the spot deep in the Earth that was the center of the actual earthquake movement. The location is some distance (depth) directly below the epicenter.

Seismic Waves. The energy waves created by an earthquake are called *seismic* waves. (The word *seismic* comes from the Greek word *seismos*, which means "to shake.") Seismic waves carry this energy outward

FIGURE 9.2 • Earthquakes around the World

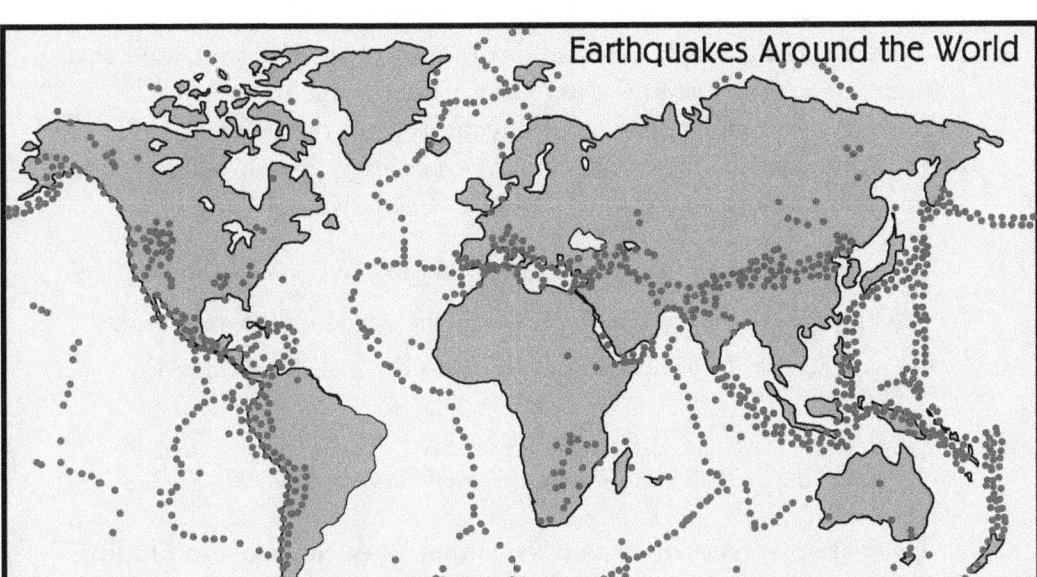

in all directions—like ripples expanding in a pond from the spot where a pebble landed in the water. When seismic waves reach the surface, the ground shakes and buildings collapse.

Magnitude. An earthquake's magnitude is a measure of the amount of energy released by the earthquake. This energy is released into the seismic waves. The bigger an earthquake's magnitude, the greater the damage it will cause. Magnitude is measured on the Richter scale.

Aftershocks. Aftershocks are smaller earthquakes that follow a major earthquake and occur in the same general area. Some aftershocks follow a major quake by hours, some by months. After a major quake, rock layers deep underground still bang and grind against each other as they adjust to the new boundary between the plates. Those adjustments create the aftershocks.

What Are Seismic Waves?

First, it is normal and common for some physical disturbance, such as the smashing of rocks and the movement of plates, to send out energy waves. Clap your hands together. That creates a physical disturbance in the air that sends out energy waves that you can hear—sound waves, in this case. Slap a wall in your house. Someone in the next room not only could hear that energy wave through the wall but also could feel those energy vibrations sent through the solid beams of the wall.

Seismic waves are the same—only *bigger*. Seismic waves vibrate the ground just as a sound wave will vibrate the air and your eardrum. Seismic waves travel through rock and dirt instead of air. A seismic wave that transfers its energy into the water can create a tsunami.

Seismic waves radiate out in all directions from the point of rock and plate movement. Because seismic waves so closely match ocean waves, scientists use the same terms to describe seismic waves.

- Period (T): the time between beginning and end of one complete wave.
- Amplitude (A): the size of the movement in the ground as the wave passes.
- Frequency (f): the number of waves that pass one spot in a given period of time.
- Speed (V): how fast the seismic waves travel. Seismic waves can race through the Earth at up to 4 miles per second (14,400 mph).

There are two types of seismic waves that an earthquake can produce. In this way seismic waves are different than ocean waves. It is important for scientists to know about each of these types of waves because they cause different kinds of damage to structures and because they tell us different things about the interior structure of the Earth.

Pressure Waves (P-Waves)

Pressure waves produce back-and-forth motion along the direction the wave is traveling. They expand and compress the rock as they pass. Pressure waves roar away from an earthquake's center at up to 4 miles per second (14,400 mph). Pressure waves travel fastest through solid rock, slower through soil, and slower yet through liquid (only 1.5 miles per second [mps] through water). But P-waves will travel through both solids and liquids.

Shear Waves (S-Waves)

Shear waves act more like regular ocean waves. Whereas P-waves move the ground back-and-forth in the direction that the wave is moving, S-waves move the ground either up and down (the way an ocean wave moves water) or side to side (like an ocean wave turned on its side). Shear waves are more powerful and cause far more damage than P-waves, shaking the ground more forcefully up, down, left, and right like a rampaging Brahma bull. Shear waves are like a pit bull dog who has grabbed the Earth in its mighty jaws and shakes back and forth as hard as it can.

These waves are also slower, traveling through rock at a maximum speed of 2 mps. Most important, S-waves can't travel through liquids. They can only travel through solid rock.

Scientists care about these different kinds of waves for two reasons. First, they have to understand the different kinds of earthquake waves so they can design safer buildings to withstand these different kinds of movement and stress. Second, these waves tell scientists a lot about the inner structure and composition of the Earth. Every earthquake sends out both P-waves and S-waves. Seismic listening stations around the world record them.

For example, an earthquake rumbles through central California. Seconds later the P-waves reach recording stations in Los Angeles and San Francisco and are recorded. Then S-waves follow a few seconds behind. Four minutes later the waves have traveled 1,000 miles, and a seismic recording station in Colorado registers the earthquake. Thirty minutes after the earthquake initially struck, its P-waves have finally traveled all the way through the Earth and have reached a recording station in western Australia. Whereas 150 stations record the quake's P-wave, only thirty record its S-wave.

By knowing how long the wave took to reach different stations and how strong the wave was when it finally reached each station, scientists can learn something about the kind of rock that lies inside the Earth on a line between the earthquake's location and each recording station around the globe.

Pressure waves travel faster through rock and slower through liquid. So, the longer it takes for P-waves to reach a certain station, the more molten (liquid) rock must lie along the line between those two points.

If a station recorded both P- and S-waves, it means only solid rock lies between the earthquake's location and this station. (Shear waves won't travel through liquids.) Using the recordings by hundreds of stations for thousands of large earthquakes, scientists have been able to build an accurate map of what the inside of the Earth must be made of. Much of what scientists now know about the interior composition of the Earth they learned through studying the P- and S-waves that nature herself provided during earthquakes.

BELIEF: Earthquakes are random occurrences.

The morning news never announces when an earthquake is scheduled to occur. Every earthquake comes as a surprise, as something not expected. After an earthquake, the buildings on one block lie in smoldering ruin. Those on the next are left untouched. It seems that both the occurrence of earthquakes and the effects of earthquakes are totally random. Right?

Yes and no. The location of earthquakes is not random at all. Earthquakes happen along fault lines. Maps exist that locate virtually every fault line on Earth. Those fault lines occur along plate boundaries, and 90% of all earthquakes occur along the fault lines that mark the plate collision boundaries that ring the Pacific Ocean. Scientists know the fault systems and general areas where almost all the earthquakes over the next 50 years will most likely happen.

Scientists know the direction and speed of every plate's movement. They know which fault systems are under the most stress and are therefore the most likely candidates for a major quake. They know the location and strength of millions of past earthquakes. They can actually now say what the probability is that a major earthquake will occur along a specific fault within the next 10 years, 20 years, and 50 years.

What scientists don't know and can't predict is the exact timing of earthquakes and their exact epicenters. Scientists can say that there is a 70% probability that a major earthquake will occur within 90 miles of Istanbul, Turkey, within the next 30 years. But that doesn't tell residents which side or part of Istanbul should be most worried or how big the earthquake will be. It doesn't help them decide which week or month—or even which year—they should plan to be away from the city.

So when a quake actually hits, it *seems* to be an unanticipated surprise—even though it isn't. Every year scientists gather more data and are able to inch closer toward actual prediction of major earthquakes.

The Richter Scale and Earthquake Prediction

Scientists couldn't really study earthquakes until they had a way to measure them. An American scientist named Charles Richter provided that system when, in 1935, he created the Richter scale. Scientists needed to know how much energy an earthquake produced, but they had no way to directly measure that. Richter decided that they only had to measure the amount of ground motion each earthquake produced. That would give them a way to compare different earthquakes, since the more energy an earthquake released, the bigger would be the ground movement it created.

His Richter scale is a measure of the amount of ground movement produced by an earthquake. With Richter's system, the magnitude of an earthquake can be expressed as a simple number (a 1.6, or 4, or 5, or

7.8, for example) and compared to the magnitude of other quakes. The Richter scale is called a *logarithmic* scale. Each whole number (4, 5, 6, etc.) represents an earthquake exactly ten times as powerful as the number below it. Thus a 5 quake is 10 times as powerful as a 4 and 100 times as powerful as a 3, but only one tenth as powerful as a 6.

Using the Richter scale, scientists have been able to study earthquakes and their energy. They have found that bigger earthquakes are created when more rock breaks at the same moment. If 5 miles of rock are shattered along a fault line deep underground, that event will typically produce around a 2.5 earthquake. If 300 miles of rock are crushed at the same time, it will result in more Earth movement and will create a 7.0 earthquake. In this way, scientists can now relate the size of the actual rock-smashing event to the amount of surface ground movement it will produce.

They have also been able to determine how much energy is released by different size earthquakes. An 8.7 earthquake produces as much energy as the explosion of 70 million tons of TNT. A 9.0 earthquake is equal to about 200 million tons of TNT.

Scientists have new tools that they hope will help them better predict and understand earthquakes. They can use lasers and GPS (Global Positioning System) satellite stations to monitor minor bulging and shifting of the ground surface over fault lines that could indicate the buildup of deep forces that will trigger an earthquake. Using modern communications technology, scientists have created networks of monitoring stations and seismograph stations around the world to record and study even the tiniest of quakes and tremors.

Scientists are also searching for signs that might precede and signal an imminent quake. Some suspect that the ground emits ultra-low frequency (ulf) vibrations before a quake. Ultra-low frequency signals are at too low a frequency for us to hear—just as dog whistles send out a sound vibration at too high a frequency for human ears to hear.

Other scientists search for foreshocks (like aftershocks, only *before* instead of after a major quake). Small earthquakes happen every few seconds somewhere in the world. Scientists are hoping that in the days and hours before a major quake they will be able to detect swarms, clusters, or some unique pattern of these tiny quakes that will announce the upcoming major quake. If these scientists succeed, every time they see the correct pattern of foreshocks, they will be able to accurately predict an upcoming earthquake.

Still other scientists study many of the reported strange observations just before earthquakes: U-shaped candle flames, swarming earthworms, animals that howl and become frightened, usually quiet animals (pandas) that scream and throw food, snakes that refuse to go into their holes, schools of fish that suddenly align themselves all in the same direction. What do these animals sense? Why don't they sense it *every* time there is going to be an earthquake? If we knew, we might be able to use our pets as an early warning system for earthquakes.

Some research has suggested that electromagnetic waves may precede—or even cause—earthquakes. Scientists are constructing monitors to search for these signals. Ball lightning (literally, glowing basketball size spheres of lightning called St. Elmo's Fire) has often been spotted just before an earthquake. So, it is possible that earthquakes have electrical and magnetic properties we have never thought to look for. Maybe they could become earthquake warning signals.

Earthquakes are still not predictable. But they are understandable, and much work is underway that might—in a few years' time—produce a system for accurately predicting them.

BELIEF: Earthquakes are a sign of something going wrong, some undesirable chaos in the Earth.

Earthquakes happen all the time—almost 140 each hour of each day, over 1 million each year. Indeed, 70 to 80 occur each week in Sonoma County, California (about 60 miles north of San Francisco). Years go by without any of these earthquakes being big enough to be felt. The number and size of last week's earthquakes is reported on the local newspaper's weather page each week.

Earthquakes are a normal part of what happens when crustal plates move—just like volcanoes. The plates of our planet's crust are forever shouldering past or against each other. That's how our planet works. Earthquakes are a very natural and necessary part of the orderly and successful functioning of our planet.

Still, earthquakes can be amazingly destructive and dangerous. The 1906 earthquake that leveled San Francisco was fifteen times more powerful than the biggest nuclear bomb ever built. The biggest U.S. earthquake struck along the New Madrid (Missouri) fault in 1811 and measured approximately 9.2. (Seismographs and the Richter scale had not been invented in 1811, so there was no way to determine the exact magnitude.) The deadliest earthquakes have struck in China. The Shaanxi earthquake in 1556 killed 830,000. The T'ang Shan earthquake in 1976 killed 240,000. India has also been rocked by killer quakes. The Calcutta quake in 1737 killed over 300,000.

The December 26, 2005, tsunami that killed almost 230,000 across the countries bordering the Indian Ocean was triggered by a 9.0 undersea earthquake. Twenty-one recorded earthquakes have each caused more than 50,000 deaths.

BELIEF: Earthquakes don't change the land.

Actually, plate tectonics is the underlying force that moves continents and land masses around the face of the globe and reshapes the land. Plate collisions—created by plate tectonics—cause all earthquakes.

Still, each major earthquake visibly, measurably changes and rearranges the land. Pieces of the continents slid past each other. Hunks are lifted up or shoved downward. These effects can be dramatic during a single earthquake.

During the 1906 San Francisco earthquake, the land around Pt. Reyes, 50 miles north of the city, shifted 21 feet. The land that was next to Pt. Reyes a few thousand years ago is now 20 miles down the road. During a 1923 earthquake in Japan, the floor of Tokyo Bay rose 10 feet. Several shipping channels had to be moved and dug out so that ships could get through. Nearby Izu Peninsula was shoved 14 feet west.

An 1819 quake in India dropped five small harbor islands by as much as 30 feet. All but the top turrets of a fort on one of those islands disappeared below the waves in a few seconds. An earthquake destroyed the Cyprus trading port of Kourion in A.D. 365.

The New Madrid, Missouri, earthquake in late 1811 changed the course of the Mississippi River. Several whole lakes were lifted so high that they drained of water. The quake created four new lakes where dry land sat only hours before. People felt that quake from Canada to New Orleans. It destroyed 150,000 acres of timberland. It flattened three whole towns. Only a few people were killed in that quake. Of course, in 1811 only a few hundred people lived in the region. Now almost 15 million do. The same quake today would be devastating.

Large magnitude earthquakes dramatically change the local landscape. Most of the 1 million earthquakes each year are too small to create noticeable landscape changes. But the 8,000 moderate earthquakes and the several major quakes each year definitely do.

WONDERS OF THE LAND

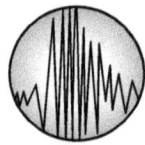

— TOPICS FOR DISCUSSION AND PROJECTS

Here are activities, research topics, and discussion questions you can use to expand upon the key science concepts presented in this chapter.

Research and Discuss. Many people live in areas that are prone to earthquakes. Why don't they move? Why live there? Compare earthquakes to two other major disasters: tornados and hurricanes. Just in the United States, where does each of these disasters strike? How often? Which of the three does the most damage? Which causes the most deaths? Which do you think is the most dangerous of these three? Why?

An Activity. Let's imitate an earthquake. Wrap course sandpaper around a block of wood. Tape a second sheet of sandpaper (face up) onto a table or work surface. Tape a rubber band to the top of the block and gently pull the block across the sandpaper sheet by pulling only on the rubber band. Be careful not to lift the block. Simply pull it steadily across the sheet of sandpaper.

What happened? Was the motion of the block smooth or jerky? The two pieces of sandpaper created friction between the block and the table just as the rough edges of crustal plates do when they try to force their way past each other. As you pulled steadily on the rubber band, tension built up. When the tension grew big enough to overcome friction, the block sprang forward—just as a plate of Earth's crust will. When that happens, we get an earthquake.

Research and Discuss. What is your experience with earthquakes? Have you ever felt an earthquake? Interview someone who has lived through a major earthquake. What did they hear? See? Feel? Remember? How long did it last? Imagine yourself being in the middle of a big quake and describe what you see, feel, and hear. As an alternative, describe some other natural disaster you have experienced.

An Activity. Make chocolate fudge sauce (or chocolate sauce) in a pan on the stove. (Use any convenient recipe for your fudge, but *not* a microwave recipe.) Watch the surface of your hot fudge sauce as it boils. (Your recipe will call for you to bring the fudge to a "rolling boil.") Sauce rises from the bottom (next to the burners), reaches surface, and cools enough to form a thin scum (crust). Then that scum moves across the surface of the pan just as the tectonic plates of Earth move across the planet's surface.

The fudge sauce crust doesn't flow as a unified whole. It's broken into parts—like plates—that move independently. Where the fudge sauce coming from two directions runs into each other (where two plates collide), a trench forms as the fudge is subducted back down into the boil-

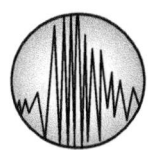

ing interior of the pan. Study the thin scum that forms as your fudge sauce cooks, and you'll have a good sense of what Earth's crustal plates do. And the best part of this experiment: you get to eat the fudge sauce after it cools!

Research and Discuss. Drop a pebble in a pan of water. Waves of energy form and move out in a circular pattern. Earthquake waves move in the same way and cause land to rise and fall just as the waves in a tub cause water to rise and fall. But there are two kinds of earthquake waves. Research earthquake P-waves and S-waves. How do scientists tell them apart on a seismograph? Do they have different effects once they reach the surface? What do scientists learn from studying these waves? How do scientists use the recording of these waves at different seismic recording stations to locate the epicenter and depth of an earthquake?

An Activity. Under certain conditions, soil can act like a liquid. This is called *liquefaction*. Buildings on such dirt collapse. Unfortunately, earthquakes can easily create those conditions. Let's do a liquefaction experiment. Fill a large metal pan—like a large loaf pan—with sand. Set the pan on a table. Now pour in enough water so that the water level rises almost up to the surface of the sand. Stand a brick vertically in the sand and wiggle it down in a little bit (like a tall building).

Now let's create an earthquake. Very gently, repeatedly, tap the end of the pan with a mallet or hammer and watch the brick building. The sand gets squishy and the brick falls over. That's liquefaction. The P-waves of an earthquake can make ground that has a high water table suddenly act like a liquid. Anything depending on that ground for support topples. Research liquefaction and describe what kind of ground is most susceptible. Has liquefaction created damage in any of California's earthquakes?

An Activity. Scientists record earthquakes on a device called a seismograph. Let's see how a seismograph works by building a highway seismograph. You will ride as the front-seat passenger in a car, preferably on a bumpy road. You will need to bring a pad of lined paper and a felt-tip pen with you.

As you ride, hold the pad of paper against the dashboard with one hand. Hold the pen in your other hand with that arm held out straight. The tip of your pen should just touch the paper. As you ride slowly, trace a line from left to right across the page.

Notice what happens when you hit a bump. Your hand moves up and down making a seismographlike recording. When the road is smooth, your line is fairly straight. When you hit a bump, the pen wiggles. The bigger the bump, the bigger the wiggles of your pen. You are recording on a piece of paper the road conditions you have driven over. A seismo-

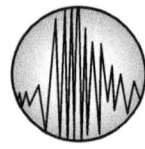

graph does the same thing, only it records the vibrations in the Earth, not the bumps in a road.

SUGGESTED READING FOR STUDENTS

Branley, Franklyn. *Earthquakes*. New York: HarperCollins, 2005.

Grace, Catherine. *Forces of Nature*. Washington, DC: National Geographic Society, 2004.

Lampton, Christopher. *Earthquake*. New York: Lerner Publishing Group, 1998.

Matthews, William. *Volcanoes and Earthquakes*. New York: Harvey House, 1995.

Moores, Eldridge. *Volcanoes and Earthquakes*. New York: Barnes and Noble Books, 2003.

National Geographic Society. *This Violent Earth*. Washington, DC: National Geographic Society, 2003.

Nicolson, Cynthia. *Earthquakes*. Ontario, Canada: Kids Can Press, 2002.

Osborne, Mary. *Earthquakes in the Early Morning*. New York: Random House Books for Young Readers, 2001.

Ritchie, D. *Superquake*. New York: Crown, 2002.

Simon, Seymour. *Danger! Earthquake*. New York: William Morrow & Company, 2002.

———. *Earthquakes*. New York: William Morrow & Company, 1997.

Sutherland, Lin. *Earthquakes and Volcanoes*. New York: Reader's Digest Children's Publishing, 2003.

Van Rose, Suzanna. *Volcanoes and Earthquakes*. New York: DK Publishing, 2004.

Walker, B. *Planet Earth: Earthquakes*. New York: Time-Life Books, 2002.

Watt, Fiona. *Earthquakes and Volcanoes*. London: Usborne Books, 1999.

SUGGESTED WEB SITES

National Earthquake Information Center. http://www.usgs.gov/data/geologic/neic/index.html

—— SUGGESTED READING FOR TEACHERS

Alexander, David. *Natural Disasters*. London: UCL Press, 2003.

Bolt, B. *Earthquakes*. New York: W. H. Freeman, 2004.

Gribben, J. *This Shaking Earth*. New York: Putnam & Sons, 1998.

Lauber, Patricia. *Volcano: The Eruption and Healing of Mt. St. Helens*. New York: Simon & Schuster, 1996.

Morton, Ron. *Music of the Earth: Volcanoes, Earthquakes, and Other Geological Wonders*. New York: Plenum Press, 1996.

Van Rose, Susan. *Volcano and Earthquake*. New York: Knopf, 1998.

Vogel, Carol. *Shock Waves through Los Angeles*. New York: Little, Brown, 1996.

Walker, Sally. *Volcanoes*. Minneapolis, MN: Carolrhoda Books, 1998.

10   Living Things

MYTHS ABOUT HOW LIVING THINGS SHAPE THE LAND

Life is an important topic for humans. We are all *alive*. All the plants, insects, animals, trees, and people around you are alive. We cherish our lives and fear losing them. Every culture has pondered the meaning of life, how life began, and the purpose of our lives. Every culture has devoted mythic energy to explaining the origin of human life. Life abounds on this planet and has morphed into countless forms and individual species.

Myths abound that explain how the various creatures of Earth—and especially humans—came to exist, came to possess their particular sets of traits, and came to inhabit their niche in the world. Typically, some god or creator molds the first humans from earth (clay, dirt, etc.) and breathes life into them. Sometimes, the first humans are born from a fallen goddess. Plant life is sometimes created from or by this same goddess (Gaia). In one African myth the creator creates a giant rainbow snake that then creates the grasses and trees that the creator's people will need.

While interesting—and even important—a discussion of the meaning of life seems to have little to do with Earth Sciences. Biology and anthropology are studies of life (present and past). But what does this profusion of life have to do with a study of the land? Does life affect the Earth? Do living things in some way change the land itself? The land supports life, but do living things affect or change the land?

Life covers the land like the fuzz of a fungal moss covers the dirt of a laboratory Petri dish. Even in the driest of deserts, life finds a way to survive and to exist. Do all those life forms cumulatively and singly alter the land? In a myth presented earlier (Chapter 5), Eagle directs the animals to create mountains by scooping earth from one place (creating California's wide Central Valley) in order to pile it up into towering mountains (the Sierra range) in another. The animals radically change the land, itself.

Does that really happen? If so, which life forms significantly affect Earth's land? Do beavers? Ants? Dandelions? Humans? Grizzly bears? Earthworms? Bark beetles? Can we measure how life has changed the Earth?

Few, if any, myths deal directly with life's impact on the land. However, a number of stories include that impact as part of the story's development. The myth presented here is such a story. This story's theme centers on how trees leaned to contain fire. Its plot revolves around selfishness and thievery born from desperate need. But in that theft, various animals and trees opt to remake the landscape to suit their own purpose. The land is radically changed by the events of this one day and its wild chase.

"How Beaver Stole Fire from the Pines," A Myth from the Nez Percé People of the Pacific Northwest

Once, before there were any people in the world, the different animals and trees lived and moved about and talked together just as human beings do today. In those days, the pine trees had the secret of fire and guarded it jealously so that—no matter how cold it was—they alone could warm themselves.

At length, an unusually cold winter came and all the animals were in danger of freezing. They begged the pines to share their secret of fire. But they would not. Almost every animal tried to steal the secret. But they could not.

Finally, Beaver devised a plan.

At a certain spot along the meandering Grande Ronde River (in Idaho), the pines planned to hold a great council. They built a large fire to warm themselves after bathing in the river's icy waters. Guards were posted to keep all others well away from the council site so that no one would get close enough to steal the secret of fire.

But Beaver had covered himself with mud and hidden under the river's bank before any of the pine guards had spread out to take their assigned places. None of the pines saw him hiding there.

When a live coal from the fire rolled down the bank, Beaver seized it, hid it in a leather pouch that he tucked into his breast, and ran away as fast as he could.

The pines raised an alarm and cried out for all to chase and catch him. They lifted their roots and thundered after Beaver. Beaver could swim faster than he could waddle on land. So when the pines drew close, Beaver splashed into the river and used his broad tail to straighten the river so that he could speed away downstream.

Once well ahead of the pines, Beaver climbed out of the water and waddled cross-country, allowing the river to meander and wiggle as it had always done.

But the fire secret was so important that the trees would not give up the chase. Mile after mile they lumbered after Beaver. When they again drew close, Beaver dove back into the river and used his broad tail to straighten its channel and again sped away from the pines.

Thus it is that, even today, the Grande Ronde River flows straight in some places and meanders wildly in others—still flowing in the path that Beaver created for it as he fled with the secret of fire.

Other animals and trees rushed to help Beaver escape with the precious secret of fire. Prairie dogs furiously dug holes, turning a wide meadow into soft dirt and sand that made the pines stumble and trip. Other trees rushed in to block the river's flow and spread its banks to form wide marshes that slowed the pines.

But still the pines raced after Beaver, growling their threats. After running a long way many pines grew so weary that they could run no farther. Most of them stopped in a great dense body along the riverbanks, where they remain to this day, forming a growth so dense that hunters can hardly get through.

The bravest and strongest pines, however, kept up the chase. But even these eventually grew too tired to continue. One by one they gave out and remain scattered at intervals along the banks of the river in the places where they stopped.

One tall cedar ran at the forefront of the remaining pines. Although he realized they would never catch Beaver by speed, he hoped that they might catch him by stealth *if* they could see where Beaver went and where he hid the fire secret. The cedar and several powerful pines pushed up dirt into a tall hill. The cedar climbed the hill, where he could see for many miles just in time to see Beaver dive into the Big Snake River where the Grande Ronde enters it.

Filled with despair, the cedar watched as Beaver crossed the river and gave the fire secret to birches and willows waiting on the other side of the Big Snake. The cedar wept as Beaver gave fire to the oaks and elm trees that spread across the meadow.

Before Beaver could share the fire secret with any of the animals, his coal burned out. Only the trees had been given the secret of fire. So it is that when we want fire, we still have to get it from the trees, for—while every tree holds the secret of fire locked inside it—they never shared that secret with any of the animals.

Heartbroken at the loss of his secret, the cedar could not make himself go any farther and stopped there on top of Lookout Hill, where he still stands to this very day. That the chase was a very long chase is evidenced by the fact that there are no other cedars for a hundred miles upstream from the spot where that cedar stands. The old people still point him out to the young and say, "See? Here is Old Cedar standing in the very spot where he stopped chasing Beaver."

THE SCIENCE OF HOW LIVING THINGS SHAPE THE LAND

The following beliefs are either directly stated or strongly implied in the presented myth. Here is what modern science knows about the aspects of life's effect on the land explained by each belief.

BELIEF: Life existed before the land.

Where did life come from? How did it evolve on this planet? Traditional myths and major religions have all addressed this question. The myth presented in Chapter 1 clearly claimed that life existed before the land. Why bring it up here? Because life is a part of the land. Change life and you change the land. Life affects the land in countless ways. To understand the land, we must look at life's effects on it. That means we must glance briefly at where life came from, and especially at when and how it got here.

Around 3.5 billion YAG one-celled life forms first expanded across the oceans. They appear in the fossil record beginning around that time. It took several billion years beyond that before life forms evolved into complex organisms. The first plant that successfully made the transition from ocean to land did so around 600 million YAG. Grasses, ferns, trees, and bushes quickly spread across the land. Land animals soon followed.

Life on the land is fairly new. The continents existed without life on them for 3.5 billion years. Life has covered the land like a green blanket for less than 1 billion.

Where did those first single-cell oceanic critters come from 3.5 billion YAG? Most people in the sciences believe that life spontaneously emerged from the soup of chemicals that were available in the surface waters of the early oceans. Researchers at George Washington University in St. Louis, Missouri, and at the University of California, San Diego, have recreated conditions in the early oceans and early atmosphere in the laboratory. They each then added artificial lightning (electric shock). Within days the water changed color. Organic compounds formed. Among these were amino acids, the building blocks of proteins and of DNA. They created life—simple, rudimentary, but still life!

Some, however, believe that life on Earth came from outer space. A famed meteorite found in Antarctica contained frozen bacteria alien to Earth. These bacteria were not alive when they reached Earth. But they had been alive while drifting in outer space. Isn't it possible that some other meteorite in the distant past could have delivered live bacteria or other single-celled organisms to Earth to begin life here?

NASA scientists are still exploring Mars and think it is likely that life once existed there. Europa (a moon of Jupiter) and Io (a moon of Saturn) both have frozen oceans. Could life exist there as well as here? And if those four bodies in our small solar system (Earth, Mars, Europa, and Io) have supported life, then isn't it possible that life exists in other places and that life on Earth came from somewhere "out there?"

We may never know for sure. But we do know this: land existed before the oceans, before the atmosphere, and definitely before life emerged on this planet. The belief is wrong. Life on Earth did not exist before the land. In fact, life on land didn't arrive until the land was over 3 billion years old.

Once life arrived on this planet, it became the dominant force on Earth. Life is a powerful, almost unstoppable force. As the saying goes, "Life will always find a way." New lava flows from the Kilauea volcano in Hawaii and kills everything in its path. Lifeless black lava rock smolders as far as you can see. Two years later small plants have already rooted in cracks in the volcanic rock. Lizards scurry past. Birds flit from rock to rock. Lines of ants march through. In 10 years, the place is a lush tropical paradise again. You'd think no plants could invade the barren moonscape of a new lava flow. But life always finds a way.

BELIEF: Plants can affect and change the land.

In the myth, trees as well as animals changed the landscape to help Beaver escape. Is that concept valid? Do plants change the land?

The answer is an emphatic yes. The changes to our planet wrought by plants are stunning and vast.

Microorganisms

Let's start with those "harmless" one-celled plants (plankton) that first inhabited Earth's oceans around 3.5 billion YAG. At that time the atmosphere consisted primarily of three things: carbon dioxide, water vapor, and nitrogen, with traces of hydrogen and other gases expelled by volcanoes.

Carbon dioxide is a prime greenhouse gas that we naturally exhale and that combustion engines spew into the air. It is one of the pollutant emissions we are trying most to control. An early atmosphere of carbon dioxide did exactly what we are worried about our atmosphere doing. It held in the sun's heat and warmed this planet. The sun was not as hot 2 or 3 billion YAG as it is now. The Earth needed to retain its heat back then. Carbon dioxide in the atmosphere is what did it.

Then single-celled plants bloomed in the vast oceans of the world. They consumed carbon dioxide from the atmosphere and expelled oxygen. For the first time the atmosphere began to fill with oxygen. With more oxygen and less carbon dioxide, the atmosphere was able to hold in less heat. The biggest, longest ice age in the history of this planet began 2.5 billion YAG. Many scientists think it happened primarily because oxygen replaced carbon dioxide in the atmosphere. Plants brought on an ice age that lasted for many millions of years.

Oxygen in the atmosphere is considered *"highly reactive."* That is, it wants to chemically bond with other elements. The process is called *oxidation*. Fire is a form of oxidation. So is rust.

Once in the atmosphere, oxygen began to chemically react with elements in rocks. The thick layers of bright red rock found in western cliffs are red because the iron in them was oxidized (just as a rusted iron chair has a reddish color). Iron-rich layers of rock laid down before 3 billion YAG are not red. There was no oxygen for the iron to react with, and thus those layers are a dull blue-gray. Ocean plants changed continental rock layers by pouring oxygen into the air.

But these microscopic, one-celled microorganisms have changed the land in other ways. There are species of microorganisms that actually dissolve (consume) rock. There are many organisms (algae and lichens, for example) that leech specific minerals and chemicals out of rocks—thereby changing the composition and physical strength of the rock. Many of these same organisms crowd into tiny cracks, joints, fissures, and crevices in a rock face. Over time they enlarge these openings and speed erosion and weathering. Microorganisms break down and destroy rocks.

Plants

Grasses, bushes, trees, and ferns all have roots. These roots worm their way into openings in a rock as tiny as a pore and act as power drills, forcing their way deeper into the rock, cracking the rock wide open. Growing plants can force their way up through even the narrowest crack of fissure and force their way through rocks and cement. We have all seen weeds crack cement driveways and sidewalks. They do the same thing to rocks.

Plants break rocks. Trees have the longest and strongest roots and do the most damage. Still, even tiny grassroots can split small stones and pebbles. The roots of growing plants can also leech minerals out of rocks, thus weakening the rocks and changing their chemical composition.

Soil

So far, we have seen some incredibly powerful ways in which plants change the land. But we now come to one of the biggest and most profound effects of plants: They create dirt—or more correctly, soil.

Plants create soil. Soil did not exist until there were plants. Before plants worked their way onto dry land, there was only rock, sand, and clay.

What is soil? Soil is decomposed organic matter (dead plants) mixed with clay and sand. Leaves fall. Grasses die. Trees die, their trunks fall, and the trunk and roots rot. This layer of decomposing organic matter is mixed with clay and sand by a host of tiny critters (led by worms, ants, grubs, beetles, and bacteria) that burrow and work in the soil. When most people think of soil, they include the microorganisms that digest and decompose the organic matter and the worms and other burrowers that do the mixing and that create paths for oxygen and water to filter deep into the soil.

When you look out your window, what you mostly see is soil and the plants that live in the soil. That's our image of the Earth. However, soil didn't exist until plants came along.

The Earth is just over 8,000 miles in diameter (12,750 km). That's about 4,000 miles from the center to the surface. The top 20 to 40 miles of that (1%) represents the crust. In most places the soil extends down between only 10 and 40 feet! That's only 0.019% of the thickness of the crust and only 0.000184% of the thickness of the Earth! The crust is 99.98% rock.

Let's put some perspective on those numbers. Pretend there are 10,000 people who are going to play a game. You and I are the captains about to choose up teams. I represent the part of the crust that's rock. So I get 9,998 people on my team. You represent the soil, so you get only two people on your team.

Since I have almost all the players, I'm sure to win. Right? You'd say, "Maybe. Maybe not." It depends on what game we're playing and on who my two players are. If you've have Hercules on your team, you suddenly have a decent chance.

The same is true for soil. Soil may represent only 0.019% of the crust, but that 0.019% of the crust is the *top* 0.019% of the crust. Soil is at the surface. Rock is mostly buried underneath the soil. That makes soil important. So, what does soil do that makes it so important? Two things: it supports life on the land, and it protects rock underneath from wind, rain, and other forces of erosion and weathering.

Plants need soil to grow in and to supply the nutrients they need. But the soil is created from the plants when plant matter is recycled by microorganisms, worms, ants, and other decomposers. It makes you wonder: which came first, the chicken or the egg, that is, the plant or the soil? In this case, plants came first. They cheated and started in the ocean and slowly worked their way onto land, where they created soil.

What else do plants do that affects the land? Plant roots protect and stabilize the soil so that it won't be eroded and washed away—so that the soil, in turn, can protect rocks from weathering. It's all a very cozy arrangement. Plants help break up the rocks. Then microorganisms and worms mix decomposing plants with sand and clay to make soil, which covers the rock and allows more plants to grow, and which protect the soil from erosion so that the soil can protect the rocks from weathering.

But plants aren't through yet. They have changed the rock layers of our crustal plates in two other ways. First, dirt and some plant matter are carried away by wind and water and deposited as sediment. Sediment layers have had a different mix of materials since plants inhabited the land. That means that the sedimentary rocks created from the layers of sediment are different now than they were before plants and dirt entered the sediment stream. Plants have changed the composition of sedimentary rocks. That also means that plants have changed the composition of metamorphic rocks, since most metamorphic rock comes form sedimentary rock.

Finally, plants have added several layers into the sedimentary rock that have become particularly important to humans in the past several hundred years. Coal and oil deposits come from plant matter. Ferns and grasses that grew thick in Jurassic swamps (and were close to worthless at the time) are now being pumped out of the ground and into your car at $2.80 a gallon as gasoline. It is amazing what a little heat, pressure, and 70 million years can do to increase value.

The belief is correct. But it didn't go nearly far enough. Plants have altered the atmosphere and surface layers of this planet in profound and fundamental ways. What you know and think of as the Earth is primarily the result of the changes brought on by plants.

BELIEF: Animals alter the land.

In the myth, Beaver and the prairie dogs altered the land to help Beaver escape. Is that just a wild story, or do animals really do that? We have seen that plants have had an enormous impact on the land. Have animals done as much?

Let's start with small animals in the ocean. Zooplankton are tiny creatures that live in the surface waters of the ocean and eat phytoplankton (floating ocean plants). Most species of zooplankton have thin shells covering their bodies. The primary ingredient in these shells is called *calcium carbonate*. When zooplankton die, their tissue-paper thin shells settle to the bottom of the ocean. But there are billions of zooplankton. Hundreds of tons of zooplankton shells drift to the ocean floor every day, falling like a gentle rain through the black waters of the deep ocean. These shells become a major element in the sedimentary rock layers that cover oceanic plates.

Sediments rich in calcium carbonate tend to produce limestone. Limestone is the predominate rock in many sedimentary layers of both oceanic and continental plates because of these zooplankton. Tiny ocean animals have changed the composition of the world's sedimentary rocks. Of course, that also changes the composition of much of the world's metamorphic rock as well.

On land, animals also do their part in transforming the land. Tiny bugs (beetles, ants, worms, grubs, etc.) along with bacteria digest dead organic matter and turn it into soil. In ecology, they are called *decomposers* because their job in an ecosystem is to decompose (break down) dead organic matter and turn it into soil so that it and its nutrients can be recycled back into new plants.

Worms, ants, moles, and other burrowers dig tunnels. Those tunnels allow air and water to percolate and infiltrate deep into the ground. This is good for plants. But it also increases the amount of water that reaches and erodes rock layers below. Worms are by far the most important of these burrowers. An average acre of ground has a half ton of worms in it. Rich, fertile soil can support as much as 12 tons of worms per acre. That is one big pile of squiggly worms!

Larger animals graze and eat plants. That removes protection from the soil and increases soil erosion. That exposes more rock to increased rock erosion.

Beavers, the most famous of the animal world's earth engineers, chop down trees and build dams. They create ponds and small lakes that change stream flow and sediment patterns. Their projects change vegetation around the lake. But these effects are local and extremely small when viewed on a worldwide scale. Large mammals have a smaller impact on the land structure than do tiny creatures and microorganisms.

Humans

We have all heard that human activity changes (pollutes and destroys) the land. Unfortunately, it's true. There are four ways in which humans change the land.

First, we "*over*" do it. We *over*cut the forests, clear-cutting large areas of forest and leaving the hillsides with no erosion protection. Humans have been overcutting trees since the days of the early Greeks. We overcut to build ships, to build houses, to make paper, to clear land for farms, and to clear land for cattle ranching. We humans clear cut hundreds of thousands of acres of forest every year.

We *over*graze and *over*farm. From the earliest colonial days, Americans have acknowledged that we graze too many animals on too little land. The result is always the same. The vegetation is destroyed and the land is left barren. Erosion rates skyrocket. Colonial leaders in Boston ranted about the practice in the early 1700s. Navaho sheep ranchers in Arizona and New Mexico have faced the problem over the past 30 years. Everyone agrees about the problem. No one can solve it.

Ever since farming was invented some 7,000 years ago, humans have *over*farmed the land. We clear-cut mile after mile of forest and prairie to make room for farms. We plow the fields, removing all vegetation that could protect the topsoil from erosion. We plant the same crops year after year and deplete the soil of all its essential nutrients. What was fertile, productive land soon becomes barren and unable to support what is planted on it. Examples from the American Dust Bowl days of the early 1930s were mentioned in the chapter on wind erosion. Where vegetation is removed, the topsoil soon disappears, erosion increases, and the amount of land useful to humans shrinks a little more.

Second, we build. Humans are builders. We build houses, offices, stores, factories, roads, interstate highways, parking lots, malls, and movie theaters. Everywhere we turn, people are building something. Every time we dig a hole in the backyard, every time we pave a new street or sidewalk, every time we build something on the land, we change natural drainage patterns and almost always increase erosion. Major projects have the greatest impact. Building cities can actually change climate and wind patterns as well as water flow patterns.

Removing a mountain, building tunnels, dams, or city housing developments, all noticeably change the land. Our projects change the way the Earth absorbs water and the way heat is reflected into the atmosphere. Fifty years ago, when Las Vegas, Nevada, had only 30,000 people, the city enjoyed pristine, dry (10% humidity) summer air. Now its smoggy summer humidity often approaches 60%! The climate has radically changes because people built and planted.

Third, people mine. We are diggers as well as builders. Both open pit and deep shaft mines change groundwater patterns and increase air and water penetration into the deeper layers of rock. We also "mine" water by pumping groundwater to the surface. In many areas this has caused major land subsidence.

Finally, humans are dumpers. We dump our wastes and trash on the land, in the water, and into the air. Airborne pollution increases the acid content of air and of rain. Both speed rock erosion. Water pollution affects aquatic plant and animal life, as well as stream flow and sediment rates. Solid waste leeches into groundwater aquifers and makes huge tracts of land unsuitable for other uses.

Whether or not human-caused pollution and other human-caused changes have a bigger effect on the Earth than the impacts of the other groups of living organisms is not the point. Human activity is the only one we can change. Research has clearly shown that human activity has impacted the Earth in a way that is not good for human existence. Our own activity makes it harder for humans to survive. We call this *negative impact*. It would be wise for us to seek ways to alter our activity to reduce the ways we are affecting and changing the surface of the Earth that we depend upon.

The belief is right. Animals do change and affect the land and the planet. One way or the other, however, the planet will survive for billions of more years. The question is whether humans will survive with it.

— TOPICS FOR DISCUSSION AND PROJECTS

Here are activities, research topics, and discussion questions you can use to expand upon the key science concepts presented in this chapter.

Research and Discuss. Research "soil" and "dirt." Is there any difference between these two terms? Is there a difference in your mind? How would you explain that difference? What makes some soil rich and perfect for planting and other soil barren and unable to support crops?

An Activity. Make some good soil. First research the ingredients you will need to combine to make soil. Write your ingredients into a recipe, listing each ingredient and the quantity you plan to use in order to make a 2-gallon batch of perfect soil. Try to include everything your soil will need in order to be top-quality fertile soil. You can compost your own organic material (leaves, grass, etc.) or you can buy a small amount from someone in your area who already composts. (If your community separates yard waste for trash pick up, your waste management company will make compost available.) Mix a small (2-gallon) batch of your soil and test it by planting a few seeds in it. Did they grow easily and quickly?

Research and Discuss. Pick one animal and one plant species and research their impact on the land. How do they affect, alter, or change the land (or prevent change in the land)? Which animal and plant will you pick? A mammal? An insect? An earthworm? A pine tree? A weed? Besides using the Internet and the library, remember to interview local experts: garden shop owners, civil engineers, park rangers, and so on.

An Activity. Build a model or diagram of one human impact on the Earth. Any human activity that affects the land will do. It might be something we do, build, dig, develop, throw out, or use. In your display, show the scope of that activity as well as its impact on the Earth.

Research and Discuss. Research pollutants and pollution. What makes something a pollutant? What is the difference between a pollutant and a nutrient? Is it possible for something to be both? Are there any "natural" pollutants? That is, are there any compounds, chemicals, or materials that are identified as pollutants that are produced in nature? What makes pollutants harmful? What do they harm? Are pollutants bad for *all* parts of an ecosystem? Are there some species that benefit from one or more known pollutants? Which species? How do they benefit?

Research and Discuss. Life on this planet started in the oceans and crept onto land about 600 million YAG. What was the first living thing to move onto land? Research early land life forms. Was it an oceanic weed? A kelp? A crocodile? A shrew? Try to build a description of how

living things spread across the land. What did land look like 600 million YAG? Was there dirt? Volcanoes? Sand? Mud? Rock?

An Activity. Create your own myth about how life started and evolved on land. (Start your story with life already existing in the oceans.) What will you use as the first life form to move onto land? Why did the life form do it? What was the motive? What did the creatures want? What happened to them? Is there a villain (force of evil) in your story? What powers and abilities does your chosen species (character) possess? What will you create to make your story exciting?

Research and Discuss. Oxygen attacks iron and other metals in a process called *oxidation*. Rust and fire are also forms of oxidation. What is oxidation? What happens during oxidation? What can be oxidized? Research oxygen and its effect on metals and rocks. How much oxygen is there? Is the amount of oxygen in the atmosphere increasing or decreasing? Why is oxygen so "aggressive" in the way it combines with other elements?

Plants produce oxygen and, thereby, helped bring on the first of Earth's ice ages. Research the oxygen cycle. What consumes oxygen? What produces it? How is "new" oxygen released into the atmosphere? What happens to oxygen in the atmosphere? How much of all available oxygen is tied up in water (H_2O)? How much oxygen is locked into compounds with other elements? How much of it is with silicon? (Silicates are the most common mineral in Earth's crust.) How is oxygen released from these chemical compounds? Try to create and draw an oxygen cycle diagram showing where oxygen is and how it moves through the environment.

SUGGESTED READING FOR STUDENTS

Amos, Janine. *Pollution*. New York: Steck-Vaughn, 2003.

Arthus-Bertrand, Yann. *The Future of the Earth: Sustainable Growth for Young Readers.* New York: Harry Abrams Publishing, 2004.

Castelfranchi, Yuri. *History of the Earth*. London: Barron's Educational Series, 2003.

Cochrane, Jennifer. *Land Ecology*. New York: Franklin Watts, 1997.

Donald, Rhonda. *Air Pollution*. New York: Scholastic Library Publishing, 2001.

Graham, Ian. *Soil: A Resource Our World Depends On*. Portsmouth, NH: Heinemann, 2004.

Hirschmann, Kris. *Pollution*. New York: Thomson Gale, 2004.

Jennings, Terry. *Rocks and Soil*. New York: Scholastic Library Publishing, 1998.

Nelson, Robin. *Soil*. New York: Lerner Publishing Group, 2005.

Parker, Steve. *Microlife That Lives in Soil*. Chicago: Raintree Publishers, 2005.

Snedden, Robert. *Rocks and Soil*. Chicago: Raintree Publishing, 1998.

Stevens, Lawrence. *Ecology Basics*. Englewood Cliffs, NJ: Prentice Hall, 1996.

Stewart, Melissa. *Soil*. Portsmouth, NH: Heinemann Library, 2003.

SUGGESTED READING FOR TEACHERS

Cairns-Smith, A. *Seven Clues to the Origin of Life.* New York: Cambridge University Press, 1999.

Chapin, Stuart. *Principles of Terrestrial Ecosystem Ecology.* New York: Springer, 2002.

Collinson, Alan. *Pollution.* New York: Simon & Schuster, 2002.

Dumanoski, Dianne. *Our Stolen Future.* New York: Penguin Group, 1997.

Emiliani, C. *Planet Earth.* New York: Cambridge University Press, 2003.

Miller, Gary. *Ecology.* New York: W. H. Freeman, 1999.

Smith, Robert. *Elements of Ecology.* Sacramento, CA: Benjamin-Cummings Publishing, 2002.

Appendix: Additional Resources

WEB SITES

The search term *earth science* produced over 9 million hits on each of the three major search engines checked. There are 100 university graduate degree programs in Earth Sciences and 200 undergraduate programs. Over a dozen federal governmental agencies and over 50 state-level agencies study, regulate, and control aspects of the land. Each has its own Web page that describes and reports on its research and studies. There are literally thousands of valuable, reliable, information-filled sites on the Web. The few sites listed here cover a wide spectrum of Earth Science fields and are some of the best and most dependable.

American Geophysical Union. http://earth.agu.org/kosmos/homepage.html

American Museum of Natural History. www.amnh.org/rose/hope

California Institute of Technology Geological Sciences. www.gps.caltech.edu

Cambridge University Earth Sciences. http://rock.esc.cam.ac.uk/main

Earth Sciences Library (a good reference site for links to other sites). www.vlib.org/EarthScience

Geophysical Survey of Canada. http://agcwww.bio.ns.ca

Geoweb. www.pacificnet.net/-gimills/main

Global Environmental Systems Simulation. http://tribeca.ios,com/;atdobran

APPENDIX

Institute of Geology at Scripps. http://igpp.ucsd.edu

International Institute for Geophysical Information. www.itc.nl/

NASA Earth Sciences Division. www.Earthobservatory.gov

NASA EOS IDS Volcanology Team. www.geo.mtu.edu:80/eos

On-Line Resources for Earth Sciences. www.csn.net/-bthoen/ores

Physical Sciences Gateway site—good links to other sites. www.psigate.ac.uk/newsite/earth-gateway.html

Rice University Earth Sciences. www.glacier.rice.edu

Science.com site on Earth Sciences. http://dir.yahoo.com/science/Earth_Sciences/Geology_and_Geophysics/

Stanford University Earth Sciences. www.pangea.stanford.edu/

UC Santa Cruse Earth Sciences. www.es.ucsc.edu/

United States Geological Survey. www.usgs.gov/index

University of California, Berkeley Earth Science. www.lib.berkeley.edu/EART/Earth Links.htm

World Data Systems. www.ngdc.noaa.gov/wdcmain.html

GENERAL EARTH SCIENCE BOOK REFERENCES

Andel, T. van. *New Views of an Old Planet*. New York: Cambridge University Press, 2001.

Ballard, Robert. *Exploring Our Living Planet*. Washington, DC: National Geographic Society, 1993.

Bolt, T. A. *Inside the Earth*. San Francisco, CA: Freeman, 1999.

Brown, G. C. *Understanding the Earth*. New York: Cambridge University Press, 2002.

Cattermole, Peter. *Building Planet Earth*. New York: Cambridge University Press, 2000.

———. *Encyclopedia of Earth and Other Planets.* Oxford: Andromeda, 1998.

Chernicoff, S. *Geology.* New York: Worth, 1995.

Dixon, D. *The Planet Earth.* Chicago: World Book Encyclopedia of Science, 1999.

Downs, Sandra. *Shaping the Earth: Erosion.* Brookfield, CT: Twenty-First Century Books, 2001.

Emiliani, C. *Planet Earth.* New York: Cambridge University Press, 2003.

Garner, H. *The Origins of Landscapes.* New York: Oxford University Press, 1994.

Good, John, and Kenneth Pierce. *Interpreting the Landscape.* Moose, WY: Grand Teton National Historic Association, 1996.

Gregory, K. J. *Earth's Natural Forces.* Oxford: Andromeda, 2000.

Keary, Philip. *Global Tectonics.* Malden, MA: Blackwell Science, 1996.

———. *An Introduction to Geophysical Exploration.* Malden, MA: Blackwell Science, 1995.

Lutgens, F. *Essentials of Geology.* London: Allen and Unwin, 2001.

Meissner, Rolf. *The Continental Crust.* San Diego, CA: Academic Press, 1996.

———. *The Little Book of Planet Earth.* New York: Copernicus Books, 1999.

Montgomery, C. W. *Earth: Then and Now.* New York: William Brown Co., 2001.

Morton, Ron. *Music of the Earth: Volcanoes, Earthquakes, and Other Geological Wonders.* New York: Plenum Press, 1996.

Mungall, C. *Planet under Stress.* New York: Oxford University Press, 2001.

Patent, Dorothy Hinshaw. *Shaping the Earth.* New York: Clarion Books, 2001.

Phinney, Robert, ed. *The History of Earth's Crust.* Princeton, NJ: Princeton University Press, 1993.

Press, Frank. *Earth.* New York: W. H. Freeman & Co., 1997.

Skinner, Brian. *The Dynamic Earth.* New York: John Wiley & Sons, 2000.

Stokes, W. Lee. *Essentials of Earth History.* Englewood Cliffs, NJ: Prentice Hall, 2002.

APPENDIX

Swanson, Diane. *The Day of the Twelve-Story Wave*. Atlanta, GA: Longstreet Press, 1997.

Weiner, J. *Planet Earth*. New York: Bantam Books, 1996.

Willie, Peter. *The Way the Earth Works*. New York: Wiley, 1996.

—— BOOK REFERENCES ON EARTH STORIES

Addo, Peter. *How the Spider Became Bald*. Greensboro, SC: Morgan Reynolds, 1993.

Allan, Tony. *Gods of Sun and Sacrifice: Aztec and Maya Myth*. London: Duncan Baird Publishers, 1997.

Andrews, Tamra. *Dictionary of Nature Myths*. New York: Oxford University Press, 1998.

———. *Legends of the Earth, Sea, and Sky*. Santa Barbara, CA: ABC-CLIO, 1998.

Beck, Brenda, ed. *Folktales of India*. Chicago: University of Chicago Press, 1987.

Bierhorst, John, ed. *The Red Swan*. New York: Farrar, Straus and Giroux, 1976.

Bruchac, Joseph, and M. Caduto. *Keepers of the Earth*. Golden, CO: Fulcrum, 1988.

Bryan, Ashley. *Ashley Bryan's African Tales, Uh-Huh*. New York: Atheneum Books for Young Readers, 1998.

Caduto, Michael. *Earth Tales from around the World*. Golden, CO: Fulcrum Publishing, 1997.

Curry, Jane. *Back in the Beforetime*. New York: Margaret K. McElderry Books, 1987.

Elder, John, ed. *Family of Earth and Sky*. Boston, MA: Beacon Press, 1994.

Erdoes, Richard. *American Indian Myths and Legends*. New York: Pantheon Books, 1984.

Gray, J. E. *Indian Tales and Legends*. New York: Oxford University Press, 1961.

Haklik, Jan. *Spirits of the Snow: Arctic Myths*. London: Suncan Baird Publishers, 1999.

Hamilton, Virginia. *In the Beginning: Creation Stories from around the World*. San Diego, CA: Harcourt Brace Jovanovich, 1988.

Kanawa, Kiri Te. *Land of the Long White Cloud: Maori Myths and Legends*. New York: Pavillion Books, 1997.

Krishnaswami, Uma. *Stories of the Flood.* New York: Roberts Rinehart Publishers, 1994.

Leach, Maria, ed. *Funk and Wagnalls Standard Dictionary of Folklore, Mythology, and Legend.* New York: Harper & Row, 1972.

MacFarlan, Allan. *American Indian Legends.* New York: Heritage Press, 1968.

Medlicott, Mary. *The River That Went to the Sky.* New York: Kingfisher Books, 1995.

Merriam, C. Hart. *The Dawn of the World: Myths and Tales of the Miwok Indians of California.* Lincoln, NE: University of Nebraska Press, 1970.

Millman, Lawrence. *A Kayak Full of Ghosts.* Santa Barbara, CA: Capra Press, 1987.

Offodile, Buchi. *The Orphan Girl and Other West African Folk Tales.* New York: Interlink Books, 2001.

Radin, Paul. *African Folktales.* New York: Schocken Books, 1983.

Robertson, Dorothy. *Fairy Tales from the Philippines.* New York: Dodd, Mead & Company, 1971.

Romulo, Liana. *Filipino Children's Favorite Stories.* North Clarendon, VT: Tuttle Publishers, 2000.

Simpson, Jacqueline. *Scandinavian Folktales.* New York: Penguin Books, 1988.

Storm, Rachel. *Myths of the East.* London: Southwater, 1999.

Suwyn, Barbara. *The Magic Egg and Other Tales from Ukraine.* Englewood, CO: Libraries Unlimited, 1997.

Van Wolde, Ellen. *Stories of the Beginning.* Harrisburg, PA: Morehouse Publishing, 1996.

Vogel, Carole. *Legends of Landforms.* Brookfield, CT: Millbrook Press, 1995.

Index

acid rain, 113–114, 119
acids, 113–114, 117
    amino, 193
    and caverns, 119–121
African myths, 4, 24, 86, 128, 189
African Plate, 10–12, 31, 92, 176
aftershocks, 177
aggregate, 53
air currents, 131–133, 132f
Alaska, 161
Alaskan (Native) myths, 147
alluvial fans, 117
alpine glaciers, 151
Alps, 33, 92, 159, 176
aluminum, 14, 77
Amazon River, 116
amber, 78
American Southwest desertification, 141
amino acids, 193
amplitude (A), 178
Andes Mountains, 91, 95
animals, 193
    as decomposers, 198
    impact on land of, 197–200
    in myths, 4–6, 86–88, 148–150, 170–172, 190–192
Antarctic continental glacier, 150, 161
Antarctic Plate, 10

Appalachian Mountains, 13, 56, 92, 95
Arabian Peninsula, 121, 138
Arabian Plate, 31
Aristotle, 170
Asian myths, 170
Atacama Desert, 136–137
Atlantic Ocean, 12–13, 33, 173
    Gulf Stream in, 157–158
    mid-Atlantic ridge of, 10, 34, 92
Atlantis, 64, 169
atmosphere
    circulation patterns of, 131–133
    Earth's spin and, 133
    formation of, 7–8, 17, 29, 39, 194
atomic number, 62
atoms, 61–62, 76
Australian Plate. *See* Indian-Australian Plate

Baja Desert, 135–137
ball lightning, 182
basaltic shield volcanoes, 34–36
basalt rock, 31, 55
basins, 96–97, 137
bauxite, 79
Bay of Siam (in myths), 106
beavers, 198
    in myths, 190–192
bed loads, 115

INDEX

Big Bang theory, 3
block faults, 89, 93
borax, 79
Borneo myths, 71–72
Bryce Canyon, 57
building, impact of, 199

calcium carbonate, 57, 197
Calcutta earthquake, 182
calderas, 38, 43
California Channel Islands, 135
California earthquakes, 174, 175f, 182–183
calving, 155
Canada
  ice ages in, 155
  oldest rocks in, 7
canyons, 118
carats, 78
carbon, 77, 79
carbon dioxide, 158, 194
carbonic acid, 114, 117, 119
Caribbean myths, 106
Cascade Mountains, 33
caves and caverns, 106, 117, 119–121
center moraines, 153, 159
chemical erosion, 119–121
chemical formulas, 73
chemical weathering, 113–114
Chili
  deserts in, 132, 136–137
  fjord in, 160
China and earthquakes, 182
coal, 57, 77, 197
coastal deserts, 137
Colca River Canyon, 118
collision of plates, 10–11, 13, 31–33, 91–92
  and earthquakes, 173–176, 182
Colorado plateau, 93
composite volcanoes, 36–37
continental crusts, 9, 14, 32, 58
  rocks in, 54
Continental Drift, 10
  and glaciers, 158
continental extension, 96

continental glaciers, 150–151, 156, 160–161
continental plates, 10–11, 33, 63, 91–92, 96
coral, 78
core of the Earth, 7, 14, 28
  seismic waves and, 16–17, 178–179
coyotes in myths, 86–88
Crater Lake, 38, 93
creation myths, 4–6
crevasses, 152, 163
crust of the Earth, 7–9, 14, 16, 196
  earthquakes and, 173–176
  elements of, 73–74, 74f
  movement of, 9–14, 17
  volcanoes and, 28–29
  See also plates
crystallization, 17
  diamonds and, 77
  in metamorphic rock, 58
  mineral structure and, 73–76
crystals
  defined, 74–75
  formation of, 76–79
  minerals and, 73–75
  myths about creating, 69–72
  science of creating, 73–80
Cumberland Gap, 118
currents, air, 131–133, 132f

Dayunisi (in myths), 5
Death Valley, 132, 135–137
decomposition, 195, 198
Delaware Water Gap, 118
deltas, 116
desertification, 140–141
desert rivers, 116–117
deserts, 136f
  latitude and, 132–133, 136
  meaning of, 127, 135
  waves, 139–140
  wind and, 134, 135–140
development, impact of, 199
Devil's Tower, 37, 94
diamonds, 77–79
differentiation, 7, 74

Index

dirt. *See* soil
dissolved loads, 115
draperies, 120
dumping, impact of, 199
dust blasting, 134
Dust Bowl, 127, 135, 199
dust storms, 134, 138

eagles in myths, 6, 86, 88
Earth
    changing orbit of, 156–157
    core of, 7, 14, 28
    first life on, 8–9, 192–193
    formation of, 6–9
    as giant furnace, 28–29
    inside of, 14–17, 15f
    mantle of, 7, 14–15
    seismic waves and, 16, 178–179
    size of, 196
    spin of, 133
    tilt angle cycle of, 157
    See also crust of the Earth; plates
earthquakes
    cause of, 172–174
    impact on land of, 182–183
    location of, 174–176, 177f, 179–180
    measurement and prediction of, 180–182
    myths about, 169–172
    occurrences of, 179–182
    science of, 172–183
El Chichón, 33, 41–42, 93
electromagnetic waves, 182
elements, 73–74, 74f, 76–77
emeralds, 70
epicenters, 176
erosion
    in caves and caverns, 119
    chemical, 119–121
    living things and, 196, 198–199
    mountains and, 94–96
    sedimentary rock and, 56
    water, 113–118, 140
    wind, 134–135, 138, 140
Eurasian Plate, 10–12, 31, 93, 95, 173, 176

Europa, 193
evaporation, 112–113

face (of a glacier), 152
fault lines, 174–176, 180, 182
    California, 175f
faults, 92–93
feldspar, 75
"Fire Goddess, The," 25–27
fjords, 160
flooding, 105–106, 117
floodplains, 117
fog and mist, 106
folded faults, 92
fossilization, 78
fossils, 54, 56–57, 63, 192
frequency (f), 178
    ultra-low (ulf), 181

gabbros, 55
Gaia, 4, 189
Galapagos Islands, 34
garnets, 58, 78–79
gasoline, 197
gasses, 7
    greenhouse, 157–158, 194
    in rocks, 55–56, 63–64
    and volcanoes, 30, 32–34, 36–38
gemstones
    defined, 74–76
    formation of, 76–79
    myths about creating, 69–72
    occurrences of, 79–80
    science of creating, 73–80
geysers, 39
"Gift of the Menehune, The," 107–110
glaciers
    age of ice in, 161–162
    description of, 150–154
    formation of, 154–155
    ice ages and, 155–158
    impact on land of, 158–160
    light absorption by, 151
    locations of, 160–161
    movement of, 162–163
    myths about, 147–150

INDEX

noise of, 162
science of, 150–163
valleys of, 159–160
global air currents, 131–133, 132f
global warming, 158
Glomar Challenger, 10
Gobi Desert, 132, 135–137
"Goddess of Mahi River, The," 50–52
Gondwanaland, 11
GPS (Global Positioning System), 121, 181
grain, 58
Grand Canyon, 57, 118
Grande Ronde River (in myths), 190–191
granite, 55, 75
graphite, 77, 79
gravity, 95
   and Earth's core, 28
Great Lakes, 160
Great Salt Lake, 160
Greek myths, 50, 170
greenhouse gas, 157–158, 194
Greenland continental glacier, 150, 158, 161
ground loads, 134
groundwater, 113, 117
   in caves and caverns, 119–120
Gulf Stream, 158, 164

Half Dome, 159
half-lives, 62
hardness and gems, 76
Hawaiian Islands, 29, 33–34, 95, 136
Hawaiian myths, 24–27, 50, 107–110
head (of a glacier), 152
heat. *See* temperature
Hekla, 37
Himalayan Mountains, 12–13, 33, 86, 92, 95, 176
"Holmes's Conveyer Belt," 16, 16f
Horseshoe Falls, 116
hot spots, 33–34, 41
"How Beaver Stole Fire from the Pines," 190–192
human beings, impact of, 198–200

Huron myths, 4–6
hurricanes, 135
hydrocarbons, 57, 63

ibises in myths, 148–150
ice
   in glaciers, 152, 155, 161
   pressure on rocks, 114
   rivers of (glaciers), 150–151
ice ages, 156–158
icebergs, 154, 161
Iceland, 34
Icelandic myths, 148
igneous rocks, 40–41, 55, 59, 63–64
India and earthquakes, 182–183
Indian-Australian Plate, 10, 12, 17, 92–93, 173, 176
Indian myths, 50–52, 70, 86, 170–172
Indian Ocean, 92, 183
Indus River area desertification, 141
interior basins, 137
Inuit myths, 4
Io, 193
islands, 13
isotopes, 62

Jackson, Stonewall, 49
jade, 70
Japan and earthquakes, 183
Japanese myths, 86, 170
jet stream, 133

Kahawali (in myths), 25–27
Kalahari Desert, 132, 135–137
Kilauea volcano, 44, 55
Klenova, Maria, 64
Krakatoa, 32, 38, 43

Laka (in myths), 25–26
Lake Bonneville, 160
land
   defined, 8
   Earth center and, 14–17, 15f
   Earth formation and, 6–9
   impact of animals on, 197–200
   impact of earthquakes on, 182–183
   impact of glaciers of, 158–160

impact of plants on, 194–197
impact of volcanoes of, 29
impact of water on, 113–117
impact of wind on, 133–135
movement of, 9–14, 17
myths about origins of, 1–6
negative impact on, 200
science of, 6–17
landslides, 114
Las Vegas, Nevada, 199
Latvian myths, 50
lava, 30–31, 33–34, 36, 92–93
layers of rock, 57
   See also sedimentary layers
life, beginning of, 8–9
   See also living things
limestone, 57–58, 197
   in caves and caverns, 120–121
"Lion's Earthquake, The," 170–172
liquefaction, 185
lithosphere, 14–16, 58
living things
   animals, 193, 197–200
   in caves and caverns, 120–121
   myths about, 189–192
   origins of, 192–193
   plants, 192–197
   science of, 192–200
loads, 115–116, 134
logarithmic scale, 181
Long Valley, 38
loons in myths, 4–5

magma, 15–16, 59
   defined, 30
   plate separation and, 92
   plugs, 36, 55
   volcanoes and, 28, 30–34, 36–37, 39–41
magnitude (earthquake), 177, 180–181, 183
Mahi River (in myths), 50–52
"Making of the World, The," 4–6
mantle of the Earth, 7, 14–15, 173
   seismic waves and, 16–17, 178–179
   volcanoes and, 28

Maori (New Zealand) myths, 24, 170
marble, 58
Mars, 29, 193
Matterhorn Mountain, 92, 148, 159
Mauna Kea, 94
Mauna Loa, 36, 94
Mayan myths, 4, 70
Menehune (in myths), 107–110
metamorphic rocks, 40–41, 57–59, 63, 197
meteorites, 193
Mexican deserts, 135–137
mica, 75
microorganisms, 194–195
mid-Atlantic ridge, 10, 34, 92
minerals, 70
   in caves and caverns, 120
   defined, 73–76
   precious, 79–80
   in rocks, 53–54, 56–57
   volcanoes and, 29
mining, impact of, 199
Minnesota, 31, 160
Mississippi River, 116, 161, 183
Missouri earthquakes, 182–183
Missouri River, 160
Modoc Indian myths, 86–88
Mohorovicic Discontinuity (Moho), 15–16
molecules, 76–77
molten rock, 14, 31
   See also magma
moraines, 152, 154, 159–160
"Mountain Making," 86–88
mountains
   changes in, 94–96
   deserts and, 136
   erosion and, 94–96
   formation of, 13, 90f
   myths about creating, 85–88
   plate tectonics and, 89, 91–93
   science about creating, 89–97
   valleys and, 96–97
   volcanoes and, 93–94
"Mountains of Gold and Jewels," 71–72
Mt. Everest, 18

INDEX

Mt. Fuji, 32, 37, 86, 93
Mt. Hood, 93
Mt. Kailas, 85
Mt. Kilimanjaro, 93
Mt. Pinatubo, 32, 37, 42–43, 93
Mt. Shasta, 86, 93
Mt. Sinai, 85
Mt. St. Helens, 32, 36–37, 93
Mt. Vesuvius, 37–38, 93
mudslides, 114
mythology. *See* African myths; Asian myths; Borneo myths; Caribbean myths; Greek myths; Hawaiian myths; Icelandic myths; Indian myths; Inuit myths; Japanese myths; Latvian myths; Mayan myths; Native American myths; New Zealand myths; North American myths; Pacific Northwest myths; Russian myths; South American myths; Thailand myths; Tibetan myths

Namib Desert, 132, 137
Nasca plate, 95
Native American myths, 4–6, 50, 70, 86–88, 105, 107
nebula, 6
negative impact, 200
neutrons, 61–62
Nevada Desert, 136–137
New Madrid fault line, 176, 182–183
New Zealand myths, 24, 148, 170
Nez Percé myths, 190–192
Niagara Falls, 116
Nigerian myths, 4
Nile River, 116
nonpolar glaciers, 161
North American glaciers, 156, 160
North American myths, 50, 147
North American Plate, 10–12, 31, 33, 96–97, 173
North Atlantic gyre, 164
Northern Hemisphere
    circulation patterns of, 131–132
    ice ages in, 155, 157
Nuclear Test Ban Treaty, 17

obsidian, 55
oceanic crusts, 8–10, 14, 16, 32, 57–58
oceanic plates, 10–11, 33, 63, 91–92, 197
oceans, 111
    and glaciers, 154
    and origins of life, 193–194, 197
    See also Atlantic Ocean; Indian Ocean; Pacific Ocean
oil, 197
Olympus Mons, 29
orbital eccentricity, 157
Oregon, desert in eastern, 136
origins of land, 3–21
overcutting of trees, 198
overfarming, 199
overgrazing, 198
oxidation, 194
oxygen, 14, 77, 194

Pacific Northwest myths, 24, 190–192
Pacific Ocean, 32–33, 36, 91, 176, 179
Pacific Plate, 10, 12, 95
Pangaea, 11–12, 92
Papago Indian myths, 50
pearls, 70, 78
"pedestal rocks," 134
Pele (in myths), 24–27
peridotite, 55
period (T), 178
petroleum, 57
phytoplankton, 197
Pico de Orizaba, 93
Pi (in myths), 107–110
planetisimals, 7
plankton, 194
plants
    first, 192–193
    impact on land of, 194–197
plateaus, 93
plates, 10–13, 11f, 12f
    earthquakes and, 173–176, 182
    sinking of, 96
    tectonics and, 89, 91–93, 173, 183
    volcanoes and, 28, 30–33

See also collision of plates; continental plates; oceanic plates; separation of plates
plugs (rock), 36, 55, 94
pollution, 113, 199
Popocatepeti, 93
precession, 157
precipitation, 112
pressure
   Earth core and, 14
   earthquakes and, 173
   faults and, 93
   gems, crystals and, 76–79
   glaciers and, 155
   ice and, 114
   metamorphic rock and, 57–58, 63
   volcanoes and, 30, 32, 36–37
   in weather systems, 133, 137
pressure waves (P-waves), 178–179
protons, 61
protostar (Sun), 6
pumice, 55
pyroclastic flows, 38–39, 42

quartz, 55, 77
Queen Maries Peak, 37

radioactive elements, 14, 17, 28
rain, 113–114
   wind and, 131–134, 140
Rajputana Desert, 141
Red and Black Deserts (in myths), 130
Red Sea, 13, 33
Richter scale, 177, 180–181
rift valleys, 11, 16, 31, 91, 96
"Ring of Fire, The," 32, 36, 176
rivers, 13, 115–118
   desert, 116–117
   of ice (glaciers), 150–151
Riverside, 117
"Rock of Chickamauga, The," 49
rocks
   age of, 54, 61–62
   basalt, 31, 55
   cycles of, 59–60, 60f
   defined, 52–53
   expansion of, 28
   groups of, 54–58
   history of Earth and, 54, 63–64
   ice and heat and, 114
   leeching and, 195
   minerals in, 53–54
   molten, 14, 31
   myths about creating, 49–52
   oldest, 7
   ongoing formation of, 59–61
   outcroppings, 50
   oxidation and, 194
   "pedestal," 134
   plants and, 194–197
   plugs of, 36, 55, 94
   science of creating, 52–64
   volcanoes and, 40–41
   See also magma
Rocky Mountains, 13, 93, 95
roots of plants, 195–196
rubies, 69
Russian myths, 4, 128–130

Sahara Desert, 132, 134–138
salt, 74
San Andreas fault line, 174–176
San Bernardino, 117
sandblasting, 134, 138
sand dunes, 138–140, 139f
sandstorms, 134, 138
San Francisco earthquake, 182–183
sapphires, 70
schist, 58
scouring, 115
scraping of plates, 33
sea level, 13
   glaciers and, 156
seals in myths, 5
sedimentary layers, 56–57, 63, 95, 196–197
   in caves and caverns, 119–120
sedimentary rocks, 40–41, 56–59, 63, 95, 197
seismic waves, 16, 176–179
seismographs, 185–186
separation of plates, 31, 92, 96
Shaanxi earthquake, 182
shadow deserts, 136–137

INDEX

shale, 58, 78–79
shear waves (S-waves), 178–179
shields volcanoes, 34–36
Ship Rock, 37, 94
Siberian myths, 128
side moraines, 153, 159
Sierra Mountains, 33, 91, 95
silicates, 77
silicon, 14, 77
silicon dioxide (SiO_2), 9, 30–31, 34, 36–37, 43
slate, 58, 79
Sleeping Bear Sand Dunes, 140
slip face (of sand dunes), 138–139
snow and glaciers, 154–155
sodium, 14
soil (dirt), 9, 17, 29, 195–196
    animals and, 198
    earth layer of, 53
    volcanoes and, 41
solid waste, impact of, 199
Sonoran Desert, 132, 135
soufflé volcanoes, 37–39, 41–43, 91
source (of a glacier), 152
South American myths, 4, 106, 148–150
South American Plate, 10–12, 31, 95
Southern Hemisphere, 132
Southwest Casa Grande myths, 70
speed (V), 178
stalactites, 120
stalagmites, 120
St. Elmo's Fire, 182
streams, 115–118
subduction, 33, 57–58, 91, 95
    gems and, 79
    zones, 11, 16, 32
subsidence, 96
sulfur dioxide, 113
sulfuric acid, 119
Sun, 6
    Earth's distance from, 17
    ice ages and, 156–157
    rocks and, 114
    wind and, 131
"Sun, Water, and Wind," 129–130
Sunda Straight, 43
surging glaciers, 162

Surtsey island, 29
suspended loads, 115–116, 134
Swiss Alps. *See* Alps

T'ang earthquake, 182
teapot volcanoes, 36–37, 41–43, 91
tectonic forces and movement, 11, 13, 16, 56
    basins and, 96
    earthquakes and, 173, 182
    mountains and, 89, 91–93
temperature
    gems, crystals and, 76–79
    inside the Earth, 7, 14–15, 28
    metamorphic rock and, 57–58, 63
    surface rocks and, 114
    volcanoes and, 28–29
Termier, Pierre, 64
terminal moraines, 153, 155, 159–160
terminus (of a glacier), 152
Thailand myths, 106
"Touchy Ibis, The" 148–150
Thomas, George, 49
Three Sisters, 93
thrust faults, 92–93
Tibetan myths, 86
Tibet plateau, 93
Titanic, 161
toads in myths, 5
tornados, 135
tortoises in myths, 5–6
trees in myths, 170–172, 190–192
tropical wind conveyor belt, 132, 136
tsunamis, 39, 43, 177, 183
Turkey (Istanbul), 175
turtle volcanoes, 34–36, 41

Ubar, 121
ultra-low frequency (ulf) vibrations, 181
uranium, 62

valley glaciers, 151, 152f, 160, 161
valleys
    glacial, 159–160

and mountains, 96–97
See also rifts valleys
Venezuelan myths, 106
Vesuvius. *See* Mt. Vesuvius
Villa Luz Cavern, 120
viscosity, 30, 32–34, 36–37
volcanoes
    active, 32f, 32–33
    creation of, 30–34
    dangers of, 41–43
    Earth's balance and, 39–40
    heat of, 28–29
    impact on land of, 29
    monitoring and predicting, 40
    myths about, 23–27
    rocks and, 40–41
    science of, 27–43
    types of, 34–39, 35f
Vulcan, 23

water
    canyons and, 118
    in caves and caverns, 119–121
    cycle of, 111–113, 112f
    impact on land of, 113–117
    myths about, 105–110
    origins of, 8, 17, 29, 110–111
    science of, 110–121
    volcanoes and, 39
    volume and location of, 111
waterfalls, 116
water table, 119–120
waves
    desert, 139–140

electromagnetic, 181
ocean, 114–115
seismic, 16, 177–179
weathering forces
    chemical, 113–114
    mountains and, 94–96
    of water, 113–117
    of wind, 134
weather systems, 133, 137
Web sites
    on earthquakes, 186
    on glaciers, 164, 166
    on volcanoes, 46
    on wind, 144
Wegener, Alfred, 10
West Australian Desert, 132, 137
Wiamea River Valley, 118
wind
    creation of, 131–133
    deserts and, 135–140
    impact on land of, 133–135, 140–141
    myths about, 127–130
    science of, 131–141
wind rose, 142
wind storms, 135
wobble, 157
worms, 198

Yamana myths, 148–150
Yellowstone Valley, 38
Yosemite Valley, 148, 159
Yurok myths, 107

zooplankton, 197

About the Author

KENDALL HAVEN is a master storyteller, former research scientist, and author of many books for Libraries Unlimited and Teacher Ideas Press. He lives and works in Fulton, California.

www.ingramcontent.com/pod-product-compliance
Lightning Source LLC
Chambersburg PA
CBHW080936300426
44115CB00017B/2841